# A VIEW FROM NEW DELHI

# A VIEW FROM NEW DELHI

*Selected Speeches and Writings*

## by Chester Bowles

NEW HAVEN AND LONDON, YALE UNIVERSITY PRESS, 1969

Library of Congress catalog card number: 79-102052
Standard book number (clothbound): 300-01233-0
Standard book number (paperbound): 300-01234-9
Printed in the United States of America by
The Carl Purington Rollins Printing-Office of
the Yale University Press, New Haven, Connecticut.
Distributed in Great Britain, Europe, Asia except for
India, and Africa by Yale University Press Ltd., London;
in Canada by McGill-Queen's University Press, Montreal;
and in Mexico by Centro Interamericano de Libros
Académicos, Mexico City.

*We have inherited a big house, a great world house in which we have to live together as black and white, Easterners and Westerners, Muslims and Hindus, Gentiles and Jews, Catholics and Protestants, a family unduly separated in ideas, culture and interests who, because we can never again live without each other, must learn, somehow, in this big world to live with each other.*

—DR. MARTIN LUTHER KING, JR.

# Contents

PREFACE    1

SECTION ONE    AN AGENDA FOR NATION BUILDING

1. Five Essentials of Nation Building   ..   7
2. The Sterile World of Slogans   ..   19
3. The Developing Nations' Most
   Urgent Need   ..   24
4. Priority for Human Dignity   ..   33
5. The Question of Personal Involvement   42
6. Education: Cornerstone of a Just
   Society   ..   50
7. A Key to Rapid Economic Growth   ..   59
8. Prospects for Indian Agriculture   ..   73
9. The Critical Importance of a
   "Balanced Diet"   ..   85
10. Prospects for India's Family Planning   ..   90
11. Confidence: Essential Ingredient of
    Progress   ..   105

SECTION TWO    ECONOMIC ASSISTANCE AND
INTERNATIONAL COOPERATION

12. What Foreign Aid Can and Cannot Do   119
13. Partners in Economic Growth   ..   134
14. The Crucial Importance of Foreign
    Exchange   ..   147

SECTION THREE    THE DEMOCRACIES OF INDIA
AND AMERICA

15. Gandhi's Influence on World Affairs   ..   157
16. Candid Comments on Indo-American
    Relations   ..   166
17. America's New Focus on India   ..   174
18. Recent Trends in Indian-American
    Relations   ..   179

SECTION FOUR  THE POLITICAL DYNAMICS OF
THE NEW ASIA

19. Let Us Keep the Cold War Out of
India                                    ..        187
20. China and India: Problems and
Prospects                                ..        195
21. Nuclear Power: Danger or
Opportunity ?                            ..        209

SECTION FIVE  INTERPRETING AMERICA

22. The Unfinished American Revolution  ..        219
23. Holidays and Heroes                   ..        224
24. The United States Has Problems, Too ..        236
25. The Evolution of America's Foreign
Policy                                   ..        248
26. What Kind of World?                   ..        266

# Preface

As I view our troubled world, three questions emerge of primary importance.

First, can the United States and the Soviet Union reach agreement on the effective control of nuclear weapons before we destroy each other and much of the world as well?

Second, can the population explosion be brought under control?

Third, can we somehow learn better to understand our world neighbors and to increase their understanding of us?

This book is addressed to the third of these challenges: our ability to understand and to communicate not only with our fellow citizens but with the peoples of Asia, Africa, Europe and Latin America.

This question involves a paradox.

In recent years we have developed fantastic communications technologies which enable people of all nations to see and hear each other on television halfway around the world, and to communicate directly over long distance telephones.

Yet tens of millions of educated Americans, most of whom spend several hours a day reading newspapers and magazines and watching television, remain as grossly uninformed about how other people think and feel as most foreigners are about us.

This situation reflects not only the complexity of our present-day world but also the unfortunate fact that the communications systems which give responsible organizations and individuals the power to *inform* also provide propagandists and demagogues the opportunity to *distort* and to *deceive*. Consequently, even presumably well-informed people cling doggedly to capsule impressions of other lands and cultures that are often gravely distorted.

Among hundreds of millions of foreigners, including most Indians, the mention of America brings to mind a land of cowboys, C.I.A. agents, movie stars, millionaires, divorcees, muggers and gangsters, with automated machines gradually taking over the work of human beings.

When most Americans think of India (which is not very often), they visualize a land of babies, monkeys and cows; of dust, heat and famine; of maharajahs, polo players and cobras; an economic bottomless pit and an international basket case.

Moreover these stereotypes tend to feed on themselves. The relatively few American visitors who stay for more than a week in India almost invariably leave with the positive impression of a great people working against formidable obstacles to maintain a free society and to establish a greater measure of economic and social justice for its citizens. Unhappily, most Americans stay for only a few days, and the tendency is to remember whatever incidents or scenes fit their preconceptions and to dismiss whatever evidence appears to clash with them.

Instead of correcting the established stereotypes, the press and television, with some notable exceptions, tend to reinforce them. News reporting under the best of circumstances is more concerned with dramatic disasters than with humdrum accomplishments. Even the most conscientious foreign correspondents soon discover that copy presenting an exotic, Kiplingish view of India is more likely to appear on the front page of their paper than a carefully documented account of rapid progress in rural electrification.

When the monsoon rains failed in 1966 and again in 1967 the food crisis in India was extensively reported in the world press with dire prophecies of millions of emaciated people who would soon be dying in the streets. Some foreign reporters assigned to describe the impending catastrophe are said to have asked the first people they met at the airport, "Where can I find the nearest bodies?"

The fact that India, thanks to massive wheat shipments from the United States and an extraordinarily efficient administrative effort of its own, managed in both years to avoid a famine was not considered "news."

The breakthrough in the production of food grains in India which first became evident in the crop year of 1967, and which was even more dramatic in 1968, may be judged by historians to be one of the dozen or two most important events of our era. Yet the story of a suddenly awakened peasantry eagerly adopting the newly developed hybrid seeds, applying for large quantities of fertilizer (nearly fifty times the amount used six years ago), learning how irrigation may be used more effectively and organizing rural cooperatives is still largely unreported in the world news media.

Consequently, not one "well-informed" American in a thousand knows that a "green revolution" has occurred; on the contrary, anyone who suggests that India, the so-called "bottomless pit," may be self-sufficient in food by 1971 or 1972 may expect to be labeled a crackpot (as indeed I have on several occasions).

Many years of experience abroad, much of it spent in Asia, has convinced me that the one best hope for peace and political stability in Asia lies in the willingness and ability of the major Asian nations—Japan, India, Indonesia and Australia—to work together toward common goals. The ability of strategically located India, with one sixth of all mankind and a deep commitment to democracy, to control its population, to feed its people, to expand its industry and to maintain its political unity is likely to be decisive.

If the United States is to contribute significantly to this development, it is essential that India develop a better understanding of the United States and the United States learn to understand India.

Consequently, during my eight years' service as Ambassador to India, I spent much of my time speaking to university students and government, labor, farmer and business organizations.

In the course of this effort I traveled tens of thousands of miles to every corner of India and talked to millions of everyday people. In addition, I contributed a regular column to the *American Reporter,* a publication of the United States Information Service with a circulation of 400,000. The column was also regularly reprinted in the Indian newspapers with a daily circulation of about 2½ million.

The speeches, articles and columns which have been brought together in "A View From New Delhi" represent my efforts as American Ambassador to give the Indian people and their government a better understanding of America's objectives in world affairs, the workings of our American democratic system and what we have learned by costly trial and error about economic development.

At the same time I have attempted to give the younger generation of Indians, to whom my writings and speeches were largely directed, greater confidence in their country and its future.

Whatever the value of my efforts, I am convinced that the problem of communications among people, both domestic and foreign, is, next to the control of population and nuclear weapons, the most important subject on earth.

Unless we can replace the current stereotypes with a better understand-

4

ing of each other, our world is headed for increased turbulence and bloodshed. If this occurs, the democratic dream of a more integrated world in which people of all nationalities, creeds, colors and religions learn to work together in peace will remain beyond our reach.

Chester Bowles

*Essex, Connecticut*
*July 10, 1969*

SECTION ONE

# An Agenda for
# Nation Building

*We have built infra-structure which will enable us to become a modern economy. We have built institutions to train the scientists and technologists who are the nerve-cells of such an economy... Compared to our starting point, we are in a much stronger position be it in agriculture, in industry, or in the social services.*

—Prime Minister Indira Gandhi

# 1. Five Essentials of Nation Building

*In a lecture at Delhi University in 1963 Ambassador Bowles outlined five requisites for rapid and balanced growth in a developing country: capital, incentives, skills, family planning, and national purpose.*

IN THE eighteen years since the end of World War II more than one billion and a half people in Asia, Africa and Latin America have embarked on an unprecedented adventure in nation building.

The objectives of this effort are broader than the building of roads, the development of industries and the production of more food. By and large they have been characterized by a sense of social purpose which is remarkable in itself.

With few exceptions the emerging nations, which have won their independence and carried out their domestic revolutions, have done so in the name of the universal values of personal liberty, racial equality, and the broad sharing of the benefits of development.

Although these values are often neglected in practice, they constitute a basic commitment which, I believe, reflects the deepest aspirations of a vast majority of mankind.

This commitment is so genuine that even totalitarian governments with little regard for individual rights feel obliged to pay homage to it as a matter of political necessity. One example is Mao Tse-tung's cynical acceptance in 1954 of the Panch Sheel as the future basis for Indo-Chinese relationships; another is Chou En-lai's endorsement of the libertarian principles of Bandung in 1955.

In addition to their common vision of the future the newly independent peoples face many common problems. For instance,

almost all are poor. They have had little or no access to the benefits of scientific technology. Almost all are undernourished. Many
are ill. Few are able adequately to educate their children.

Yet overriding these awesome difficulties is their fierce determination to improve their condition. The historian Arnold Toynbee
underscored this point in a recent article. "Our age will be remembered," he wrote, "not for its horrifying crimes or its astonishing
inventions but because it is the first age since the dawn of history
in which mankind dared to believe it practical to make the benefits
of civilization available to the whole human race."

As a result, the economics and politics of development, once
of interest to scholars, have moved to the top of the world's
agenda. The leisurely pace at which the United States and Europe
developed during the 19th century is no longer adequate to keep
ahead of the rising global demands for a better existence. This
means that governments will be pressed to strain every muscle and
to employ every resource to insure the economic growth and the
political and social justice which their people now expect
and demand.

Nor is the modern challenge of development confined to the
so-called "backward" continents of Asia, Africa and Latin
America. Within many of the most productive nations of Europe
and America there are still shocking contrasts of wealth and poverty
which are crying for attention. This is true in rural Greece, in
southern Italy, in parts of southern France, in certain sections
of the United States and in much of the USSR. Indeed, no major
nation can claim fully to have eliminated poverty or to have provided each of its citizens with the basic essential of every free society—
equality of opportunity regardless of race or religion.

Among the less developed nations we find a wide variety of
problems and opportunities. In much of Latin America, for instance, a major obstacle to the political and economic growth that
is basic to all free societies lies in the stubborn reluctance of the
more privileged groups to move with the times. Less than one
and one-half per cent of the people possess more than half of all
the land of Latin America; many own more than 15,000 acres.

In only a handful of Latin American countries is there an effective
income tax; in fewer still are there adequate limitations on the use
of scarce foreign exchange to pay for non-essential luxury imports

or even on the export of domestic capital for "safe keeping" abroad. Consequently, national per capita incomes which may appear satisfactory in themselves often hide shocking differences in income that breed bitterness and frustration among the under-privileged majority.

In Africa the major obstacles to rapid national development are different. Most rural land, for instance, is owned by the tribes and allocated to individual families on the basis of need and competence—a system which in many areas is now evolving naturally into modern democratic cooperatives. Since there is little entrenched wealth, opposition to taxes based on the ability to pay is not a serious problem. For years to come the major barrier to rapid growth in Africa will be lack of education, basic skills, administrative and management experience, and personal incentives.

In Asia we find still another set of difficulties, which vary widely from nation to nation. Among these, in several countries, are soaring population growth in relation to resources, rural apathy rooted in generations of exploitation or neglect, and among business groups an emphasis on trading and speculation rather than creative enterprise.

From this brief review it appears that every nation, rich or poor, has its own special agenda of unfinished business to which its government must soberly address itself. Our present task, however, is to isolate those special factors that affect the process of nation building in the less developed continents.

The experience of recent years has demonstrated that there are five requisites for rapid and balanced growth in a developing country. The first of these is material, while the other four relate to public attitudes and human capabilities. These five essentials are:

1. Adequate capital from both domestic and foreign sources.
2. Enough goods and services to persuade people to contribute the personal effort that development requires.
3. Adequate skills for management, administration, production and citizenship.
4. A willingness and ability in overcrowded nations such as India and Pakistan to curb a rapid population increase.
5. A unifying sense of national purpose with effective communication between the people and their leaders.

It was these five elements which permitted the amazing resurgence of Europe and Japan from the rubble and despair created by World War II. It is their creation in the developing nations of Asia, Africa and Latin America that must now be the first order of business for those who would raise living standards within an orderly political framework.

L ET US examine these five essentials in order, starting with the question of investment capital for development.

Inevitably most of the capital requirements of any nation must be met from indigenous resources, through increased private savings or through various forms of taxation and other governmental limitations on consumption.

While private savings in most developing nations will ultimately provide the major source of capital, deep-seated community attitudes usually have to be changed before this source can effectively be tapped. Only in a reasonably secure social and economic environment can people be persuaded to part with their gold ornaments, excess acreage and other traditional forms of financial security.

In most less developed nations, therefore, the capital requirements for the initial stages of the growth process must be met largely by the government drawing on a wide variety of tax sources. For instance, land taxes can be progressively increased on large holdings. This not only raises revenue; at the same time it encourages the development of more efficient family-sized farms. Sales and excise taxes can provide additional revenue and serve as a means for directing investment into selected capital projects.

Incomes can also be taxed on a progressive basis. The argument that a reasonably progressive income tax reduces the incentive for private investment does not stand up in practice. More than half a century ago when the United States first introduced such a tax, the cries of anguish were loud and clear. There is no evidence, however, that the income tax has damaged the productive capacity of the United States. Instead it has brought about a democratic redistribution of incomes which had created the mass purchasing power that has prodded our economy to ever higher levels of production.

There are clear limits, however, on the amount of domestic

capital that can be accumulated through taxation and restricted consumption. Those taxes which are easy to collect, like excise taxes and sales taxes, fall most heavily on the people least able to pay, and therefore reduce the purchasing power necessary to maintain minimum standards of living. The taxes which would benefit the economy most, like the income tax, are notoriously hard to collect. Moreover, because so few people in the developing nations have large incomes, this tax source is limited.

Although the export of raw materials may offer another major means of capital accumulation, such exports in themselves do not assure the broad-based economic development which we are seeking. The exports of coffee, tin, oil and other basic materials, for instance, have earned generous incomes for many Latin American producers. But because only a meagre fraction of the total income from these exports has sifted down to the people who work in the fields and mines, the gap between rich and poor has been steadily growing. In spite of the vast oil wealth of West Asia, the majority of the people still live in dire poverty.

In view of these limitations it is not surprising to find that almost every nation that has succeeded in modernizing its economy has had the advantage of loans and grant from more advanced countries. The pace of United States development in the 19th century, for instance, was speeded by massive amounts of private capital from Europe. By 1912, foreign investment totalled more than $ 6 billion—a huge sum for those days.

We must, however, keep this matter of foreign capital assistance in clear perspective. While it is a vitally important element in developing an adequate rate of economic progress in a democratic environment, ultimate success depends on the energy and effectiveness of the government and people of the recipient country.

For instance, the United States has provided loans and grants for many countries, which because they failed to carry their share of the burden, have remained in the economic doldrums. On more than one occasion we have seen our assistance used by reactionary governments to sustain the status quo against the forces of economic and social change which we had set out to encourage.

The nations in which United States assistance has been least effective have many common characteristics. In most cases the local tax structure has been inefficient and inequitable. Capital funds badly needed at home have been allowed to go abroad. Luxury imports have eaten up foreign exchange.

There has often been corruption in the government and lack of interest in the kind of development that benefits the masses of the people. Semi-feudal systems of land tenure have often suppressed the initiative of the cultivators and thereby impeded agricultural production, at the same time creating a bitter sense of injustice throughout the countryside.

On this essential point our experience is clear. Foreign capital makes a meaningful contribution to national development only in those countries which are willing and able to mobilize their own resources. In such cases foreign aid may provide the decisive margin for success. When the necessary effort is lacking, the effects of foreign aid may be virtually nil.

Much of the recent opposition to foreign economic assistance in the United States is misinformed and misguided. Its origin lies, however, in the valid conviction that my country has no obligation to provide funds for governments that fail to put their own economic and social houses in order.

I have profound sympathy for this view. Indeed, as a member of the United States Congress I proposed the establishment of operating standards that would relate our economic assistance to the capacity and willingness of the recipient country to use it and its own resources effectively.

Except in the most unusual political circumstances, I am convinced that economic assistance given on any other basis cannot possibly accomplish its only valid objective which, to repeat, is the creation of dynamic independent nations which offer their people increasing prosperity and opportunity within the framework of their own traditions and culture.

The challenge to develop better plans and techniques is a major one. The combined gross national income of the developed nations now totals $900 billion annually*. If one per cent of this amount were loaned or given each year to the less developed nations, the gap between the rich nations and the poor nations would be eased in a way that would profit both giver and receiver, add to

* This figure, based on 1961-1962 U.N. statistics, is now considerably higher.

the self-respect of each, and make our world an infinitely safer and better place for us all.

THIS brings me to the second of our five essentials of national growth; the need for adequate and equitably distributed rewards for hard work and initiative.

As we have seen, there is a political limit to the amount of taxation, austerity, or maldistributed wealth which people are willing to accept without either adopting evasive devices which corrupt the system and diminish confidence in the integrity of the government, or throwing the government out of office.

Totalitarian systems, to be sure, can enforce a higher rate of capital accumulation through a merciless squeeze on producers who are denied consumer goods while simultaneously being urged by blaring loudspeakers to make greater and still greater efforts in behalf of the state.

But even in the most rigid police state, slogans and loudspeakers have their limitations, as the Soviet Union has been learning by hard experience. After working for forty years to organize its national agriculture on a mass basis, the small kitchen gardens which Soviet farmers can really call their own still produce much more efficiently than the rigidly organized state farms where adequate personal incentives are lacking. Industrial workers in the Soviet Union are now offered wage and bonus benefits whose differential exceeds that of the American wage scale. Soviet factory production has responded to these incentives.

Thus, we see that regardless of political ideology, capital for development can be accumulated effectively over the long run only when all of the people stand to gain some immediate and tangible benefits. No developing nation with these factors in mind can afford to dismiss consumer goods and social services as frivolous embellishments which may be withheld in the interests of capital accumulation; on the contrary, such incentives, however modest in amount, act as an essential generator in increasing national wealth.

Moreover, the production of consumer goods such as bicycles, shoes, clothing, pots, pans, simple household equipment, flashlights and self-help housing schemes provide an essential source of jobs which in most developing countries cannot be provided in adequate amounts by heavy industry.

If the nation-building process is to succeed, the individual must be given an opportunity to improve his standard of living, as well as a sense of belonging of personal dignity and faith in the integrity and ability of his government.

W E NOW turn to the third essential for national development—skills for management, for production, and for citizenship. Administrative skills are, of course, in short supply in all developing nations, particularly so in those which are newly independent. Even where there is a competent civil service, as in India, there are too few people with experience in bold and creative policy making.

Equally serious is the lack of technical skills in most developing nations, particularly in Africa. For years to come there will not be enough competent doctors, teachers, engineers, architects, labour leaders, and other specialists to meet the increasing demand.

Like capital, these administrative and technical skills must be developed in large measure by the country itself with some assistance from its more advanced friends. Foreigners in public administration are usually out of the question for political reasons and there are simply not enough competent technicians available for service abroad. Foreign experts therefore should be used as a scarce resource and largely for the purpose of training local specialists.

Fortunately, a small amount of foreign technical assistance, like limited doses of foreign capital, can have a major impact on the developmental process. This is true, however, only if the host country makes substantial efforts on its own behalf to provide competent people for training, and to place those people who have been trained in positions of responsibility where their skills can have a continuing effect on the economy.

If newly trained technicians are assigned routine jobs where their initiative is crushed and if they are not encouraged to train their subordinates, no amount of foreign technical assistance will have a significant impact.

In democratic countries whose governments are based on the consent of the governed, the social change which accompanies development also requires the creation of new political and social skills among the citizenry as a whole. Skill in citizenship is more than just the ability to mark a ballot. It is the skill to dissent without revolution, to accept the compromise that may be necessary for a consensus while maintaining a sense of personal independence, and to cooperate with others for the improvement of one's village or nation.

Where these basic political abilities exist, there is potential for vital, democratic growth; where they are lacking, we can ultimately expect either turmoil or totalitarianism.

The colonial era has retarded the growth of these essential social and political skills in most of the less developed nations while simultaneously creating demands for changes in structure, direction and priorities which would tax the administrative capacities of the most advanced nations.

All of this underscores the importance of education as a first step in creating a sense of participation and individual responsibility among the masses of the people. A literate person can discover through the printed word the possibilities that life offers him. The vision of what he can accomplish for his family and himself serves as a most powerful incentive. The literate person can read instructions and develop simple technical skills through understanding rather than through rote learning.

Most important of all, the literates can be made aware of their rights and duties as citizens so that they need no longer be at the mercy of the deeply-rooted, tradition-conscious elements of their society which stand in the way of the political, economic and social changes which they seek.

Japan's phenomenal post-war growth would have been impossible, in my opinion, if it were not for the fact that over 98 per cent of her people can read and write. In most developing countries the figure is still under 30 per cent.

THE FOURTH of our five essentials of development—family planning—is of immediate, special importance in those emerging nations where a massive and growing population is pressing against limited natural resources. In many countries the problem does not yet exist.

Moreover, even in the more crowded nations there is little immediate danger of the mass starvation predicted by Malthus. With adequate fertilizer and more advanced techniques India, for instance, could triple its production of food from the present cultivated areas; and its opportunity for greatly expanded fisheries has scarcely been touched.

The real economic cost of continued rapid population growth in such already crowded nations as India, Pakistan, Ceylon, Indonesia and China stems from the drag it places on the increase in per capita incomes. In such countries a rate of economic growth which might otherwise give the average citizen a satisfying sense of progress only enables him to stand still.

Although India's national income over the last decade has grown at a rate nearly four per cent annually, the population increase of two and one-half per cent has reduced the per capita income increase to less than one and one-half per cent.

A major effort is now under way to bring India's population into better balance. In 1930 the birth rate was 48 per thousand; it is now 41.5 per thousand. In areas such as urban Bombay where a determined effort at family planning has been made over a period of years the birth rate is about 30.

Some authorities believe that if programmes and techniques now available are carried out effectively the birth rate by 1985 can be reduced to 25 per thousand against an anticipated death rate of 14. If this ambitious goal could be reached, India's present per capita increase in income will be doubled. If the birth and death rate can ultimately be brought into balance and the population stabilized, the present 4 per cent average annual increase in national output, compounded from year to year, would have a dramatic impact on living standards.

THE FIFTH and final essential involves the environment in which development takes place. The four prerequisites which we have just considered—capital, incentives, skills and family planning— cannot operate in a cultural or political vacuum. Each new nation must consider them within the framework of its own past experience, its present needs, and its own vision of the future.

Only when it does so can it develop the sense of national purpose which draws a diverse people together and provides a bridge of mutual understanding and respect between them and their leadership.

The United States is still in the process of realizing the political vision which the founders of our nation so eloquently proclaimed nearly two centuries ago. Our Declaration of Independence from Great Britain asserted that "all men are created equal." Its author, Thomas Jefferson, believed that "all eyes are opening to the thoughts of man... the mass of mankind was not born with saddles on their backs, nor a favoured few, booted and spurred, ready to ride them by the grace of God."

This deep belief in the importance of individual dignity initiated the world's first major anticolonial revolution and experiment in political democracy. Although our traditional objectives are not yet wholly secured, each succeeding generation of Americans has worked to broaden its base of individual freedom and opportunity.

India has her own vision of what she is determined to become. Gandhi saw that "what is good for one nation situated in one condition is not necessarily good enough for another, differently situated. India has got to develop her own economies, her own policy."

The keystone of the Indian vision is a belief in the supreme value of the individual human being. "In modern terms," Gandhi stressed, "it is beneath human dignity to lose one's individuality and become a mere cog in the machine. I want every individual," he said, "to become a full-blooded, fully developed member of society."

The deep suspicion of "bigness' and strong sense of social conscience which is reflected in the strict democratic teachings of Gandhi will continue directly and indirectly to shape Indian development for generations to come.

In the hands of leaders who are devoted to the cause of the whole nation, such vision is an effective instrument for progress. If the leadership can communicate a sense of purpose to the people so that it becomes a treasured national possession of them all, the battle for development can be won.

THESE then are the five basic essentials for rapid and balanced growth in a developing country, for growth which engages the energy and enriches the lives of every citizen.

Although I have been tempted to add a sixth essential—a pragmatic non-doctrinaire approach to economic growth—this prerequisite, implicit in our entire discussion thus far, will be discussed in the next chapter.

Developing nations which seek answers to their complex problems in some neatly packaged ideology are almost certainly doomed to failure. Capitalism as defined by Adam Smith and Communism as defined by Marx, Engels, Lenin and Stalin have become largely irrelevant in our complex modern world. The tasks of national development are difficult enough in themselves without confusing them further with emotionally charged slogans and political hand-me-downs from another era.

In meeting the challenge of national development India may on occasion borrow certain concepts and techniques from abroad— from Western Europe, from Sweden, from Yugoslavia, from Japan, and from America. Yet I believe that India will draw primarily on her own inner strength, experience, and traditions, relating these elements in her own way to the five essentials which I have described.

# 2. The Sterile World of Slogans

*In a series of columns in the* American Reporter *during 1966, 1967, and 1968 Ambassador Bowles urged economic planners to forgo outworn ideological slogans and to adopt pragmatic approaches to the problems of development.*

OUR MODERN world is moving too fast for slogans. No sooner is a new one conceived and popularized than events make it irrelevant. Indeed not only the slogans, but the ideologies which gave birth to them are largely irrelevant as well.

Consider Karl Marx, who insisted that the western world would come apart at the seams under the impact of urban class conflict and who virtually ignored the problems of the peasantry.

Marx's beliefs were the logical response of a great and good-hearted man to the economic and social evils of his time.

All around him he saw factory workers being exploited. He saw them living in city hovels with their children suffering from malnutrition. He saw them at the mercy of huge, impersonal industrial complexes with which they could neither bargain nor reason.

But with all his brilliance Marx had an important and costly blind spot. What he failed to see was the plight of the millions of European peasants whose existence was at least as precarious as that of the urban industrial workers.

Because he did not understand rural people, he failed to sense their passionate desire to own the land they tilled and their bitter hatred of the landlords who controlled their lives just as completely as the lives of the industrial workers were controlled by the owners of mines and factories.

Consider Lenin, who, building on Marx, saw the world doomed

to an eternal struggle between the colonialist exploiters and the exploited. In his Resolution of November 7, 1917, he urged the peasants of Russia to rise against the landlords and to take possession of the land they had tilled for centuries.

It was only after this decision had been translated into action that Lenin was satisfied that "the Revolution is now irrevocable."

But after Lenin came Stalin, and with him an era of forced collectivization and unprecedented mass suffering for the tens of millions of peasant families who lived on the land.

Consider Mao Tse-tung, who now threatens to destroy China in a wild effort to fit the slogans which he created forty years ago to a frustrated nation striving desperately to feed and clothe itself.

Mao based his revolution on the peasants, and the political result was explosive. In response to the Leninist slogan "land to the tillers," millions of young Chinese peasants and agricultural labourers flocked to join Mao's Communist armies.

It was the solid support of these peasants with visions of owning their own land that made possible his military victory over the Nationalist forces.

Yet soon after the victory had been won, Mao Tse-tung abruptly revised his policies. Fearing as Stalin had the political implications of a nation of small land owners, he moved ruthlessly to herd the tens of millions of newly freed peasants into highly organized communes which could readily be controlled by the central government.

In this way the same revolution which first offered land to the landless people of China was used to force the recently emancipated peasantry into a new form of bondage, more oppressive and more efficient by far than the one they had known before.

In the Soviet Union the recent trend has been in the opposite direction. Even though Soviet farmers still work huge collective farms, each is now allowed a small plot of his own, the produce of which he may use or sell as he sees fit. These small plots are highly productive.

History has proven that Marxism is unbalanced in its assumption that the farmer could be ignored in the process of revolutionary development. History has also demonstrated that Marxism is mistaken in its belief in the inevitability of "class struggle."

Marx maintained that in each nation a ruthless confrontation between the "exploited workers" and the "ruthless capital ists" were inevitable. Indeed, he firmly believed that it was only through the triumph of the urban "proletariat" that a society could be established in which the worker would be assured economic justice.

How astounded Marx would be if he could now visit modern industrial countries such as Sweden, Japan and the United States.

Instead of an "exploited proletariat" he would find workers with the power to bargain with their employers for higher wages and improved working conditions through their own organizations and on a basis of full political equality. He would see that even the lowliest can now rise to the top through ability and hard work.

Consequently, Marxist ideology, like all static and rigid dogma, is declining in its relevance to the task of the modern world, and the communists themselves are finding it of less and less value as a workable economic theory to fit the rapidly changing conditions of the twentieth century.

Nor has it been only the communist leaders who have gone astray. Take Adam Smith who built a whole theory of economics on the assumption that all problems could be solved by turning them over exclusively to the "market". Government, he thought, had a legitimate role to play except to conduct foreign policy and national defence.

Even our great radical democratic leader, Thomas Jefferson, saw no place in the future scheme of things for cities or for urban life. Jefferson's views on agriculture turned out to be almost as wrong as Marx's views on industrial capitalism.

TODAY, planners in both the developed and developing coun- tries are moving rapidly towards a new pragmatism. Their economic judgments are no longer based on ideological consis- tency but rather on the simple question: "What approach will pro- duce the most benefits for the most people?"

In today's world any government, regardless of its ideology, must accept responsibility for a wide variety of social and economic activities which, in the public interest, cannot be left to individual judgment.

At a minimum these activities include a national educational system, national public health programmes, communications, and transport, a national land policy, the allocation and collection of taxes, and the maintenance of law and order.

The second factor involves the developmental process. In any modern society, totalitarian or democratic, capitalistic or socialist, progress must necessarily be made by trial and error.

In a totalitarian society the inevitable mistakes which flow from this process are made and corrected in private behind a blackout provided by a government-controlled press.

In a democratic society, with its free press and wide open debate, mistakes in organizing and administering, economic and social development cannot be covered up.

In a democratic nation which chooses to follow old-fashioned, inflexible concepts of socialism that call for a maximum of direct government control, the government is exposed to a constant drum-fire of political harassment and criticism.

As each of its mistakes is eagerly denounced by a politically hungry opposition, civil servants and administrators become timid and freeze into rigid attitudes.

Thus, the already cumbersome process of bureaucratic decision making is further slowed and a damper placed on the vigorous spirit of innovation and experiment which in our modern era of advanced technology is a prerequisite of industrial expansion and individual progress.

This leads me to the following conclusions:

1. The record demonstrates that totalitarian socialism can produce steel mills, power plants and nuclear bombs. However, these gains are made at heavy cost in human dignity and social justice and with considerable inefficiency, notably in agriculture and in the consumer goods industries.

2. Democratic societies in which the government attempts in the name of doctrinaire socialism to direct almost all phases of economic life are doomed to stagnate under the inevitable outpouring of frequently irresponsible criticism.

3. The modern, realistic road to social and economic progress calls for the government to:

> Establish after democratic debate, a series of socially desirable national goals with standards by which to judge performance.

Encourage by means of incentives maximum production with penalties for economic behaviour which is contrary to the national interest. These incentives would include land ownership for the maximum number of rural familes, with government-guaranteed, low-interest loans for cultivators and small businessmen. Within this socially-oriented framework leave maximum scope for private initiative with competitive prices. When the government finds that it is necessary to go into the business of production, delegate this production to autonomous, government-owned corporations (such as our American TVA) each with its own board of trustees and management staff who are responsible to the government only for an efficient performance in the public interest.

In the last ten years the record shows that the most impressive increases in national production have taken place, not in the totalitarian nations, but in those countries which have combined adequate but not oppressive government control with maximum scope for private initiative.

Whether a country is large or small, whether it is developed or in the process of developing the outworn economic concepts of Marx, Lenin, Mao Tse-tung, Jefferson and Adam Smith are no longer relevant.

The meaningful questions for our modern age are the *pragmatic* ones: Does this specific technique benefit the community? Does it increase production? Does it open up new opportunities for more people?

The record shows that by and large people who live in democratic, pragmatic, socially conscious societies enjoy the highest living standards, and the greatest measure of individual freedom and social justice.

# 3. The Developing Nations' Most Urgent Need

*The greatest need of a developing country is a pragmatic balance between the public and private sectors. These articles by Chester Bowles appeared in the* New York Times Magazine *of April 12, 1964 and the* American Reporter *of July 27, 1966.*

AMONG thoughtful leaders in Asia, Africa and Latin America a soul-searching discussion of economic and political principles is now in progress.

How, they ask, can the rapid industrial growth which is essential to their national development be assured within a framework of social justice? Are these two objectives in perpetual conflict or can some means of achieving them simultaneously be found? And always in the background is the question that Lincoln asked: "Must a government of necessity be either too strong for the liberties of its own people or too weak to maintain its own existence?"

Although to Westerners the search for answers often seems contentious, utopian and unrealistic, it constitutes for the most part a genuine debate among honest and committed men who have undertaken an unprecedented task with uncertain guidelines.

In their younger years when they were struggling to free their countries from colonial rule, many of these leaders considered Marxism a ready-made solution to all social, economic and political problems. Now, as Presidents, Prime Ministers, parliamentarians and planners faced with the practical problems of creating viable new nations, they find the techniques of communism increasingly irrelevant to the day-to-day realities with which they are faced.

Since my return to India last July, I have met with many groups of students, among whom all shades of political opinion were represented. Although the give-and-take has often been vigorous, I cannot recall a single question that reflected a rigid Marxist conviction. Ten years ago in such discussions Marxism would have been the point of departure on almost every issue.

Yet the growing awareness among many Asian, African and Latin American leaders of the sterility of Marxism as a political-economic doctrine only creates a dilemma. While recognizing the material accomplishments of the private sector in Western Europe, Japan and the United States, these leaders are also conscious of the excesses which have invariably occurred during the adolescent stage of capitalistic growth. In their minds the black markets, the corruption, the speculation and the tax evasion which they associate with capitalism and which they now see flourishing in their own back-yards, are intellectually, politically and socially unacceptable.

It is these considerations that lead young Asian and African governments to seek an approach to economic and social development which will permit the rapid economic growth their populations demand without the social cost which our age condemns. While they no longer believe that the balance they want will be found in Marxism-Leninism or in Maoism, they are convinced that it does not lie in unrestrained capitalism either.

A GAINST this background of a restless and increasingly pragmatic search for answers let us consider a series of basic principles which may ultimately point the way to the dynamic economies of growth within a framework of social justice which leaders of the new nations are so earnestly seeking.

We may start with an obvious fact: In any developing nation, government must play a central and critically important role. Only through government planning, government capital and government supervision can many of the basic tools be provided which are required to start things moving—and moving in the right direction. For instance, the so-called infrastructure—the roads, rail transport, schools, power and the communications networks—are in large measure a governmental responsibility.

Even in the United States where private enterprise has played such a vital role, government has often been forced to carry a heavy share of the burden in these areas. One of the first acts of our new national Congress in the seventeen-nineties was to provide Federal subsidies to expand our merchant marine. In the eighteen-thirties the Erie Canal, the first effective transportation link between the east coast and the fast-developing new west, was built with public funds—borrowed in large measure in England.

Thirty years later the privately owned and managed American railroads were given massive Federal grants of public land to finance the unprecedented programme of railroad construction which so rapidly spanned the American continent.

Following the outbreak of World War II, the United States Government promptly took over the planning, control and much of the management of the economy. Today our Federal, state and local governments continue to subsidize railroads, shipping, airlines, housing, all levels of education, much scientific development, a large percentage of our agricultural output, hundreds of power plants and other enterprises.

Many American business leaders who shudder at the very thought of government owned and managed enterprise are now among the most enthusiastic recipients of government subsidies.

The nations of Africa, Asia and Latin America at the dawn of a new age, face a continuing emergency. Their people, pressed by poverty and aroused by the promise of the new technology, are in a hurry and anxious to catch up. In such circumstances, government planning, investment and management will inevitably have an even greater role to play than in the United States, where the foundations for more growth were created in the more leisurely atmosphere of the past.

Yet the experience of the last 15 years has demonstrated that, in a democratically-oriented developing nation, there are practical limits to the share of the industrial load that the government can effectively carry.

For instance, in the emerging nations of Asia, Africa and Latin America, administrative experience is rarely adequate even for such basic needs as education, electric power and transportation. The amount of capital that can be raised by taxation or government borrowing from the underprivileged majority is limited, and the well-to-do minority is very small. In many cases the left-over traditions of the colonial civil services place more emphasis on regulating the people than on creating opportunities for them to prosper and grow.

In regard to the direct management of government enterprises, democratically-oriented governments face an additional hurdle: In every industrial operation growth is dependent on thousands of day-to-day decisions, large and small, many of which require a trial-and-error approach. Any industrial manager who is unwilling to risk mistakes will almost certainly fail to create an efficient and expanding operation.

Here we run into a paradox. In a thoroughgoing police state this essential risk-taking process can proceed unhampered by opposition attacks. The managers of private enterprises in a democratic nation are also politically free to seek answers through experimentation, without regard for the second-guessers. When the inevitable mistakes occur, they are marked off against more profitable operations elsewhere.

But when mistakes are made in the public sector plants of a democratic society, the political opposition may be expected to belabour the party in power with charges of incompetence, corruption and worse. These attacks in turn undermine the administrative process on which further development depends. Civil servants anxious to avoid political chastisement for actual or alleged errors freeze into rigid attitudes. The already slow process of bureaucratic decision-making is further slowed and a damper placed on the vigorous experimentation which is essential to industrial expansion.

In the United States a few years ago the Ford Motor Company invested some $300 million in building a car called the Edsel, which, as it turned out, very few people wanted to buy. The company balanced its losses on the Edsel against more favourable investments elsewhere and that was the end of the story. I shudder to think of the political uproar that would have occurred if the ill-starred Edsel had been built by a government agency under a Democratic or Republican Administration. The party in power might have lost the next election.

Since conditions vary widely among the developing nations of Asia, Africa and Latin America, there can be no precise formula to govern the size and domain of the public sectors. But because of the awesome problems facing their governments, an increasing number now undertake in the public sector only those essential enterprises which cannot be financed through other means.

Nor is there a precise formula specifying how public enterprises can best be managed. The tendency in many new countries is to assign management responsibilities for publicly owned industries directly to the relevant ministries; thus steel mills are placed under a Heavy Industries Ministry, power plants become the responsibility of a Ministry of Power and so on.

The experience of Western countries with large public sector industries indicates that they inhibit creative and responsible management. Even the Soviet Union is now delegating considerable authority to the plant level and relying more on managerial initiative than on ministerial control.

Mr. C. Subramaniam, when he was India's Minister for Steel and Heavy Industries, initiated a bold experiment in decentralized management at two large public sector plants in India. His justification for this step contained an axiom which can well be applied to public sector enterprises in any nation. "The idea that public sector management can be so hedged about with checks and balances that mistakes cannot occur is mistaken. Effective management will always make interim mistakes. Mistakes are the price of progress. It is the end result that counts."

GOVERNMENT in a developing nation, as we have seen, has the primary task of setting national economic and social objectives, providing the capital and direction for the basic infrastructure, and creating other essential production facilities for which private capital may be lacking.

This leaves a vast area of the economy open for a vigorous private sector operating within a clearly defined framework of national objectives and social and economic justice. With the right balance of profit incentives and with respect for the public interest experience demonstrates that privately owned and managed industries can make a decisive contribution to national growth and well-being that cannot be duplicated by government.

Private enterprise can enter every nook and cranny of economic life. It can draw out and thrive upon small pockets of indigenous capital and skills which would otherwise remain untapped. Its competitive characteristics can help generate initiative, research and the development of new products and methods which invigorate the whole economy. It can provide opportunities for individual advancement to people whose chief assets are intelligence, experience and energy.

In addition, the prospect of reasonable incentives and political security can attract substantial amounts of private foreign capital, which in most developing nations are sorely needed to supplement foreign exchange reserves. To this may be added foreign experience in complex industries and modern marketing techniques that may sharply reduce the cost of distribution.

The self-regulating characteristics of the private sector are an additional factor which many developing countries are only beginning to appreciate. Privately owned and managed plants operating within the framework of the national plan more or less automatically shape production along the lines most acceptable to the consuming public. If people want bicycles, their willingness to pay for them provides a powerful inducement to their manufacture.

Conversely, the public's dislike of a special model is an automatic curb on additional production, at least of that particular bicycle at that particular price.

The fact of the matter is that no government is flexible enough to adjust itself effectively to consumer preferences which may vary from place to place and from year to year. The self-regulating market system guides the allocation of capital and skills to those products and services which the public wants, in the style and quality that it prefers. What appears on the surface to be a wasteful process of trial and error, as small entrepreneurs feel out the need of the public, is in fact a vital process of experimentation and growth.

Although this system of "control by the market" is usually associated with the democratic nations of the West, it is interesting to note that here as in other economic situations, the communist nations are being forced to adopt similar means. As the U.S.S.R. moves increasingly toward a consumer-oriented economy, its Government faces a growing dilemma. How can a totalitarian economic system with tight control from the top provide the wide and inviting consumer choices which are necessary to stimulate progress? In other words, what can the Soviet Government substitute for the relatively free market system of the West?

I believe that experience will demonstrate that there is no workable substitute. If this is so, the communist nations, as in the case of worker and management incentives, will again be forced to aban-

don dogma and to adopt the marketing mechanism of free consumer choices as the ultimate guide to consumer production. Although
this may cause Karl Marx to turn over in his grave, it will not be
for the first time.

THIS brings us to another point of profound significance. In
describing the potential role of private enterprise in a developing nation, I stressed that it must operate within a framework of
established national objectives and economic and social justice. But
how can such a framework be provided without creating a maze of
controls that foster the very stagnation we are striving to avoid?

The market mechanism is by no means a guarantee that free
enterprise will always function even in its own best interest, much
less in the public interest. Price-fixing monopolies can exploit
the public. Dishonest practices can lead to black markets and
tax evasion. Labour can be exploited. The task of a developing
nation, therefore, is not to forgo the creative aspects of free enterprise for fear of its excesses, but rather to find the means to discourage these excesses without discouraging responsible initiative.
This means that side by side with adequate profit incentives there
must be realistic rules laid down by government to ensure that
private energies will be devoted primarily to creative enterprise
rather than to speculation, and that the broader public interest will
be given the highest priority.

Through the process of democratic debate and adjustment we
in the United States have gradually established a system of regula-
tory laws and agencies which in the public interest police the activities of almost every segment of our private sector. Legislation
such as the Sherman Antitrust Act, the Food, Drug and Cosmetic
Act, the Clayton Antitrust Act, minimum-wage laws, tax laws and
workmen's compensation laws have served to domesticate American
capitalism, and to help turn it into a socially responsible force for
national growth.

We have succeeded in this delicate task of regulation without
stifling the initiative of our entrepreneurs. As a result most American
businessmen have come to see that what is good for the public is,
in the long run, also good for them.

FROM this discussion certain basic principles emerge. Private enterprise in a moral sense is neither more nor less to be preferred than public enterprise. With genuine encouragement, on the one hand and responsible regulation on the other, the private sector can provide a major share of the economic dynamism which is essential to national growth.

This means that the government can be freed for the primary task that it alone can accomplish—the spelling out of national priorities and the plans best calculated to reach them plus the creation of the all-important economic infrastructure of education, mass transportation and those basic industries for which private financing is unavailable.

Such a balance also allows struggling new governments to limit their political responsibilities for the day-to-day operation of much of the country's economy. This relieves them in a major degree from the harassment of an opposition in search of political issues.

Questions in regard to degree and emphasis will arise in different ways in different countries. They can only be settled by trial and error and by enlightened discussions.

What all developing nations must eventually achieve is a realistic balance between government planning and government investment in the essential infrastructure on the one hand, and the encouragement of a fast-growing, socially responsible private sector on the other.

Mature nations with socialistic objectives such as Britain and Sweden have long since struck such a balance. Having lost their doctrinal concern over private enterprise, they have learned to encourage it, to give it scope, while moulding it to the national objectives.

I believe that liberal-minded American businessmen may have a special role to play in the quest of the new nations which I have described. In our country the struggle to relate a rapid growth rate to individual dignity is an old and familiar one. Although Teddy Roosevelt and his trust-busting, Woodrow Wilson and his New Freedom, and F.D.R. and his New Deal may have faded into history, most American businessmen have learned to work successfully within the framework of social justice which these great leaders helped to create.

If our present generation of businessmen is in turn prepared to carry this philosophy abroad, the effect on industrial development in the emerging nations could be dramatic. Indeed, I am eager for the day when more American businessmen will be prepared to say to the governments of these nations:

"I am anxious to come to your country, to invest my money there, and to become a partner in your national development. Although I naturally expect the right to earn a reasonable profit, I want much more than that.

"For instance, I want to see you use the authority of democratic government for the benefit of the many rather than for the privileged few.

"I also want to see you distinguish in your tax system between the profits earned, on the one hand, by producing the goods that your country needs while simultaneously creating more employment for your workers, and speculative profits on the other, from land and other commodities which create neither national wealth nor jobs.

"I want to see your government build a solid infrastructure of electric power, transportation and schools.

"I want to see you crack down hard on tax evaders, black marketeers and those who sell government favours. I want to see you encourage by your legislation rising wages keyed to rising productivity rates and improved working conditions. I want to see you forbid the mislabelling of products, misleading advertising and price rigging.

"I want to see you help your farmers to buy the land they till so that their growing prosperity will make them better customers for the goods I am eager to produce and sell.

"I want to see you do these things because only then will you create the political and economic climate in your country which will provide a sound foundation for my own investment."

When the American businessmen begin to talk in such terms abroad, they will find themselves welcomed as creative participants in an economic revolution which can bring new opportunity, dignity and prosperity to the hundreds of millions of Asians, Africans and Latin Americans who are weary of sterile dogma and eager for pragmatic answers.

# 4. Priority for Human Dignity

*In an article in the September 1965 issue of the Inter-national Development Review Ambassador Bowles suggested that developing nations should channel the potential energies of idle men into more people-oriented developmental schemes.*

YEARS OF work and study in the developing nations have led me to two disturbing conclusions; first that economic planning in many developing countries is dangerously unrelated to economic and political realities, and second, that unless a better balance can be struck between material and human needs, intensified political unrest is inevitable.

Since the early 1950's, planners have concentrated largely on power plants, steel mills, refineries, railroads, bridges and the training of thousands of engineers and agronomists. With a few notable exceptions, they have given an ominously low priority to the welfare of the underprivileged masses whose hopes and fears, satisfactions and frustrations, are the key not only to political stability but to the developmental process itself.

In most cases this imbalance reflects the doctrinaire assumption that a choice must be made between hydro-electric dams and slum clearance, between more railroad cars and more shoes. The resulting decision to downgrade human needs is often rationalized by cliches such as "The poor have always carried the burden of development and always will," and "We are closing our ears to the demands of the present in order to build for the future."

In 19th century Europe and Meiji Japan, economic development was in fact achieved by denying the impoverished majority the means of better life and by diverting capital savings into the building of an industrial infrastructure. In the Soviet Union under Stalin this formula was carried to a ruthless extreme in the systematic regulation of every phase of economic and social life.

In the early stages of national development in Japan and European nations there may have been no alternative; in the communist countries there was no effective means of protest. But today we are living in a totally new political environment in which increased literacy, modern communications and the consequent awareness of new techniques are rapidly raising popular expectations.

As a result, we may expect to see new energies bursting up from the bottom of the social pyramid. Whether these movements in a particular nation degenerate into a snarling nationalism under right-wing military leaders, or become dominated by China or the USSR, or develop along constructive lines will be determined in large part by the amount of economic improvement, social justice and personal participation which each citizen experiences.

Does this mean that the developing nations must choose between long-term investment in steel mills or power plants, on the one hand, and more consumer goods on the other?

On the contrary, I believe that in many developing countries massive increases in consumer goods and services can be achieved side by side with burgeoning industrial growth. What is more, I believe that this can be done without significant inflationary pressure.

One of the least happy facts of human evolution is that even the harshest economic experiences must be relied and the most costly lessons relearned. Consider, for instance, our own recent economic experience:

Just thirty-three years ago fifteen million hungry, desperate, unemployed Americans were walking the streets in search of non-existent jobs, passing grocery stores overloaded with spoiling food for which there were few purchasers.

For three long years this incredible situation had gradually been developing with no significant effort to correct or even understand it. As our economy stood on the brink of collapse, most privileged Americans were content to remark that although the spectacle was indeed distressing, we could be sure that sooner or later "natural forces" would again combine to restore a reasonable economic balance; in the meantime, the primary need was for public patience.

By 1939 Franklin D. Roosevelt's New Deal had enabled us to expand our production, put several million people back to work, introduce a large measure of social and economic justice into American society, and establish a positive role for our Federal government in economic affairs. Yet the most basic problem of all remained unsolved: in spite of our still massive unfulfilled human needs, one out of every six able-bodied men and women was still unable to find a job.

Faced with this paradox, some influential economists concluded that our economy had permanently lost its capacity for rapid expansion. From now on, they said, a substantial amount of unemployment would have to be tolerated, while we applied ourselves to the task of sharing more equitably the limited production that we had.

Despite this widespread assumption of permanent economic scarcity, President Roosevelt called on the American people, shortly after Pearl Harbor, to produce five million tons of shipping a year and fifty thousand airplanes. Many of our economists and virtually all our businessmen agreed that while this might be a useful psychological gambit with which to worry the Japanese and the Germans, as a practical matter it was reaching for the moon.

But again the Cassandras proved wrong. Within two years we went well beyond Mr. Roosevelt's targets to produce twenty million tons of shipping and nearly one hundred thousand planes. Moreover, at the height of the war effort in 1942, 1943 and 1944 we added to our massive military output more civilian goods than in any previous years.

Thus under pressure of a world war Americans came to see what we had failed to understand in peacetime: that there is no earthly reason why unfulfilled human or capital needs should exist side by side with idle manpower, idle tools, idle skills and idle capital.

MANY planners and political leaders in developing countries assert that the American experience which I have described is irrelevant to the situation which they face. According to their thesis, raw materials and skills are so scarce in their countries that any significant increase in the production of consumer goods for the masses would inevitably slow down the development of heavy industry, power plants and transport. And even if more consumer goods could be added to current production, it could only lead to runaway inflation.

In my opinion, these objections are defeatist and mistaken. On the contrary, I believe that an improvement in living standards will introduce into the lives of the people a new element of hope and purpose which can actually increase the rate of industrialization with no significant growth in inflationary pressure. The solution lies in mobilizing the idle manpower, tools, and machinery and unused indigenous resources that are now readily at hand to provide the additional elements needed for more balanced national development.

If the common man in Asia, Africa and Latin America were pressing for a flood of complex and costly consumer durables such as refrigerators and washing machines, it would be a different matter. In that case his demands could be met only by diverting skills and raw materials from heavy industry. His present needs, however, are relatively simple and can largely be met from resources that are in abundant local supply.

Every villager and urban worker, for instance, would like an extra dress or sari for his wife. There is unlimited need for shoes. Most rural families would like to replace their leaky, inflammable straw roofs with tile, to buy two or three new beds, a smokeless stove, better cooking equipment and most of all a clean home built of good lumber, stone or bricks.

Each of these needs can be met with materials and production skills which are now at hand. Even if we should add more transistor radios and bicycles, the drain on foreign exchange and the diversion of indigenous resources from heavy industry would be insignificant.

Moreover, in many industrializing countries sophisticated machinery lies idle for a large part of the time because there is not yet sufficient consumer purchasing power to absorb the volume of output which it is designed to produce. Fuller use of these plants and equipment would result from increased personal incomes together with governmental policies that encourage rather than inhibit growth.

Another major opportunity lies in the field of housing. Although visitors to developing countries are often impressed by the number of new building projects which surround many cities, a closer look would reveal that most of the building is for upper middle income families while the needs of the slum-dwellers are largely ignored. Yet when asked why the slum problem is not tackled more boldly, many planners answer, "Because there isn't enough cement, bricks and lumber."

When we faced a comparable situation in America during the war, we put first things first. If some families had to move in with their mothers-in-law, we determined that it should be those who already had the most space. Therefore, regulations were established which provided that no home could be built that cost more than $6000; and no commercial or government building could be constructed with scarce building materials unless it could be demonstrated that it contributed to the national welfare.

If developing nations were to adopt an equally egalitarian approach, it has been estimated that the existing amounts of cement, lumber and steel would provide clean, adequate new housing with running water for five or six times as many families and at the same time create additional jobs for lakhs of workers. Moreover, in most countries there is no reason why the present supply of building materials cannot be shar lyincreased. Ample supplies of clay for brickmaking are available in most areas, and cinder blocks can often be produced even more cheaply than bricks.

A similar challenge is posed by the paradox of idle manpower and natural resources side by side with massive capital needs. As the eminent Columbia University economist, Ragnar Nurkse, pointed out, "By far the greater part of a country's real capital structure consists of objects that require local labour and local materials for their production or construction."

For instance, almost every rural area of Asia and Africa is in urgent need of better roads, of dikes to hold back the flood waters, irrigation canals, schools and health clinics, which would contribute directly to improved standards of living and require virtually no expenditure of foreign exchange. Yet the means to produce these improvements are now lying idle on every side—landless labourers without jobs, half-used tools, indigenous raw materials and undeveloped skills.

In Tunisia, Morocco, Mexico, Pakistan and several other countries hundreds of thousands of unemployed workers have been mobilized in public works projects to meet this situation. Through skilled and dedicated leadership, good organization and a wise choice of projects, remarkable gains have been achieved— with the wages in some cases provided by the sale of surplus American PL 480 wheat and cotton.

In India a start along these same lines has been made in Rajasthan and West Bengal. With imaginative planning and able administration four or five million unemployed or partially employed Indians could be given jobs for at least half of the year, with the bulk of their wages paid in PL 480 surplus foods.

Moreover, the opportunities for expanded public works are not confined to rural areas. In every city there are sewers to be dug, streets to be widened, fresh water systems to be introduced.

In crowded, restless Calcutta the Metropolitan Planning Organization, with the assistance of a Ford Foundation team of American specialists, has offered a breathtaking vision of the possibilities. The Metropolitan Plan calls for rebuilding vast sections of Calcutta, clearing away the slums, and modernizing the transportation system. Once underway, this programme could employ tens of thousands of people for several years and ultimately turn one of the world's most tragic slum cities into a place of relative dignity, comfort, and good feeling.

In Venezuela, the housing deficit is being tackled by the government in cooperation with private efforts launched by development-conscious businessmen. The effort includes a rural housing programme which provides homes on a no-down-payment, 20-year mortgage basis within reach even of some semi-employed workers. Complementary sanitation and community development programmes augment the ranks of those employed in the housing effort, provide an outlet for the talents of the literate lower middle-class, and build responsible citizenship among the aid recipients.

UNFORTUNATELY, the governments of most developing nations mistakenly assume that money spent to provide employment on people-oriented projects of this kind is money which cannot be spent on industrial development. Yet the evidence seems to me conclusive that vastly increased employment of men and locally available materials in public works and in the production of consumer goods not only does not hinder development in other sectors, but in fact makes an essential contribution to overall economic growth.

What of the second argument of those who oppose bolder development planning—that expanded consumer goods production and heavy government spending on public works will inevitably lead to inflation ?

No one questions the need to prevent runaway prices in a developing country or anywhere else. However, inflation should not be permitted to become a political bogyman that blocks the process of economic growth. If Japan, Germany and other war-torn countries had allowed fear of inflation to dominate their post-war planning, millions of workers would still be idling in the ruins of Hamburg and Tokyo or standing in government bread lines.

Inflation occurs when rising incomes after taxes are not matched by comparable supplies of attractive consumer goods at fair prices. One way to keep prices from soaring is to remove the excess income by massive increase in taxes. The other is to provide a flood of consumer goods on which the excess income can be spent.

Too much emphasis on the first of these techniques condemns large sections of the people to squalor, unemployment and despair, while heavy stress on the second lowers unemployment, raises living standards and creates an atmosphere of hope, national participation and dedication. Moreover, the production of more consumer goods means that a normal tax rate will produce substantially higher income tax returns.

Simple types of consumer goods which require readily available indigenous materials are ideally suited to soaking up the added incomes which a bold programme of human resource utilization would generate. The net result will be more for everyone, and a generally quickening tempo of economic development.

Food, of course, is the most basic of all consumer goods, and ample supplies are needed to forestall inflation, to provide a better life for the masses and to assure more vigorous economic growth. As in the case of public works, however, there are no inherent contradictions between increased food production, greater employment, the use of idle resources, the manufacture of more consumer goods, and industrial development as a whole. In fact all of these elements of a dynamic society can be made to support and stimulate one another under the guidance of a bold and creative national leadership.    Let me illustrate this mutual relationship with several examples.

A N IMPROVEMENT in rural productivity is one of the major keys to large-scale increase in national purchasing power—increases which, in turn, will stimulate demand for many new lines of urban-produced consumer goods.   In order to realize profits, industrialists in many developing countries have looked primarily to the high-priced, upper-class city markets, capitalizing on the demand in those markets for durable consumer goods—refrigerators, electrical appliances and other products of high-income living standards.   Even a slight rise in rural income can generate good profits for producers of goods such as shoes, clothes, processed foods, and pots and pans—goods in demand by the whole of the population, not just a privileged minority.

A rise in rural productivity also means a more, better and cheaper foods and fibres for urban as well as rural consumption. When food costs fall, the worker has more to spend on other goods.   Most of the world's population is waiting for the chance to buy an extra pair of shoes, a toy for a child, a roof for the house, a bar of soap.   When that demand is released by lowered food costs, entire economies can receive a major boost, and life becomes a little more hopeful and attractive for the millions who have had to scrape too long just to stay alive.

Increased food production means that foreign exchange, which many developing countries must now spend to import additional food supplies, can be invested to industrialization.   Developing countries which are already self-sufficient in food can expect to earn additional exchange by exporting whatever extra food they can produce.

Another example is the way in which public investment in projects like canal-building and roads contribute directly to increased agricultural production as well as employment.   Water from the canals raises the yield of the fields.   The new roads make it possible for the farmer to bring in fertilizers, which again increases his yields, and to market his produce more cheaply.

Moreover, as cultivators use more pesticides and fertilizers (creating incidentally, demand for industrial goods), the initial need may be for more labour, not less.   The expansion of agricultural output also means more jobs in the production of tools, materials, and simple machinery as well as more employment in the marketing of the agricultural output.

Additional farm production will be forthcoming only if the cultivators are given clear incentives to work longer hours and to use the new farming techniques. This means giving each cultivator a direct personal stake in the success of his farming operations—which in turn means ownership of his own land. It also means assuring him a fair minimum price for his produce and providing him with a choice of consumer goods at fair prices on which to spend his increased income.

The communists have failed in agriculture largely because they neglected these basic incentives. Japan, on the other hand, provides a dramatic example of the integral relationship among individual land ownership and increased agricultural output, consumer goods production, employment, industrialization, and a general improvement in the lot of the common man.

The key elements of Japan's extraordinary economic success was a comprehensive land reform programme and the introduction into the rural areas of small manufacturing plants using indigenous materials.

The Japanese experience underscores the fact that every move that helps to improve the lot of the masses of people—urban as well as rural—broadens the market for manufactured goods. It also demonstrates that inflationary pressure can be contained by matching the extra income created by expansion of capital investment and such free service as public schools with ample supplies of consumer goods plus a moderate, progressive tax system.

Let me conclude by stressing once again that I am not urging developing countries to forgo heavy industry for more consumer goods, nor am I suggesting an exercise in inflationary brinkmanship.

But I deeply believe that the governments of the developing countries and those who are striving to help them can no longer afford to dismiss poverty, slums and squalor as a normal part of the Asian, African and Latin American landscape while busying themselves with the building of vast power dams in the hinterland. Idle men and idle tools must be recognized for what they are: a miserable, unforgiveable, unnecessary insult to human dignity and a brake on national growth.

# 5. The Question of Personal Involvement

*As people sense the fast growing opportunities made possible by modern technology, political turbulence grows. In these excerpts from his 1967-1968* American Reporter *columns Ambassador Bowles asserted that the only effective answer is more personal involvement in the process of production and community affairs.*

PERHAPS the most striking development of our times is the mass unrest which is now evident in almost all nations, both in those which are highly advanced and in those which are in an earlier stage of economic growth.

In India, as in other Asian, African and Latin American countries, there is widespread political turbulence, stemming from a variety of causes and expressing itself in many different ways. In China, this turbulence has gone beyond all reasonable bounds.

In the affluent United States, riots have occurred where Negro citizens feel deprived of complete equality and a full measure of opportunity, and where students press for more involvement in local and national affairs.

Although this global phenomena has inevitably created confusion and fear, I wonder if it does not reflect the churning of economic, social and political forces which hold enormous promise for mankind?

In the last generation fantastic new technologies have been tearing old societies apart and upsetting the traditional rhythm of individual lives. Thus the vast development of electric power is bringing dramatic changes to industry and easing our daily burdens.

Buses, motor cars and scooters are providing us with a new mobility. Man-made satellites high in the heavens relay pictures, news and ideas to all parts of the world.    By jet airplane, we can now fly from New Delhi to New York in less than 24 hours.

These and other technological developments have already provided better housing, better food, better health, more comfort and more leisure for several crores of people.

But even more important from a sociological and political point of view, they have created a new sense of hope in the hearts and minds of hundreds of millions more whose eyes have been opened to the possibility of advances which their grandparents had not even dreamed of.

The result is a vast wave of rising expectations sweeping across the world, encouraging people of all ages, races, occupations and nationalities to believe that poverty, ill-health and slums are in fact man-made evils which can and must be eliminated.

But let us not make the Marxist mistake of assuming that these expectations are concerned only with immediate material gain.

The American Negro is also demanding a more generous measure of dignity and self-respect; so are the Harijans of India, the slum-dwellers of Brazil, and their counterparts in every other country.

This brings us to a critically important point: every history student knows that it is not the most downtrodden and the exploited who protest most violently, but rather those who are beginning to sense the possibility of something better.

In the depths of the United States depression of the 1930's, with fifteen million people out of work, the masses were apathetic, frightened and politically immobilized.    It was when they began to go back to work and to feel a new sense of security and hope that mass unrest and violence made itself evident.

Over 130 years ago, the French student of democracy, Alexis de Tocqueville, described this process in the following words:

"Only great ingenuity can save a prince  who undertakes to give relief to his subjects after long oppression.   The sufferings that are endured patiently, as being inevitable, become intolerable the moment it  appears that there might be an escape.   Reform then only  serves to reveal more clearly what still remains oppressive and now all the more unbearable; the suffering, it is true, has been reduced, but one's sensitivity has become more acute."

De Tocqueville was saying that people who at last have caught a vision of what their lives and their children's lives might become will vigorously reach for that future here and now. I find something enormously hopeful in this rising expectation of the masses throughout the world.

THE world-wide student movement illustrates these high hopes. We should welcome the enthusiasm and desire for a better world by young people, even though we may deplore the occasional outbreak of ugly violence.

For example, on a recent trip to the United States, I visited the campus of my alma mater, Yale University, in New Haven, Connecticut, which incidently was named after Elihu Yale, one of the early British Governors of Madras when both India and what is now the United States were British colonies.

I was impressed not so much with the students' concern against the injustices of modern society—which I expected and indeed share—but by their positive, action-minded approach to the future.

Students throughout America, India, Germany, Poland, Japan, France, and almost all other countries are expressing their disapproval in a variety of ways, many of which are politically explosive and disruptive.

This widespread student activism has raised an important question for every democratic society; how can the efforts of students to promote urgently needed social change be pressed within a democratic political and social framework?

Student efforts to reorder their universities, their societies, or even the international community is a profoundly encouraging development. Concern for injustices and a willingness of millions of individuals to act on that concern is the most basic strength of a democratic society.

In America the movement is being directed against bigness: against big governments, big corporations, big labour unions, big universities and particularly their lack of involvement in the life of the countries in which they exist. Above all the movement is against our increasingly complex society, which has left the individual with a decreasing sense of identity and purpose.

The special target of the college students is the university administration which often seems to them impersonal, inflexible and arbitrarily controlled by fund-raisers, inaccessible deans, trustees and faculties that have become out of touch with the young people whom they are seeking to educate.

Consequently, students are demanding a greater share in managing their university's affairs, in the choice and development of courses, in new methods of teaching, in the selection and promotion of faculty members, and in the general administrative machinery.

They are, in effect, striving for greater participation for themselves in the educational process, in order to bring education from kindergarten to graduate school in line with their needs, ambitions, objectives and requirements.

In its longer perspective this protest of youth reflects a quest for new human values and standards to fit a new age.

Indifference cripples democracy. Only through active, purposeful participation by all its citizens can democracy legitimately be described as a government "of the people, by the people, for the people."

Certainly there was never a period in world history when bold, fresh thinking was so urgently needed. The old world, with its restrictive habits of mind and its short-sighted thinking, is now being drastically challenged by modern production and communication technology. These have opened the minds of the new generation to opportunities which are far beyond the dreams of their grandparents.

Much of the responsibility for achieving an orderly and creative transition rests on people under thirty years of age. From many years of observation I have become convinced that, with some important exceptions, relatively few men and women over forty come up with fresh and creative ideas. What they do—and many do it superbly well—is to develop more persuasive ways to restate their original concepts and to relate them to new situations.

As long as their views remain generally relevant, they can continue to make an important contribution to their fellowmen. But in an era of rapid, fundamental change they are apt to be left far behind.

For this reason we can be thankful that an increasing number of student activists in India, Europe and America are showing a keener awareness of the developing new political issues.

Unfortunately and perhaps inevitably in some cases, the less responsible students, instead of concentrating on the urgently needed changes, have focused on turning their campuses into a political battle ground.

Although such students may be claiming the privilege of dissent, in fact they often seek through militance to impose their will on a reluctant majority.

Older people may be irritated by their unruly behaviour and the blanket indictments they launch at those who are in positions of power. But whether or not these elders approve, they should not, and indeed cannot, ignore the voices of responsible young people who are determinedly seeking better answers to the problems of our anguished societies.

However, students who rightly identify with the under-privileged have an opportunity to develop new techniques for attacking poverty and backwardness and to develop strategies for peaceful social change.

The university, so often the focal point of student criticism, can be a vital force in promoting active student participation in building a more prosperous democratic society.

For example, the new thrust of American higher education, education-in-action, will allow students of economics to spend less time worrying about the theoretical dangers of deficit financing and instead to relate their work and studies to the way in which a neighbourhood can serve itself by organizing cooperative housing projects.

It is by responsibly and urgently challenging the old order and by avoiding the trap of sterile political slogans, that the greatest progress towards reducing poverty, expanding democracy and promoting development can be made.

Whether an individual lives in a developing country or a developed one, the stress, as they see it, should be on the quality as well as the quantity of life, on the development of an economic and social system through which goods and services can be distributed more justly and in which more young people, and older people as well, actually participate in the life of the community.

This, they assert, calls for more decentralized societies in which major decisions are made not by distant governments and institutions but by people who are most closely involved.

They are protesting an imperfect world brimming over with economic and social injustice. The response of those who are more fortunate than they should not be to retreat in fear, but to join with their fellow-men in seeking ways to conquer poverty and eliminate injustice.

ON ANOTHER plane, however, we often hear frustrated young Indians express this thought:

"It's true that other Asian countries, such as Japan, Malaysia, Taiwan and South Korea, have made fantastic progress in economic development. But it doesn't follow that India can match their achievements. Our national character is different."

As I listen to such gloomy observations, I am reminded of the similar scepticism with which many Americans looked to the future of their own country only a few generations ago.

In 1845 one pessimist wrote: "In the four quarters of the globe, who reads an American book? Or goes to an American play? Or looks at an American picture or statue?

"What does the world yet owe to American physicians or surgeons? What new substances have our chemists discovered? Or what old ones have they analyzed?"

However, within a few years, Walt Whitman, an eloquent spokesman for the new American democracy, published his magnificent book of poems, *Leaves of Grass*. By 1885 everyone in England was reading the books of the American author Mark Twain. Since then there has been an ever-increasing flow of art, poetry, music, writings and scientific contributions from eminent Americans.

The United States has thus belied the gloomy predictions of the pessimists. After a slow start we have opened up a great continent, created the world's most advanced industry, absorbed 40 million immigrants from Europe and Asia and provided undreamed of opportunities for tens of millions of people.

This does not mean that the American national character has basically changed. We have simply found a way to release our slumbering potential by giving an increasing number of our people in all walks of life a sense of involvement and a stake in local and national affairs.

This same dynamic potential is present in all nations—both in the East and in the West. Three generations ago, Japan was essentially a feudal society with a tradition-bound population. Led by a massive exercise of national will, Japan has literally transformed itself to become one of the four leading industrial nations of the world.

History overflows with equally striking reversals of what was once glibly described as "national character."

In the 18th century, the French were generally said to be so preoccupied with "orderliness" that they could never hope to break new ground. Contemporary historians considered the English, on the other hand to be a turbulent people.

Then, after the French Revolution, the French were described as "turbulent," the English as "disciplined".

A few generations ago the Germans were said to be so backward that railways were thought to have no future there. With unification in 1871, that country went on to become one of the most dynamic technological nations in the world.

Here in India, I now sense similar stirrings. Millions of young Indians are rightly proud of their country's great past and are eager to put their energies to work in creating a modern and dynamic India in which increased production will go hand in hand with increasing economic and social justice.

The most dramatic recent examples are in agriculture and family planning. Three or four years ago many Indian and foreign observers were asserting that rural India could never be persuaded to adopt modern agricultural practices. Yet, today we see Indian cultivators competing with one another in their eagerness to secure and use new improved seeds, fertilizers and pesticides.

In a similar spirit, India is now coming to grips with the problems created by its rapid population growth. Less than three years ago the State and Union Governments launched what is by all odds the biggest family planning programme ever attempted.

These are some of the reasons why, whenever I hear people lamenting India's alleged "inability" to reject traditional habits of mind and to create a dynamic, modern nation, I think of the eager young Indian cultivators and civil servants; of India's new generation of engineers, scientists and teachers and of the dynamic industrialists and small businessmen who are eager to build a new India—progressive, independent and self-sufficient.

What these people seek above all is a sense of involvement and personal growth in the development of their societies. They will not be content with the role of onlookers. They are determined to become political participants, striving for a more just society, one providing a greater opportunity for all its citizens.

# 6. Education: Cornerstone of a Just Society

*Addressing the Calcutta University convocation on February 14, 1964, Chester Bowles advocated an educational system which creates the skills required for a dynamic nation. He also discussed the relationship between education and economic development.*

INDIA AND America have had many experiences in common. For instance each of our countries inherited from its colonial past a system of education designed principally for a small, cultured ruling elite.

However, both nations are now committed to an educational system which creates among both young and old the skills they need to play productive roles in their societies; a system that promotes attitudes which will welcome fruitful and, when necessary, radical social change; a system that will engender the understanding required to draw diverse peoples together in the complex effort of nation-building.

A brief look at the American experience with public education may be helpful for some of the lessons which we have learned in the last century. Our mistakes as well as our successes are quite relevant to the present-day educational plans and policies of India and many other developing nations. After discussing these lessons, I would like to examine in more general terms the relationship between education and economic development.

During the 18th and 19th centuries, the colleges of America were primarily concerned with training young men for the professions of law, divinity, medicine, and government. Students at these colleges came from private secondary schools which catered to a small fraction of the people and were almost wholly devoted to preparing privileged students for admission to the colleges.

As early as 1779 Thomas Jefferson had stated, when introducing his "bill for the more general diffusion of knowledge" in the Virginia State Assembly, that public education should "avail the state of those talents which nature has sown, as liberally among the poor as the rich, but which perish without use if not sought for and cultivated."

But not until after 1840 were substantial beginnings made on providing free, public, primary education. Not until after our civil war in the 1860's was significant progress achieved in public free secondary education. And only in the closing decades of the last century did our state universities, liberally subsidized by federal grants of land, begin to shape the educational system to meet the needs of the mass of people and of the developing nation.

Indeed, not until the late 1940's, after World War II, did the American people fully recognize the vital role which education had already played and must continue to play in the economic and political evolution of our country. When the United States became seriously concerned with the problems of the developing countries of Asia, Africa and Latin America, we began to view our own history more clearly.

For the first time we understood that our educational system, which we had tended to regard as a fortuitous consequence of economic progress, had been, in fact, a dynamic and indispensable cause of our political and economic maturity. We realized, for example, that one role of our education system had been to bring together people of national origins and religions as diverse as those of India and to help them to learn to live in mutual respect.

Consequently, we now cherish the hope that the new nations can draw on our experience wherever it fits their needs and will not have to tediously re-enact all our errors.

THE first and foremost lesson our experience offers is that the curriculum—the content of education—must at each level relate to the needs of the nation. Education is the most powerful of all our tools for controlling and shaping the forces of nature and creating an orderly, dynamic and just society. It must do much more than simply satisfy the intellectual and aesthetic tastes of a minority of scholars.

Concretely, the subject-matter taught in the schools should nourish in the young people skills and attitudes which will be useful in their life and work as well as helpful in broadening their horizons.

For instance, the primary schools in the villages of India (as in rural United States, or Nigeria, or Colombia) can and should become centres of community life. The pupils should devote their attention not only to learning the basic skills of reading, writing and arithmetic, but also to the fundamentals of community organization, health, and sanitation, care of animals, and modern but simple agricultural techniques.

Each school could have its own "garden plot" in which even the youngest children learn the value of fertilizers, hybrid seeds, and irrigation and, through these, begin to develop the spirit of experiment and innovation.

Such an approach is of special importance in the early years of school because the drop-out rate is so high. Just as in the United States at the turn of this century, India is now losing a majority of its school-goers before they complete primary school. Without some practical training these youthful drop-outs lack the rudimentary skills and attitudes required to alter age-old social and economic patterns, or for that matter, to make democracy work.

A curriculum which strongly emphasizes the physical and social science and teaching of practical skills and attitudes is sometimes falsely described as "materialistic". In my view, nothing could be less materialistic than an educational system frankly designed as a means of raising human beings out of the mud, squalor and backbreaking toil in which tens of millions of them are now submerged.

To plan such a curriculum, to obtain the proper text-books and other equipment, and to train teachers to handle the new substance is an immense challenge. But to ignore this challenge or to compromise with halfway measures will gravely inhibit the nation's process of development.

In this light, the present disagreement over the meaning of Gandhi's concept of basic education is disheartening. The critical point is that the union of "hand work and head work," in which Gandhi was deeply interested, or what used to be called "mental and manual labour" in the United States, should be built into every sound education system.

THE second important lesson we learned over a long period of time in the United States is that both the curricula and the methods of instruction must stimulate the ability of each student to solve problems and to think creatively. It took us in the United States many generations to outgrow the undeviating pattern of set text-books and repetitive class recitations.

This lesson grows out of what is probably the most difficult area of educational theory: the inter-relations of motivation, memory and reasoning.

I suppose that in a society which is absolutely static—in which there is not only no change, but no desire for change—in such a society the appropriate educational system might be content with memorizing the details of the past, since no more than this would be needed as a base for present action or future plans.

Although there have been educational systems which resembled this model, in this revolutionary age of change and challenge they make no sense whatsoever. The passing of uniform examinations, testing the accumulation of data may produce prodigious feats of memory, worthy of an electronic tape recorder, but they are unworthy of the human mind. In such a system, the passing of examinations and the acquisition of degrees become a substitute for the powers of reason, and no such substitute is adequate.

In a country in which rapid economic and social change is already well under way, in which economic development and social progress are deeply felt national needs, and in which the substitution of a broadly based political democracy for a narrow ruling elite is a central objective, an educational system based exclusively on rote learning and degree-hunting spells failure.

The true hallmark of an educational system designed for a dynamic society is its emphasis upon cultivating the ability to solve problems; to sift and classify data; to stimulate curiosity; to ask critical questions; to make new combinations of old facts to challenge accepted authority and tradition; to create useful generalization; and to apply principle to cases.

I agree that this is a tall order. Indeed, it is an order which cannot possibly be filled unless the student is highly motivated to face the difficult task of using his head to think. Under these circumstances, it is too much to expect that young men and women will be so motivated unless the contents of the curriculum which guides their studies are relevant to the life which lies ahead, both for the individual and the nation.

This is just as true of the village primary school as it is of research laboratories. If the educational process is to be the profoundly important instrument of human progress that we expect it to be, it must appeal directly to the lives, and hopes of those engaged in it.

It follows that the dynamic educational system, I am describing, requires soundly trained teachers who themselves are not bound by rigid attitudes, and who will encourage their students to show initiative, imagination and insight. The curricula and teaching materials must be sufficiently flexible so that these teachers have the opportunity to welcome and reward venturesome young minds. Such minds are vital in the process of national development.

The shift of emphasis from degree-hunting to problem-solving may also require some changes in the specifications which government and business impose upon applicants for employment. To a distressing extent the pursuit of degrees, instead of being a search for knowledge, may become a desperate struggle for jobs.

As long as the possession of a degree is specified as a condition for securing a position, this is bound to be true in greater or lesser degree. But if public and private enterprise established their own tests for the skills, knowledge and attitudes truly necessary in each occupation, the focus might shift from memorizing data to learning to cope with the overriding problems of living in a changing world.

THE third significant lesson which emerges from our experience in the United States is that a nation must maintain a careful balance between primary, secondary and higher education.

The political and humanitarian pressures for universal, free primary education are nearly irresistible in many of the developing countries. At the upper end of the educational ladder, the prestige associated with universities and research institutions tends to focus attention and resources upon them. The result is that the secondary schools are squeezed between the pressures for primary and university education.

Yet, the secondary schools are the backbone of a nation's educational system. As such they must be prepared to serve three vital functions:

(a) They must provide the teachers for the primary schools;

(b) They must provide a terminal education specifically directed toward fitting the student to live in a modern, complex, technological, politically mature society;

(c) They must adequately prepare the best young minds for admission to universities consciously devoted to the development of leaders in government, business, technology, agriculture, research, the arts and professions.

This is obviously a very large assignment. It is one to which we in the United States are now devoting a nationally organized effort— especially in the sciences and social studies. There is no dodging the difficulties involved, nor denying the fact that it took us a long time clearly to recognize the problem.

At present, secondary schools in almost every developing country are only a downward extension of the universities, with little or no philosophy of their own and no concept of the purposes they could serve in the changing industrial, social and political life of the nation.

Indian educators deserve great credit for recognizing this problem. Since 1882 every commission studying education has agreed upon certain major recommendations regarding secondary education which, I believe, could serve as a model for all of the developing countries:

(1) That the secondary school should provide its students with two recognizable streams with an adequate programme for each, one for college-bound students, and one for those who go into employment after secondary schools;

(2) That vocational schools should be established for industrial skill development to care for a large proportion of secondary school age youth and post-secondary school age students;

(3) That syllabi and textbooks be re-written in the light of modern developments;

(4) That examination practices dominating the secondary schools be reformed; and

(5) That pre-service secondary school teacher training be thoroughly overhauled, and in-service teacher education be expanded in breadth and in depth.

I would summarize by saying that unless adequate attention is given not only to the number but to the quality of secondary schools, it will be impossible to reach other educational objectives. Without teachers who have had at the very least a secondary education, universal primary education becomes an empty pretence. Unless students are sufficiently prepared at the secondary level to make full use of the university opportunity, expenditure for universities becomes a misuse of public funds.

THE fourth and final lesson is one which deeply concerns us today in the United States—namely, to recruit and train enough good teachers. Obviously, the ability of a nation to succeed with the first three lessons depends in large measure on its teachers.

This involves two separate problems. First, to attract the best individuals to the teaching profession by providing adequate pay and a high measure of public respect. And second, to offer these individuals the best possible training.

Americans are only beginning to appreciate the importance of paying school teachers in a manner which reflects the value of their role in the community. Until this problem is fully met, it will be difficult to attract the necessary number of talented young men and women into the teaching profession.

A generation ago, many of our college students looked on elementary and secondary teaching as jobs for those who "can't do anything else." Even today, over half of those already in the teaching profession still find it necessary to "moon-light" —or hold a second job—in order adequately to support and provide for their families.

Happily this is now beginning to change. Although teachers' salaries are still far from what they should be, our communities are beginning to recognize the need to pay for quality if they want quality in their schools. This principle is equally valid in the developing countries in which teachers must be counted upon to play such a catalytic role.

Finally, good teachers must be well-trained for their job. This is presently the subject of a major free-for-all debate in the United States, largely as a result of James Conant's recent study of the standards and content of our teachers' training programmes.

Higher emphasis should be placed on in-service training, especially when the curricula and methods in the schools are developing and changing as rapidly as they are today. Moreover, teachers' training—whether for primary school or for advanced science or mathematics in a secondary school—must be upgraded and modernized extensively. This is as true and as urgent in India as it is in the United States.

Let me briefly summarize the four important tasks I have discussed:

1. To develop and implement curricula related to the needs of the community and the nation.
2. Through the curricula and the methods of instruction to foster the ability to solve problems and to think creatively.
3. To build a balanced educational system which provides the best possible education for students at all levels.
4. To recruit and train top flight teachers—and these are problems of enormous difficulty. But I believe that they merit the very highest priority on every developing nation's agenda.

THIS brings me to my final point and one of particular importance to the new generation of young Indians—the relationship between a dynamic and well directed educational system and the society which it serves. The creation of an educational system which focuses upon the creative powers of the human mind is a stirring challenge. In binding the force of nature to the service of man and in devising social and political institutions which permit maximum freedom to the individual while serving the common cause of humanity, it opens the doors to a new kind of world for hundreds of millions of people.

The government and the society must find the means to assure the young people who are the products of such an educational system challenging opportunities. A nation which gives priority to education as a key to development must encourage and welcome the impact which that education has on the nature of society as a whole.

This is especially important in the context of a programme of planned development such as India's. Such planning must take advantage of responsible individual initiative and must reward creative decision-making and administration.

The keynote of planning should be opening opportunities for

individuals to act responsibly rather than circumscribing their actions. For example, ministers should be able fully to rely on the wisdom and vision of their plant managers or their administrative agencies once the broad lines of policy have been established.

If a nation trains its young people to think for themselves and to solve problems and then offers them no opportunity to use these abilities, deep-seated, and I believe, fully justified resentment will be the only result.

The reciprocal relationship between education and national development is clear and direct.

To cultivate this relationship in the formulation and execution of national plans is imperative. Education must meet the needs of the nation, and the nation must be prepared to make maximum use of such a system and the students it produces.

May I add a personal comment ?

You are graduating into a world of extraordinary change, of considerable danger and of individual opportunities. Since independence, your national leaders have faced great decisions—decisions in the development of your economy, in the strengthening of your political system and in your relationship with the world. For young people of imagination, dedication, and courage, the future is an exciting prospect. I wish you good luck.

# 7. A Key to Rapid Economic Growth

*Ambassador Bowles, in a series of columns for the* American Reporter *from 1966 to 1969, asserted that the basic ingredient of rapid economic growth is the widespread ownership of rural land. He cited dramatic examples of successful development in three Asian nations as guides for other countries to follow.*

RECENTLY IN reading an American magazine I ran across an article by an American economist which expressed solid confidence in India's economic prospects, assuming a good monsoon this summer.

As I read it, it occurred to me that foreigners who have worked on development programmes in other parts of the world and who have seen at first-hand the evolution through which many new nations are passing, often have more confidence in India's economic future than many Indians.

There are, it seems to me, three principles which must be applied to assure the kind of rapid economic progress which has taken place in those new nations which have been growing most soundly and rapidly.

*First,* economic justice and greater production complement one another. It may be possible to achieve rapid advances in economic growth without economic justice, but no nation can establish economic justice without steadily increasing production.

Whatever its ideology, no government can divide and re-divide non-existent wealth and still expect to improve the lot of the average citizen.

*Second,* incentives for cultivators and businessmen are essential to persuade them to work harder and to produce more. The tax system should be geared to stimulate those economic activities which contribute to faster economic growth and to penalize speculation and other forms of non-productive economic pursuits.

*Third*, a developing nation with a large agricultural population cannot succeed economically unless it gives the very highest priority to the welfare of the rural masses.

Peasant cultivators should not be looked upon as a poverty-ridden drag on the nation. They should be considered potential customers who under favourable conditions can absorb all the goods and products that urban factories can provide.

How can a rural economy be stimulated into such dynamic action? A basic requirement is that the largest possible number of cultivators should own their own land.

This requires the enactment of laws that encourage or even force, the sale of large land holdings to tenant farmers and landless labourers.

Unless most of the cultivators are given a sense of personal participation and dignity, production will lag, democracy will be undermined and there will be no security for anyone.

India has understood this need and has moved in several ways to meet it. For instance, in ten years more than 50,000 village workers under the Community Development Programme have helped build many thousands of new schools and primary health centres and have also established the Panchayati Raj, which is laying the foundation for local democracy in many areas.

Although this is an impressive record, it is only the first chapter in India's struggle for rural democracy. The programmes which are now being introduced will almost certainly generate vast visions of further progress to come in the minds of millions of villagers.

What will follow? Will it be the release of positive forces for dynamic, democratic rural progress—or the creation of mass frustration and political unrest?

In large measure the answers will depend on the relation of the cultivators to their land which in turn involves such questions as land ownership, tenancy and the rights of landless labour.

As early as 1935 a Congress Party resolution stated: "there is only one fundamental method of improving village life, namely the introduction of a system of peasant proprietorship under which the tiller of the soil is himself the owner of it . . . ."

Thirty years later this goal is as fundamental as ever. In any developing nation "economic progress" will create as many problems as it solves unless it provides an increasing measure of social justice and human dignity for rural as well as urban citizens, however lowly or deprived they may be. And these goals in turn are closely related to the number of cultivators who are given a stake in their own land.

WHO should own the land? One articulate group argues that small privately owned holdings are "uneconomic". Increased production, they assert, can best be achieved through the middle-sized and larger landowners who have the education and the capital resources to invest in chemical fertilizers, improved seeds and modern machinery.

While they admit that disproportionate economic benefits may accrue to the larger farmers, they assert that a more reasonable share will ultimately trickle down to the small cultivators and landless labour in the form of high wages and increases in the amount of food. And in the longer run, the smaller cultivators may be persuaded to adopt the successful techniques used by their larger and more progressive neighbours.

A second school of thought asserts that this "favour the large cultivator" approach overlooks several crucial economic, agronomic, social and psychological facts.

For instance, there is no evidence that small farms with adequate fertilizer, credit and extension services are less productive than large ones in a country with a vast labour surplus. On the contrary, the owner of a small plot may be expected to work harder and more effectively than the insecure hired labour on a large holding. As for the tenant cultivators, it is futile to expect them to make a major investment in improving land which they may lose the next year.

Moreover, farm machinery which is assumed to be a special advantage available to the larger farmer does not in itself raise production; it is a labour saver which enables fewer people to till a larger area in the same amount of time.

In most developing countries the need is not for expensive farm machinery, which would add significantly to the already massive rural unemployment but to devise a system which will encourage rural people to exert greater individual initiative.

Land, they assert, is the very basis of production, and until it is more equitably shared, incomes will continue to be inequitable, the necessary sense of participation will be lacking, agricultural production will lag and political discontent will steadily increase.

Along with land ownership the cultivator must be offered low interest credit to enable him to acquire fertilizers, pesticides, better irrigation and improved seeds.  An extension service to train him in modern agricultural methods must also be available.

New small industries in the towns and villages can add additional cash incomes by providing jobs for cultivators between harvest time and the next planting.

Instead of living from hand to mouth in squalor and insecurity, as its forefathers did, the rural population becomes a major customer for sewing machines cloth, shoes, transistor radios, and a hundred other items.

A few years ago India initiated a massive programme to help provide some of these benefits to Indian cultivators.  The results throughout the country are encouraging.

Let me cite an example: On a small farm in Madhya Pradesh which I visited three years ago, a young Indian cultivator and his family were growing wheat on non-irrigated land.

His production cost per acre was Rs. 240 and his net income per acre was only Rs. 50.  Because of his limited profits he and his family were forced to eke out a bare living by working on road construction.

Last year this same young man dug a well, equipped it with a Persian wheel and began to apply new high-yielding seeds, pesticides and organic fertilizers to this same land.  As a result, his output per acre increased three fold.

From his last *kharif* crop he had a net income of Rs. 1400 per acre; his *rabi* crop netted an additional Rs. 600 per acre after he had paid all his expenses.  From his five-acre holdings he now earns a net income of Rs. 10,000 a year.

This cultivator has moved from marginal production to modern economic farming in the short space of three years.  He and tens of thousand of others like him point the way to a new future for all the cultivators of rural India.

This concept is not theory.  It is a tested approach to economic development which has already worked wonders in many parts of Asia.

O N AUGUST 14, 1945 when the Pacific war was brought to an end, Japan was in a state of chaos.

Her cities were devastated, her communications disrupted, her people demoralized, and her industrial capacity cut to a fraction of pre-war levels.

The Allied Military Government which took control after the fighting stopped was faced with a potentially explosive situation: nearly a third of the Japanese farmers owned no land at all and some 40 per cent owned so little that they were forced to rent additional acres from someone else.  Together these two groups rented almost half of Japan's cultivated land at exorbitant prices.

Rents were usually established in terms of fixed quantity of rice per unit of land irrespective of whether the farmer had a good or bad year.  The land rental averaged more than half of the crop.

In a bad year the tenant farmer was bound to run into debt, on which he paid usurious interest rates.  This meant that the politically explosive gap between the few "haves" and the many "have-nots" was constantly growing.

A generation later Japan has emerged from the confusion and frustration of defeat to rank third in economic output behind the United States and the Soviet Union.

Despite its almost total lack of domestic iron ore and limited quantities of non-ferrous metals and petroleum, the Japanese economy has been growing at the unprecedented rate of 10 per cent annually.

Japan now produces more steel than France, Britain or Italy; indeed she is exporting steel to the United States.

Japanese exports have been spectacularly successful in winning customers and earning foreign exchange in all the world's markets.

Japanese farmers produce more foodgrains per acre than any other farmers in the world.

Most of the benefits of this economic break-through have been passed on to the Japanese consumer; even in rural areas most Japanese now own television sets, washing machines and other amenities of modern life.

What made this remarkable economic success possible?

Japan started her extraordinary economic surge from a strong base: her people were almost 100 per cent literate; her workers were among the most skilled in the world; Japanese managers were pragmatic, growth-minded innovators.

To this solid base the Japanese have added major new elements. One of the most important of these was the land reform programme.

In 1946, at the urging of the Allied Military Governor, General MacArthur, the Japanese Government launched a reform programme "to ensure that those who till the land of Japan shall henceforth have an equal opportunity to enjoy the fruits of their labour."

Between 1946 and 1949 the Japanese Government bought up nearly one-third of all the cultivated land which had been in the hands of large cultivators or absentee owners. This land was then resold on easy terms to four million tenant families.

Absentee landlords were required to sell all their cultivated land. Non-cultivating resident landlords were permitted to keep two and a half acres, which they could continue to rent at a tightly-controlled rate. The maximum area any owner-operator could farm was seven and a half acres. Exceptions were limited to orchards and the less fertile land in Japan's northernmost island.

As a result, 94 per cent of the rural families of Japan became landowners and as invariably happens, land ownership provided the incentive which boosted agriculture to its present record levels.

At the same time, rural credit systems were established with efficient cooperative marketing establishments to cut distribution costs, provide cheap fertilizer, pesticides and agricultural implements.

In the industrial sector, generous tax incentives encouraged the rapid development of both large and small concerns. When the private sector was unable or unwilling to act, the government did not hesitate to build and manage production facilities.

Foreign investment was sought and welcomed; as a result it soon flowed in massive amounts. At the same time export markets were carefully studied. Products were adapted to competitive conditions and vigorous overseas selling efforts undertaken.

The importance of family planning was recognized and the birth rate lowered to its present level of less than 1 per cent annually.

What Japan has done, other Asian countries can also do. The formula, I believe, is clear:

1. The very highest priority for education, agriculture, and population control;
2. Land reform designed to release the energies of the maximum number of farmers by assuring them ownership of their own land;
3. A tax system tailored sharply to discourage land speculation and generously to reward new investments which create more jobs and raise production;
4. A government which constructively guides and encourages growth, also making sure that economic justice and freedom of opportunity are continually extended to all citizens;
5. The elimination of bureaucratic barriers to constructive private initiative.

This is the story of the unprecedented success of an Asian nation that was determined to set aside outworn economic dogmas and pragmatically to work for the prosperity and well-being of the people. Let us now turn to another example.

WHEN I first visited South Korea in May 1953 the savage fighting, which followed the Chinese Communist invasion of 1950, was just petering out and peace negotiations at long last were moving towards a successful conclusion.

The devastation created by this bitter war was an unforgettable spectacle. Cities, towns and villages were in ruins and human misery was evident everywhere. The outlook for the thirty million courageous people of South Korea was dismal indeed.

Yet today—only 14 years later—a near-miracle has occurred. South Korea is on the move with rapid but balanced modernization as the central theme.

The capital city of Seoul, with rising skyscrapers and successful businesses, is a bustling modern city. In the rural areas, an agricultural revolution is in full swing; the production of grain crops, forest products and fishing is increasing rapidly. Concrete highways and railroads are linking the countryside with towns and urban centres.

How was this miracle accomplished? It was accomplished by a combination of sound priorities, realistic planning, hard work and generous incentives designed to free the energies of the South Korean people.

From the outset the Government put first things first; education and agriculture were given top priority.

Under pre-war Japanese rule, a comprehensive educational system had been established from kindergarten to university. After the war, many new teacher training schools were added and the school network expanded rapidly. Today more than 90 per cent of the South Korean people are literate, an achievement directly related to their rapid economic development.

The first step in agriculture was a determined effort to assure cultivators the ownership of their own land. Even before the Chinese invasion of 1950, sweeping land reforms had begun to change the pattern of land ownership and tenure. By 1958 these reforms were largely completed.

With the help of fertilizer, rural credit on easy terms and increased irrigation (more than half of South Korea's cultivated land is irrigated) production on these small land holdings increased rapidly.

Soon rural industries began to develop, offering more and more part-time employment to village families. The uneven boundaries of farm plots were redrawn into rectangular shapes so that small farm tractors and other mechanisms could be more easily used. The time saved by this equipment enabled many cultivators to boost their incomes by working a few additional weeks a year in the nearby factories.

On the solid foundation created by expanding education and more intensive agriculture, the South Korean Government then launched a vigorous industrialization programme. Power, coal and other energy resources were rapidly expanded. Power-generating capacity increased three-fold.

Heavy emphasis was placed on import—replacing industries, and the increased exports of new products.

As a result, imports have remained almost constant while exports have been increased from $ 32 million in 1960 to approximately $ 250 million in 1966, with a major shift from raw materials to manufactured goods. Sixty-five per cent of all South Korean manufactured products are now being sold abroad to earn foreign exchange.

Fertilizer is one example. Before 1959, South Korea was forced to import all of its fertilizer. In 1960 and 1964, two large fertilizer plants were completed and three more were begun in 1965. By early next year, South Korea will be self-sufficient in nitrogenous fertilizer and will be able increasingly to export this basic commodity to its neighbours.

In the last five years, South Korea's gross national product has increased at a rate of 7.6 per cent a year, compared to 4.7 per cent from 1954 to 1961. The per capita national income is increasing by 4.6 per cent annually, taking into account the population increase of 2.9 per cent.

This national record has been made possible by several factors in addition to agriculture and education. Among the most important is a tax system devised to encourage enterprise and innovation backed by a greatly improved tax collecting system which has enabled the Government to expand its development budgets without significant increases in tax rates. Since 1963, monetary and fiscal reforms have effectively controlled inflationary pressures.

South Korea is a modern-day success story in nation-building. Hard work, modern technology, tough-minded fiscal policies, and wise planning is putting this important Asian country well on the road to economic self-sufficiency while opening a new era for the South Korean people.

THE Republic of China on the island of Taiwan also has a dramatic story of rapid economic development to tell. However, because New Delhi and Taipei do not have diplomatic relations, this story is not well known in India.

As in the case of Japan and South Korea, Taiwan's economic revolution began in the rural areas.

In 1905, Dr. Sun Yat-sen, father of the Chinese Democratic Revolution (which later lost its way under Mao Tse-tung), organized a "Land to the Tillers" programme to assure every Chinese cultivator the right to work his own land and to enjoy the fruits of his labours.

Unfortunately, Dr. Sun's programme was blocked by reactionary forces and it was not until the 1930's that his protege, James Y.C. Yen, was able to breathe new vigour into the land reform efforts in South China, this time supported by a programme of community development similar to the integrated programme launched by Jawaharlal Nehru in India in 1952.

In their drive for political and military domination of China, the communists effectively revived the old slogan of "Land to the Tillers." Having once attained total power, they went back on their promise and forced the Chinese rural people into tightly controlled giant "communes."

When the defeated Nationalist Government retreated to Taiwan, it launched a major effort to correct the mistakes which had contributed to its downfall on the mainland. This included a sweeping land eform programme based on the concepts of Sun Yat-sen and James Y.C. Yen.

In a series of steps, the rural districts were gradually transferred from the large landholders, many of whom lived in the cities, to the actual tillers to assure increased production and a more stable social order in the villages.

When the programme first got under way, only 36 per cent of the rural population were full-fledged owner-farmers while another 25 per cent owned only part of the land they tilled. Thus various degrees of tenancy were predominant in the rural areas, and by and large the tenants were at the mercy of the landlords.

The first step in the new land reform programme was a reduction in rents to no more than 37.5 per cent of the value of the annual crop.

In the second phase, government-owned public lands were made available to landless labourers and tenants who paid for them in instalments over a ten-year period.

In the third phase, the government financed the mandatory purchase of land from land-owners owning more than ten acres through an ingenious scheme which provided 70 per cent of the payments in land bonds and 30 per cent in stock shares of public enterprises.

As a result, thousands of landlords transferred their investments from large tracts of land to tax-favoured small rural industries. This programme has been a key factor in the rapid development of rural industry on Taiwan in the last decade.

As a result of this series of land reform measures, nearly 90 per cent of the cultivators' land is now owned by the families who actually till it. This switch of rural economic power has been accompanied by a readjustment in political power.

Rural Taiwan is largely dominated by farmers' associations. These associations provide members with technical advisory services, wide-distribution of fertilizer, pesticides and other essential commodities, plus banking services including deposits and agricultural credit. Some associations also provide coordination services for the marketing of vegetables and fruits.

Before land reform, the farmers' associations were composed almost entirely of landlords. Now they include eight out of ten of all the farm families in Taiwan.

The land reform programme in Taiwan was completed over a five-year period. It was accompanied by an intensive publicity programme through which each new step was explained and demonstrated. A government totally committed at every level—village, district, state and central—was an essential factor.

The results are dramatic: the average farm size on Taiwan is about the same as in Japan, 2.7 acres. Because ample fertilizer, pesticides, hybrid seeds and water are available the output per acre is now among the highest in the world.

Taiwan is now exporting large amounts of rice and sugar. Small rural factories provide additional income. Nearly all children are in school. Rural health services have rapidly expanded. Electric power is now available in most villages. The rural economy and social order have now become stable and progressive.

This rural revolution, generated by a vigorous programme for land distribution, has also created a growing rural market of bicycles, scooters, sewing machines and other household accessories.

Taiwanese exports now exceed its imports. Foreign economic assistance from the United States, the World Bank and other sources is no longer needed.

Taiwan has successfully solved the question of whether industry or agriculture should receive first priority in development planning. It has demonstrated once again that the primary source of this economic dynamism comes from the rural areas and that widespread land-ownership is essential in creating this sense of progress.

Taiwan's dramatic progress underscores an important point: if a similar programme had been launched on the China mainland 30 years ago, there is little likelihood that the communists could have taken over China, and India, and the world would now be enjoying a far greater measure of peace and security.

THE experiences of these three nations suggest that the ultimate answer to the explosive question "Who owns the land ?" will shape the economic and political future of Asia, Africa and Latin America.

One aspect of the question involves the need for a reasonable balance between the capital savings which go into land ownership and the savings invested in industry to create both goods and jobs. As a result the price of good agricultural land in many parts of India is already higher than in the American states of Iowa or Kansas.

Another aspect is that the very success of the new technology (involving hybrid seeds, water control, and fertilizers) is bound to create a rapidly growing and politically explosive economic gap between those cultivators who own significant amounts of land and those who work for wages or a share of the crop.

There are three possible ways to deal with these problems, each of which presents serious difficulties.

1. A developing nation may choose to launch a sweeping land reform programme modelled on those to which I have referred in Japan, South Korea and Taiwan. By assuring the widest possible ownership of the land, such a programme would provide nearly all rural families with a direct personal stake in political stability, increased production and national growth.

For example, if all of India's cultivable land could be distributed equally, each rural family would receive approximately six acres. This is twice the average land holding in Japan where the cultivators have achieved the greatest output per acre in the world.

However, in a developing democratic society, the political obstacles to a radical programme of this kind are formidable. When Prime Minister Nehru broke up the vast zamindari estates in the 1950's, he faced bitter opposition from most landowners, who held considerable political power. If land ceilings were now reduced to the low levels of Japan, South Korea and Taiwan, the political opposition would be explosive.

2. A second approach may be to decide that a sweeping land reform programme of this magnitude is not now feasible. To protect the landless labourers and tenant farmers from exploitation, they could be encouraged to develop organizations

which would enable them to bargain more effectively with the landowners for a reasonable wage or share of the crop.

Such an approach would create a different and perhaps even more explosive set of problems. With the landless labourers and tenant farmers organized on one side and the large landowners on the other, a dangerous confrontation would be created. Extremist leaders of both left and right would almost certainly manipulate this situation to promote their own political objectives.

For instance, when negotiations break down at planting and harvest time, many landowners could be expected to introduce strike-breakers. Violence would be inevitable. Meanwhile, to reduce their dependence on hired labour, many landowners would purchase labour-saving machinery to do the work that landless labourers and tenant farmers have been doing in the past. This premature rush to introduce machinery could throw many millions of cultivators out of work and further embitter the political conflicts.

3. A third possibility is a system of tax incentives and disincentives that would encourage large landowners to sell the major part of their holdings to their tenants and landless labourers and to invest the proceeds in small industrial plants in neighbouring towns. This would enable more and more families to own the land which they till and at the same time provide them with part-time factory jobs when their labour is not required in the fields.

This transfer of capital from land to factory ownership could be encouraged by a three-step programme: (a) a modest tax would be applied to land holdings under, perhaps, ten acres; (b) above this cut-off point, the land tax would rise sharply and progressively; (c) simultaneously, as in Taiwan, an announcement would be made that new industries in the rural areas could be tax free for, let us say, ten years.

This would give the larger landowner a choice between two courses of action. He can retain the holdings to which he is entitled under present law and then pay the new extra tax on everything over ten acres; or he can profitably farm the ten acres on which he pays only a modest tax, sell the rest of his holdings to tenant farmers and landless labourers and invest the proceeds in a tax-free factory, brickyard or the like. The sale of land could be financed by governmental loans on easy terms.

This latter approach has the double advantage of enabling more people to possess their own land and at the same time stimulating increased investment in small rural factories which can create millions of new jobs.

# 8. Prospects for Indian Agriculture

*On October 30, 1967 Chester Bowles wrote a detailed memorandum explaining the problems and prospects of India's agricultural revolution.*

IN INDIA, after two years of severe drought, prospects for a record grain harvest are excellent. With normal weather from now until the winter crop is harvested in March production may exceed 95 million tons in comparison to 75 million tons last year.*

A major factor in this record production has been an excellent monsoon. Rainfall has been plentiful, widespread and well-timed.

But even more important for the longer haul, this year's bumper harvest reflects the first stage of a revolution in Indian agriculture based on improved seeds, expanded credit, the increased use of fertilizer and pesticides, and better management of irrigation water.

Three or four years ago only a handful of wishful thinkers would have suggested the possibility of India becoming self-sufficient in foodgrains in the foreseeble future. Now there is some basis for hope that, with good rains and the continuing expansion of the present programme, this goal may be reached by the early 1970's.

Let us consider the background behind this development. First for the basic logistics.

At present India has some 368 million acres under cultivation which amounts to approximately 45 per cent of the total land area (only 14 per cent of the land area is cultivated in China).

Twenty-three per cent of the Indian cultivated acreage is planted in rice, 8 per cent in wheat, 28 per cent in coarse grains, 16 per cent

---

* 1957-68 proved to be a record harvest of 100 million tones with a further increase expected in 1968-69.

in pulses, 2 per cent in sugarcane, 5 per cent in cotton, one per cent in jute, less than one per cent in tea, 16 per cent in oilseeds and miscellaneous crops.

When the British left in 1947, India had 45 million acres or 15 per cent of its cultivated land under irrigation. In the last 20 years this area has grown to 85 million acres with plans for an increase to 111 million by the early 1970's. During the current crop year (April 1967 to March 1968) India expects to produce about 41 million tons of rice, 15 million tons of wheat, 27 million tons of coarse grains and 12 million tons of pulses.

THE story behind the current progress begins in the 1950's. From 1950 to 1961 Indian foodgrain production increased by roughly 37 per cent while the increase in population was 21.5 per cent. Consequently the daily diet of the average Indian had gradually increased from 1,700 calories to 2,000 calories.

These production increases were made possible not so much by improvements in agricultural techniques but rather because (1) more land was opened up for cultivation, and (2) double cropping in some areas was made possible by the new multi-purpose dams and by additional wells. *Output per acre* showed but little change.

By the early 1960's the possibility of further extending cultivated acreage had been greatly reduced. The new hybrid seed varieties were not yet available and prices were too low to encourage culti-vators to increase their investment in fertilizer and pesticides. Consequently output per acre remained low and foodgrain produc-tion levelled off at about 80 million tons annually. In 1963, much of the 200,000 tons of fertilizer (nitrogen) produced in India backed up in the warehouses because of the lack of demand.

Then came an unexpected breakthrough. In 1964 even with an 89 million ton bumper crop, prices rose sharply due to two poor harvests in the preceding years and an increase in deficit financing. Consequently, for the first time since independence Indian cultivators began to receive a significant increase in their incomes. The two severe droughts in 1965 and 1966 raised prices still further.

Although experience the world over has demonstrated that increased prices to farmers invariably leads to increased production, few foresaw the vigour with which Indian farmers would respond. Traditionally cautious, conservative, seemingly indifferent to new methods and techniques, millions of cultivators suddenly came to life. Demand for fertilizer and pesticides rose by leaps and bounds. New seeds were eagerly sought after. Measures to improve storage facilities and cut down on the rat population were welcomed.

Although the immediate explanation of this revolution in attitudes lies in increased income opportunities for the cultivators, other and less dramatic factors were also involved.

One was the technical assistance rendered by USAID and the Ford and Rockefeller Foundations. Another is the community development programme which now extends throughout India.

The latter programme, which was launched in 1952, divided rural India into 5,000 "blocks" with roughly 100 villages in each block. Each Block Development Officer has a staff consisting of experts in agriculture, public health (including malaria control), family planning, education and the like.

Although this programme was designed as a broad effort to help introduce modern ways into the rural areas, inevitably its major focus was on increased agricultural production. There is no doubt that this nationwide network of extension workers, under the guidance of dedicated young District and Block Development Officials, helped lay the bases for the present revolution in rural India.


IN DECEMBER 1965 a major decision was made by the Indian Government. With the support of the Cabinet the then Food and Agriculture Minister, Mr. C. Subramaniam, announced that India was determined to become "self-sufficient" in agriculture by 1971, and pledged the Government to provide the resources required to achieve this goal. Following the formation of a new Cabinet in March 1967 the present Minister, Mr. Jagjivan Ram, reaffirmed this commitment.

In keeping with this decision the Union Government of India allocated Rs. 293 crores ($390 million) in 1966-67 for agriculture programmes as against Rs. 219 crores ($292 million) allocated in 1965-66. In addition the State Governments allocated Rs. 200 crores ($267 million). With the Rs. 80 crores ($105.26 million) carried over from projects initiated the previous year the increase in agricultural investment by the Central and State Governments is well over 50 per cent.

This increase in agricultural investment is especially noteworthy since it occurred at a time when total Government investment was being scaled down as a result of the general economic slump following the war with Pakistan, the temporary cut-off of U.S. aid, and the severe droughts of 1965 and 1966. In the next fiscal year a further substantial increase in investment has been indicated.

What is the substance of the new programme ?

A.  *Education and Applied Research.*  For several years India's 24 agricultural degree colleges and a number of specialized institutes sponsored by the Indian Council of Agricultural Research have been conducting extensive programmes of research and experimentation. These programmes which are based less and less on theory and more and more on the practical realities faced by cultivators, are now providing India with the tools which are required to make India self-sufficient in foodgrains.

In the last ten years, 30,000 young Indians have graduated from Indian agricultural schools including the eight new agriculture universities set up with U.S. assistance. These graduates include soil biologists, agronomists, chemists, botanists, veterinarians and the like.

B.  *Fertilizer.*  The new Government programme, announced in 1965, called for a massive expansion of the Indian fertilizer industry and provided generous incentives for new plant construction. The following steps have been taken:

1. Removal of geographic constraints on fertilizer marketing and the abolition of the Government's near-monopoly control over fertilizer distribution.
2. Decision to allow fertilizer prices to be set by the market demand.
3. Provision of adequate foreign exchange to operate fertilizer plants at full capacity.
4. Institution of administrative and procedural changes to ease approval and licensing procedures for foreign private investment in new fertilizer plants.
5. Provision of increased credit to farmers regardless of where they buy their fertilizer.
6. Abolition of the requirement of Government participation in the ownership of private fertilizer plants.

These steps should make possible a continued fast growth in fertilizer production. In the present fiscal year 1967-68 (July-June) India expects to produce about 500,000 tons of nitrogen, which is an 80 per cent increase over last year. By 1970-71 plants now actually under construction are expected to raise India's nitrogen production capacity by another one million tons to a total of 1.5 million tons.

Successful conclusion of negotiations now in progress with American, British, Japanese and Italian interests would provide, if a reasonable percentage of these come through, for the construction of additional plants capable of producing another 0.7 million tons of nitrogen. This would assure total capacity of 2.2 million tons by 1972.

Production of phosphate fertilizers ($P_2O_5$) is planned to increase from 260,000 tons in 1967-68 to 550,000 tons in 1971-72.

To fill the fertilizer gap before India's own production can meet its needs, fertilizer imports have been sharply increased. In the current year 960,000 tons of nitrogen, 400,000 tons of phosphates and 300,000 tons of potash are being imported by India at a cost of Rs. 150 crores ($200 million). This is compared with 376,000 tons of nitrogen, 22,000 tons of phosphates and 94,000 tons of potash only two years earlier.

Plans for next crop year call for imports of one million tons of nitrogen and 330,000 tons of phosphates. If India's foreign exchange situation should permit imports to be further increased the added tonnage would be quickly absorbed.

C. *Seeds.* India's traditional grain varieties have been developed over the centuries by natural selection. Most of those varieties provide slow developing crops which usually limit the cultivator to one crop per season.

Moreover, most of the traditional plants were long stemmed and tended to lodge (fall over) when even limited amounts of fertilizer were applied. Consequently these varieties were unsuitable for the new production techniques which have been made possible by fertilizer, improved water supplies and pest control.

In the early 1960's Indian scientists began to realize these shortcomings and in cooperation with other governments and private foundations launched a massive down to earth effort to develop and introduce seed varieties suitable to the requirements. As a result India now has improved seeds for all five major foodgrains. An important feature of most of these new varieties is their short growing season. This permits double and even triple-cropping and consequently is giving a major boost to Indian agriculture.

In the early 1960's the Indian Government imported 18,000 tons of a Mexican short-stem variety of wheat (Sonora 64). Experimentation in Indian research centres resulted in selections specifically adapted to Indian soil and weather requirements. These were quickly multiplied and are now providing almost fantastic yields. One farmer near Delhi recently harvested in a single crop nearly 3 tons of wheat per acre from a 2½- acre plot.

Wheat seed of the improved varieties is now available to all Indian wheat cultivators. Indeed India is now exporting wheat seed to Nepal.

The rice programme is not far behind. The most successful seeds are ADT 27, a variety developed in South India, Taichung Native I and Tainan III from Taiwan, and more recently IR 8 developed at the International Rice Research Institute in the Philippines. These are all high-yielding varieties that mature in 105 to 135 days in contrast to the 180 days often required for traditional varieties; their yield is from two to four times greater.

Equally sensational examples could be cited in the production of corn (maize), milo (jowar), and millets (bajra and ragi). Together these so-called coarse grains represent about 25 per cent of India's total grain and pulse production.

Indian scientists are consistently working, and with good prospects of success, further to extend such improvements. Although there are many problems of taste, disease and insects, the plant breeders are now confident that they can keep ahead of these problems.

Last year India planted a total of 4.8 million acres with these locally produced, high-yielding seeds. For the current year (1967-68) plans call for 15 million acres. This acreage will be more than doubled by 1971.

D. *Irrigation*. In British India, most of the irrigation was provided by artificial lakes and tanks and by canal systems which drew water from the rivers.

In the early years of Indian independence the major emphasis was switched to multi-purpose dams which provided both electric power and irrigation. One of these, the Bhakra Dam in the Punjab completed in 1963, is now producing 600,000 kilowatts of electricity and watering some five million acres.

More recently the emphasis has been shifting to tube-wells which provide water from depths of up to 300 feet, and dug wells which go down 20 to 40 feet. Most cultivators prefer this well irrigation because it can be locally maintained and managed, while canal irrigation, which is controlled by the Government, does not always fit local planting schedules.

The Union and State Governments of India are now embarked on a major effort to expand this system of well irrigation. All States now provide loans to enable the cultivators to dig wells. The cost for a tube-well averages Rs. 8000 ($1051); for a dug well, Rs. 500 to 1000 ($70 to 130).

In Madras State 265,000 wells are now equipped with electric power. In U.P. more than 100,000 wells were dug in the last two years.

The Gangetic Plain is a particularly fruitful area for such development. Although it has not yet been fully explored, many experts believe that it probably contains the largest underground reservoir in the world.

Major and medium irrigation schemes are also being expanded while efforts are made to utilize existing sources more efficiently. Improved irrigation and drainage practices have the potential of supporting other modern agricultural practices that can double or even triple yields on presently irrigated lands.

Although water supplies are not always reliable, roughly 22 per cent of the arable land in India is now classed as irrigated. The substantial increase now planned will, if realized, be a significant move toward freeing farmers in the better watered and more productive areas from the uncertainties of the monsoon rains.

THE multiplier effect of increased agricultural production on the economy of India is dramatic. Let us consider, for instance, what the new agricultural technology, with adequate water, can mean to a forwardlooking Indian wheat cultivator.

On his five acres of land he formerly produced an average of 535 pounds of wheat per acre currently valued at Rs. 650 ($87) or more a ton. By using the new high-yielding seeds, irrigation, chemical fertilizers and pesticides this farmer can now increase his yield five times and his net earnings about six times.  From a single crop his comparative budgets will look like this:

|  |  | Cost by Traditionally Methods | Cost by New Methods |
|---|---|---|---|
|  |  | (in rupees) | (in rupees) |
| 1. | Plant Protection | 0 | 30 |
| 2. | Seeds | 50 | 100 |
| 3. | Irrigation, capital charges @ 20 per cent a year gross return | 0 | 300 |
| 4. | Irrigation, operating charges | 0 | 50 |
| 5. | Fertilizer | 0 | 1000 |
| 6. | Labour and bullock power | 250 | 350 |
|  |  | 300 | 1830 |

|  | | |
|---|---|---|
| Yield | 1.5 tons | 7.5 tons |
| Total Value | Rs. 810 | Rs. 4875 |
| Net Earnings | Rs. 510 | Rs. 3045 |
|  | ($67.10) | ($400.65) |

His new tube-well enables him to secure a second crop.  This will double his annual net profit to more than Rs. 6100.  If there are five in this cultivator's family, their per capita income will be four times the present Indian average.  Moreover, the cultivator using the new technology has not only increased the yield for one growing season, he has also sharply increased the future productivity of his land.

With this increase in income he begins to purchase consumer items which his family had never been able to afford—a sewing machine, bricks and roofing tiles, a transistor radio, a  bicycle, lanterns, shoes, cloth, other consumer goods and ultimately a small tractor—many of them may be produced by new  factories in the nearby rural towns.  As the rural consumer markets are further stimulated by increased demand the impact begins to be felt in far away urban centres and more money is thus invested in additional industrial production.

This agriculture-small rural industry approach to national economic growth is already responsible for spectacular economic gains in Japan, Taiwan and South Korea. Now there is reason to hope that the same dynamic process is beginning to work in India with its crucially important one-seventh of the world's population.

A LTHOUGH prospects for Indian agriculture are enormously improved in the last few years with the likelihood of still further improvement, several important questions remain unanswered:

    1. *Will a procurement system be maintained which continues to offer the cultivators the incentives for increased production which have sparked the current surge of new production?*

Although consumer food prices are now undoubtedly too high, it is agreed that a *sharp* drop would reduce production and slow down the present process of growth. The problem is to find a proper balance between prices the non-farm families pay for food and the income the farmers received for growing it. This will require determination, planning, and bold experimentation.

    2. *Can a reasonably orderly national foodgrain market be developed and maintained?*

At present food distribution in India is based on a system of State zones, with shipment of food across State lines permitted only on a Government account. This programme is designed to enable the Government to procure grains more easily from surplus States. However, inevitably it has created sharp differences in price between areas only a few miles apart.

There is now general agreement that with increased production, the zoning system will at some point become not only unnecessary but an impediment to full production. However, the Indian Government will be reluctant to eliminate the zones until it has built up adequate reserve stocks which will enable it to ship supplies to deficit areas and to stabilize prices.

    3. *Will the present pace of research be maintained?*

The development of new seeds is a sensitive and intricate process. New varieties must be developed regularly which are pest-resistant, productive and palatable to the consumers. As new blights develop, these seeds must be replaced at regular intervals with still newer varieties. Consequently any let down in the present agricultural research programme would be dangerous.

4. *Will storage facilities be adequate?*

At present, the Central Government has storage facilities for 3 million tons of foodgrains with the storage for 2 million additional tons under the control of cooperatives. Eventually India will require a system of pest-proof storage godowns (warehouses) located in all the 315 districts of India which will cut down transportation problems at harvest time, allow farmers to maintain reasonable prices and prevent losses by rodents.

5. *Will the rate of construction of fertilizer plants be maintained and expanded?*

The demand for fertilizer in India now greatly exceeds the sharply increased supply. In the next few years, the Indian Government will be hardpressed to meet this growing demand as massive imports cut deeply into India's scarce foreign exchange.

If Indian fertilizer needs are to be met at prices the farmer can pay, present capacity must be expanded. This will require large amounts of foreign exchange which can most easily come from the private sector. To induce this private investment, India must continue to encourage the investors.

6. *How will increased farm income affect the political stability of rural areas?*

This is a particularly critical problem which is bound to grow in importance in coming years.

At the time of Indian independence, many landholders under the old zamindari system owned thousands of acres each. India's leaders deserve credit for eliminating this system and establishing land ownership ceilings, terms of tenancy, limits on land rents, etc.

Although the results have been impressive, there are still serious dislocations in many areas. For instance, 38 per cent of the farm land in India is owned by 7 per cent of the farmers; 92 per cent of the farmers who own land own less than 2 acres, and 33 per cent of all the rural people own no land whatsoever.

At this point a word in regard to the optimum size of agricultural landholdings may be in order: Most Americans think of agricultural efficiency in terms of tractors and similar mechanization. However, the largest outputs of foodgrains per acre are achieved not in the

United States but in Japan and Taiwan where the size of farm is limited by law to 7 and 10 acres respectively.

The main role of mechanization is to save labour by reducing the number of men required to operate a single farm. It has been said that an Indian village could live for a week on the wheat that an American or Canadian harvesting machine leaves behind.

Consequently, unless jobs in local industries, construction firms, and commercial outlets are available, premature mechanization will throw millions of people out of work.

In most Indian States the ceiling on land owned by a single family is now about 30 acres with a provision for permanent occupancy for tenants and a limitation of 25 per cent of the crop to be paid by the tenant farmer.

In actual practice, however, it is possible for several members of one family to pool landholdings under the management of a single family member. Because records may be outdated or non-existent the rights of tenants to farm the land at a reasonable rent are often circumscribed.

In this politically explosive framework, a substantial number of the Indian farm families are already participants in a rural revolution which is creating brand new social and political pressures, particularly in those villages where the progress is most pronounced.

Landless labourers may accept their wage of two or three rupees a day without much complaint as long as they know that everyone else in their village is poor. However, when they see the landowners' incomes rising rapidly while their own rises much more slowly if at all, they become restless and resentful.

In other words, the dramatic increases in food output which are occurring—and which should continue to grow in the years ahead— may lead to sharp disparities in income which in turn may create an expanding sense of economic and social injustice.

We might add, however, that this phenomenon is not peculiar to India. In America as well as in India the solution or partial solution of old problems invariably creates new ones: this is an inevitable part of the developmental process.

INDIA has embarked on an agricultural revolution which would have been difficult to visualize only a few years ago. Throughout much of rural India, there is now a brand new confidence, a new sense of opportunity and of hope.

However, a balanced perspective is essential. Progress in the last three years has no doubt been dramatic; yet the challenge to the Indian Government and cultivators to provide the Indian people not only with an adequate diet but also with a balanced one remains formidable.

Thus far the rural breakthrough which we have described has directly affected between 10 and 20 per cent of the village areas of India. Many of the remaining Indian villages are still relatively untouched by modern technology.

Nevertheless a critically important and impressive beginning has been made which may be expected steadily to spread. With a comparable programme of family planning, there is now a reasonable prospect that India may succeed in striking a balance between population growth and food production which will enable the great majority of citizens to expand steadily both their living standards and their sense of dignity.

# 9. The Critical Importance of a "Balanced Diet"

*Ambassador Bowles emphasized that it was not only essential that each person should eat enough, but that the individual's diet should be balanced with protein, fats and carbohydrates. He discussed this important subject in two* American Reporter *columns in 1968.*

NINETEEN SIXTY-EIGHT will be remembered as the year of the "Great Agricultural Breakthrough".

In many parts of the world and particularly in India, an awakened peasantry is eagerly turning to new hybrid seeds, fertilizers, pesticides and more efficient use of irrigation water. The result is a dramatic increase in foodgrain production.

In 1953 the average Indian consumed about 1500 calories a day. This year the amount will rise to 2100 calories.

It would be a serious mistake, however, to assume from this comparison that India's food problems have been solved. As employment opportunities increase, additional calories will be required to provide more energy for daily tasks. Moreover, as incomes rise there will be increased demand for the better grades of rice, wheat and other foodgrains.

Another factor in the food situation which has not received adequate attention is the importance of a "balanced diet." In addition to foodgrains, a healthy person requires proteins from foods such as soybeans, eggs, fish, poultry; also fats from milk products and nuts; and other minerals and vitamins found in fresh fruits and vegetables.

This means that even if an individual eats enough foodgrains to provide a high level of caloric intake, he may still be subject to malnutrition if the essential elements in his diet are not available.

Mortality statistics point to such relatively minor diseases such as measles, chicken pox and whooping cough for the tragically large number of Indian children who die before they are six. But these statistics obscure the fundamental fact that most of these children lacked a balanced diet which rendered them highly vulnerable to what would otherwise not have been a severe illness.

For those malnourished youngsters who survive the hazards of early childhood, the problem is no less grave. Undernourished children do not grow as strong or as tall as they should.

An even more serious result is the debilitating mental effect which is often irreparable. The consequent loss of a most important economic asset—a nation's human resource—is irreplaceable.

A promising new means of preventing malnutrition is the "fortification" of foods. This involves the scientific enrichment of commonly consumed foods to provide the necessary fats, vitamins, proteins, and carbohydrates. This can be achieved without affecting the taste, colour or odour of the original food, and without significantly increasing its cost.

India has taken dramatic steps forward in this field. Among these is the fortification of bread produced by nine new modern bakeries. Already more than one million loaves per year of this highly nutritious bread is available in many cities and towns. This is the largest effort of its kind any place in the world.

This bread is fortified with six nutrients, including lysine, a protein component which significantly increases the protein value of bread. I am delighted to learn that the Indian Government is now exploring possibilities of fortifying a wider range of other foods including rice, wheat, salt and tea.

A second important means of combating malnutrition is through the development of low-cost protein foods. India is already among the world's leading producers of protein-rich oilseeds such as groundnut and cottonseed. After extracting the oil, the meal can be processed into edible-grade protein concentrates. This in turn can be incorporated into a wide variety of high protein products: biscuits, sweets, soups, beverages and baby foods.

The Indian Government is also producing thousands of tons of a new groundnut-based children's food called Bal Ahar, which is being distributed by CARE through school-feeding programmes which now reach several million children daily.

Thus India has taken the lead in the development of nutrition programmes that provide not only adequate calories but also the balanced intake of proteins, fats, minerals and vitamins. This effort will not only help make many crores of Indian people healthy and strong, it will provide the techniques which can benefit hundreds of millions of men, women and children all over the world.

India is proving that malnutrition, so long a critical obstacle to rapid economic development, is an evil that can be met and overcome.

THE vast oceans surrounding the subcontinent are also a rich and cheap protein source. Fish and fish by-products offer extraordinary opportunities to help balance the diets of crores of people.

Much time, effort, and money have been spent in man's effort to explore the vast regions of space miles from the earth's surface. But I wonder whether a much higher fraction of our resources should not be devoted to probing the unexplored potentialities and wealth that can be found in and under the seas which cover over 70 per cent of the earth?

Traditionally, the seas have yielded fish and have provided travel routes between continents and nations. More recently, oil, gas, and minerals have been extracted from shallow coastal waters, and chemicals such as magnesium have been taken from the sea itself.

However, the potential of the sea has only begun to be tapped, and the increasing needs for food, oil, and minerals makes the sea a rich area for further exploration and exploitation.

These modern needs are giving the science of oceanography a new impetus. Before resources in and under the sea can be exploited, the existence, properties, and environment in which they are found must be carefully studied.

Oceanography, the term used for scientific research involving the sea, is not restricted to the sea itself. It also involves studying the sea floor, the shore and the atmosphere over the ocean.

About one year ago, four Indian scientists joined a team of American scientists on a research expedition to the Gulf of Arabia.

The extraordinary vessel they used for their investigations was America's largest and most modern oceanography research ship, the *Oceanographer*. Together these scientists were working to provide data for further research, for testing new theories, and for developing man's knowledge about the sea. For example, Dr. Rama of the Tata Institute of Fundamental Research concentrated on atmospheric conditions and their effect on the annual monsoons.

Fish in great variety have always been available from the sea. Fish are rich in the proteins which are urgently needed to balance the diet of most Indians.

But fish products can provide far more than fish for the dinner table. Fish technology has developed highly nutritious, low-cost "fish meal" products made from coarse fish which were formerly discarded.

The Indian Central Institute of Fisheries Technology in Cochin, Kerala, is presently producing a type of fish protein concentrate on a laboratory scale which could provide massive inexpensive protein for undernourished bodies.

This concentrate can be baked into chapatis or combined with other foods to make tasty and nutritious dishes. At present the Government of India is considering the erection of a pilot plant to turn out this product on a scale large enough to test its potential acceptability and effectiveness in India.

India has already made great strides in increasing its sea food production through "aquaculture". In bays and inlets where the water environment can be controlled, extraordinary new opportunities for increasing "fish farms" are now opening up.

Estuaries and coastal swamps can be cheaply exploited. In Indonesia and the Philippines fish are even raised in the irrigation water of the paddy fields. Shell fish grounds or fish ponds can be managed with a small number of unskilled workers and without any large initial investment. Actively cultivated areas may yield as high as one ton of fish per hectare.

With currently available techniques, the new "aquaculture" can be profitable and successful on a massive scale in India.

India's shoreline also promises productive petroleum yields. Technological advances now permit drilling in deep water, opening up vast new areas for exploitation.

In addition to petroleum and natural gas, the sea itself contains many components which will be extracted as the need arises, and technology develops efficient means of extraction.

Both India and the United States are committed to peaceful exploration and exploitation of the sea and its potential harvest. The United Nations Committee on the Peaceful Uses of the Seabed is only one of the organizations cooperating in this effort.

America's President, Lyndon B. Johnson, has stated: "We must ensure that the deep seas and ocean bottoms are, and remain, the legacy of all humanity."

Thus from lysine in fish and other sources of protein lies the great promise of future health of the Indian people.

# 10. The Prospects for Family Planning in India

*In a memorandum prepared for a group of leading American businessmen visiting New Delhi in November 1967, Chester Bowles explained India's most pressing problem—family planning. Subsequently, in an article the next year he strongly urged the leaders of the technologically advanced nations to establish a crash research programme to develop a simple, widely acceptable, reversible contraceptive. Also in 1968, in a reply to a letter from a U.S. Congressman, Ambassador Bowles supplied pertinent statistics on India's family planning effort.*

THE FUNDAMENTAL question of food supply is gradually being solved by the agricultural revolution now sweeping India. This leaves family planning, the greatest single piece of unfinished business in the subcontinent and in Asia.

If a deterioration in living standards is to be avoided in India, effective family planning is essential. What are the prospects for family planning here?

With only 2.4 per cent of the world's land area, India supports 14 per cent of the world's population. Fifty-five thousand babies are born every day.

Each year there are approximately 21 million births and 8 million deaths. Consequently 13 million people per year are added to the current Indian population of approximately 520 million. In stark terms the problem is how to prevent 13 million births annually.

The immediate target of Indian family planning officials is to reduce the birthrate from its present level of 41 per thousand population to 25 per thousand by 1975. This would cut the growth rate in half. The long-range goal is to stabilize India's total population at around 670 million by 1985.

To achieve these objectives something like half of the 100 million couples in the reproduction age group must be persuaded effectively to practise family planning by 1975 and 75 per cent by 1985.

THE Indian Government—Union and State—is striving to reach its objective of a stabilized population by offering a "cafeteria" of techniques from which to choose.

A. *Sterilizations.* By far the most effective method of preventing births is by sterilization. It has been estimated that the number of births prevented per thousand sterilizations is three times greater than those prevented per thousand loop insertions.

Since 1964 when the programme began to get underway, there have been 2.6 million sterilizations.* In the last Indian fiscal year 1966-67, 864,237 sterilizations were performed.

About 90 per cent of all sterilizations are male operations (vasectomy) and 10 per cent are female operations (tubectomy). This method is steadily gaining acceptance.

Progress has been notably high in the State of Madras, with significant gains in the States of Kerala, Maharashtra, Gujarat, Mysore, Madhya Pradesh and Orissa. A start has been made in Uttar Pradesh, Punjab, Andhra Pradesh, Haryana, Bihar and West Bengal.

B. *Intra-Uterine Contraceptive Device (IUCD)*: The "loop" was introduced in India as a new method of contraception in April 1965. By mid-1967, 1.8 million IUCD insertions had been achieved with the Punjab, Maharashtra, West Bengal, Kerala, and Mysore accounting for a major fraction.

The number of insertions in the 1966-67 fiscal year was 915,167. The programme was slowed down because of side effects (mostly bleeding), adverse propaganda and the difficulty in reaching a significant percentage of the rural population with the limited number of women doctors available. Nevertheless, it is hoped that a total of 2.0 million insertions can be performed in this fiscal year.

C. *Condoms*: The condom is probably the most practical and effective method of child spacing for the 75 per cent of the male population which is out of touch with clinical facilities.

---

* The figure in January 1969 is more than 5 million.

The private sector in India is gearing up to produce 100 million condoms per year. The largest private plant, in Madras, is expected to reach the capacity of 75 million by April 1968; three others are improving their testing equipment and should soon be adding significantly to the supply.

In addition a new factory in the public sector is now being constructed in Kerala. The initial capacity of this plant when it starts producing in 1969 will be 144 million pieces annually, which will be doubled by the following year.

In the meantime, to help close the immediate gap between supply and demand, condoms are being imported in increasing volume from Japan, South Korea and the United States.

It is anticipated that the use of condoms will climb steeply due to extensive promotion and a subsidized sales price of less than seven paise each. Several corporations with large selling organizations such as Union Carbide, Liptons Tea, Tata Oil, Brooke Bond Tea, Hindustan Levers and Imperial Tobacco are being asked to cooperate in a distribution programme which will ultimately cover hundreds of thousands of small bazaar shops and tea houses.

By 1970-71, the current programme calls for 10 per cent of all Indian married couples of child-bearing age to use 500 million condoms per year.

D. *The "Pill"*: After a clinical trial of two years, oral contraceptive pills have been approved for private prescription.

When they were first introduced, their cost and the requirement that they be taken regularly 20 days each month made them impractical for all but the higher income groups. Now the cost is down to one rupee ($ 0. 13) per cycle, and pills are being prescribed by private doctors for some 200,000 women. USAID is providing several million cycles of pills for pilot work to determine their practicability under Indian conditions.

E. *Abortions.* A committee which was set up to review the questions of legalized or liberalized abortions has recently recommended legislation that will permit abortions wherever the mother's health is believed to be endangered. In India, where the maternal mortality rate is 6 per 1,000 this could have a major effect on the birth rate. While it is too soon to judge the potential of this approach here, the record shows, that in every country where abortion has been legalized the effect on the birth rate has been significant. In Japan, for instance, it was instrumental in bringing down the annual rate of population increase from 3 per cent in 1950 to less than 1 per cent in 1966.

Legalization of abortion is also important to control unnecessary and harmful abortions by substituting more effective means of family planning. It is estimated that one million of these illegal abortions take place each year.

F. *Raising Minimum Legal Age for Marriage*: The minimum age for women is now 15 years and for men 18 years. A proposal to raise these minimums by law to 21 and 25, respectively, is now being considered. If new legislation eventually passes, it is likely to be a compromise between the present level and the current proposal.

THE Central and State Governments and private industry have begun to offer a variety of incentives to induce married couples to adopt one or the other of these family planning techniques.

One thousand scholarships are offered each year by medical schools for women students. Each student agrees to work in the family planning programme after graduation for as long as he or she is under the scholarship. Thus far this has been a highly competitive popular programme.

Special allowances are also being paid to district family planning officers and doctors who participate in the family planning effort. Private medical practitioners are paid special allowances for sterilizations and IUCD insertions. Homœopaths and practitioners of the indigenous medical sector are also becoming involved. Provisions have been made for providing minor operation theatres for sterilization operations.

In most States husbands and wives who participate in this programme are directly compensated by the Government for expenses incurred in travelling and time lost from work.

Industry, too, is encouraging workers to participate in family planning. The Union Government compensates companies for much of the costs to their employees; the balance is an allowable deduction for tax purposes.

Consideration is also being given by the States and Centre to a much broader incentive programme directly to reach low and middle income families. It is estimated that there are 46 million Indian males of family-bearing age who have not been sterilized and who already have three or more children. In some states direct payments are being offered to those who are willing to have vasectomies.

In three-children families, where the father is unwilling to submit to a vasectomy, wives may be persuaded to accept a loop by a lesser inducement, for example, Rs. 30.

A particularly promising incentive programme is now under way in Madras and Maharashtra. A person already sterilized refers as many of his acquaintances as he can convince and is paid Rs. 10 for each referral. In Madras alone this system helped produce 230,000 sterilizations last year.

Several State Governments now permit giving the entire incentive allocation per loop insertion (Rs. 11) to the private doctor who then uses his own discretion in its dispersion. It is hoped that this will encourage the medical profession to become more actively involved in persuading people to practise family planning.

Uttar Pradesh is experimenting with the restriction of medicine and maternity benefits for governmental and other employees. For example, in June 1967 a directive was issued stating that "non-industrial women employees of the Central Government will not be eligible for additional maternity leave after April 1, 1968 if they already have three or more children."

APPROXIMATELY Rs. 10 crores ($13 million) has been allotted by the Union Government during the next four years for mass media programmes to promote family planning, of which Rs. 9.6 crores will be spent by the States. Every possible medium to spread awareness of family planning is being exploited or will be exploited. These include the following activities:

1. *Radio*: Family planning programmes are being broadcast on all 33 stations of All India Radio. Special 3-man family planning information teams have been set up at 22 of these stations.

2. *Press*: Massive amounts of information on the importance of family planning is being disseminated in the daily newspapers via feature stories, commentaries and advertisements.

3. *Films*: Twelve population control educational films of various lengths and themes have been produced for exhibition in commercial theatres. These are also being shown through the Field Publicity Mobile Vans.

One Family Planning Van for each of the 315 districts has been sanctioned and efforts are being made to put them in the field as fast as possible. The magnitude of this undertaking is underscored by the fact that even when these mobile units are all in operation, it would still take each unit several years to cover each village in its District with one presentation.

4. *Outdoor Publicity*: Using designs and slogans at the Centre, the States are now erecting signs and billboards presenting the case for family planning. A simple, easily recognizable symbol, the Red Triangle, has been adopted to help people, mainly those who are illiterate, identify the location of family planning facilities.

Buses all over India carry posters in the local language saying "Two or three children are enough". Similar posters are displayed in the cities, along the highways, and even on railway cars and locomotives.

In addition there are match box covers, printed materials, wall paintings, songs, plays and signs in buses. To overcome the barriers of distance, illiteracy and lack of mass media, the Government is even experimenting with the possibility of air dropping simple literature on villages.

Under the guidance of the Ministry of Health and Family Planning, the Posts and Telegraphs Board is cooperating by printing slogans and symbols on envelopes, preparing special postage stamps and cancelling stamps with family planning slogans. It also intends using postmen and stamp vendors to assist in the distribution of contraceptives.

T O support this vast programme, the Central Government has established new nationwide administrative machinery, which is now directed by a number of competent professionals.

In January 1966 the Ministry of Health was redesignated as the Ministry of Health and Family Planning and a separate Department of Family Planning was set up with a Secretary directing the administrative wing and a Commissioner of Family Planning directing the technical wing.

Since the actual implementation of the family planning programme is the responsibility of each State, the Central Government is working to stimulate a greater effort on the part of the States by assuring adequate financing and by providing guidelines and consultative services.

Throughout the 315 Administrative Districts in India there are now 4,569 Primary Health Centres, to which a total of 41,122 subcentres are to be attached by 1971. These constitute the administrative base of the programme.

Through this structure a comprehensive training programme has been developed in consultation with the States. This programme provides for training of 1,500 key personnel at the State and District levels in five central institutions. Of the 46 training centres authorized, 38 have been established, 36 of which are now fully staffed.

The Central Family Planning Field units have already given short-term orientation to 9,108 medical and 69,542 other technical personnel. Over 13,000 auxiliary nurse midwives and 1,700 lady health visitors are now at work, but thousands more will be needed.

The Government has also involved the Rural Community Development Organization in implementing the new programme. In five districts the intensive agriculture programme has been integrated with family planning. To support this direct extension work in the field, more than 75,000 Community Development workers have been sanctioned to promote the programe at the village level, plus 66,200 supervisors and technical assistants at the block, district and state levels.

This massive administrative effort is being backed by greatly increased funds. In the Fourth Plan Rs. 2.3 billion ($ 306 million) have been budgeted, which is a ten-fold increase from the Third Plan allocation.

Approximately 96 per cent of this will be allocated by the Central Government to the States. This includes 100 per cent financing of non-recurring expenditures and 90 per cent of recurring expenditures for the next ten years. India, with its vast population, has thus far budgeted more of its own funds for family planning on a *per capita* basis than any other country.

ALTHOUGH responsibility for stabilizing the population growth rate has been wholly assumed by the Indian Union and State Governments, private and professional, commercial and philanthropic groups are also making contributions.

One of the most active foreign supporting groups is the Ford

Foundation. Since 1959, Ford grants totalling roughly $ 6 million have been awarded to private and public organizations for research, training, integrated faimily planning/health projects and to demonstrate innovations to speed the Family Planning programme to success.

Ford's original grant to the Ministry of Health for research related to family planning helped get the programme under way. Under this grant Communications Research Centres have been set up in Bombay, Lucknow, Trivandrum, Calcutta and Gandhigram.

The programme of the Institute of Rural Health and Family Planning in Gandhigram in Madras State deserves special notice. The main purpose is to implement the family planning programme in rural community development blocks through a variety of techniques. The Institute prepares teachers to work in training services, and is responsible for an intensive health and family planning programme.

Since 1966 the U.S. Agency for International Development has been working with the Indian Government to promote information for planning and management.

The U.S. Peace Corps has also assigned one group of 50 volunteers to work under the Maharashtra and Madhya Pradesh State Family Planning Programmes. Forty more volunteers are scheduled to work in Bihar beginning in December, 1967 and another group will be assigned to the Punjab in 1968. Three hundred other volunteers working in general health related projects are spending about half their efforts on family planning.

The Population Council, Church World Services, the Christian Medical Association, the American Friends Association, UNICEF and the Rockefeller Foundation have also assisted on various facets of the family planning effort.

THE task of stabilizing India's population at around 670 million by 1985 is staggering, and at this early stage success is by no means assured. However, after years of uncertainty there is no doubt that a massive effort is now being made.

The following figures underscore the dimensions of the undertaking:

To achieve the immediate Indian objective, *i.e.* to lower the birth rate from 41 to 25 per 1,000 by 1975, will require some such "mix" as 3 million sterilizations *annually* which would eventually prevent 4½ million births, the use of condoms and other contraceptive techniques by some 15 million families to prevent 4 million births, and one million IUCD insertions to prevent 500,000 births.

It is not too much to say that the future of India will be profoundly affected by the answers to the following questions.

1. *Will the Indian Government continue to give family planning top priority?* The critical importance of family planning has now been accepted by the Central Government and in greater or lesser degrees by all State Governments. Public opinion is favourable; there is no active political or religious opposition. Budgets are expected to continue to rise as the needs expand; the governmental efforts become more effective and public acceptance increases. But with so many competing needs there is always danger of a let down.

2. *Can the necessary organization be recruited and trained?* A nationwide family planning programme of these dimensions is probably the biggest challenge that India or any other developing nation has ever faced. However, it is reassuring to remember that the Indian malaria control programme which was put together in less than a decade reduced the incidence of malaria from 100 million cases annually as recently as 1953 to less than 50,000 today.

Although this programme included the efforts of some 100,000 trained workers and the massive use of DDT, the logistical requirements of the family planning effort are substantially greater.

3. *Can the necessary public support be mustered and maintained?* This is a *key* question. India's task in curbing her population is far more difficult than the problem of becoming self-sufficient in foodgrains. If only 20 per cent of Indian cultivators can be persuaded to accept the newly-developed seeds, fertilizers, pesticides and improved irrigation, India's food problem can probably be solved.

However, to achieve India's family planning goal requires the support and cooperation of at least 60 per cent of the entire population. The dimensions of the necessary programmes of research, organization, explanation and motivation are staggering.

Although there are no significant cultural or religious barriers against family planning, there is the stark problem of opening the minds of 100 million married couples to a new and revolutionary concept.

*4. Will the more technically advanced countries apply their vast research facilities to the development of a simpler, reversible, truly effective contraceptive technique?*

On the one hand, critics from developed nations never cease telling the people of developing nations that they must somehow stop having so many babies or disaster will overtake them. Yet, with all of their vast scientific resources, facilities and expertise, advanced nations have thus far failed to come up with a contraceptive that meets the special conditions in Asia and Africa, *i.e.*, safe, acceptable, reversible, inexpensive and easy to use.

The stark reality of the world's bulging population is that while several nations are doing a great deal to control population growth, this is just *not* enough. A crash research programme for better family planning methods is needed.

The National Institute of Child Health and Development has primary responsibility within the United States Government for research in family planning. However, it obligated only $ 7.7 million in the last fiscal year for population research, and almost none of this was for improved contraceptives.

The most promising work in this field is being done by the Population Council, founded by John D. Rockefeller 3rd and supported by Rockefeller Foundation and Ford Foundation funds. In Western Europe, where research and development facilities are also widespread, the effort is minimal.

The annual research investment needed to develop at a fast pace contraceptives more widely acceptable to families of the developing nations is said to be on the order of $ 150 million. Although this is more than ten times our present expenditures, it is less than two per cent of the annual research budget for military equipment.

Contrary to the Malthusians, the danger now facing India and other developing countries is not that the people will starve to death— India's food production could be increased fourfold—but rather that the schools, housing, doctors, hospitals, and consumer goods required to raise the living standards of a rapidly increasing population will simply be unavailable.

A few years ago anyone suggesting that India would be self-sufficient in food by 1972 would have been considered a dreamer. Today there is a reasonable prospect that this goal will be achieved.

Unfortunately all this effort may largely be wasted without a comparable breakthrough in the technology of contraception. High hopes for achieving a balance between world population and food output will be shattered unless efforts to check population growth are instituted on a crash basis.

If the scientists of the technologically advanced nations are able to meet this challenge, they will have made an enormous contribution to a politically stable and economically viable world.

U PON receiving a request for agricultural and family planning information from a Member of the U.S. House of Representatives, I sent the following report with more detailed figures in spring 1968:

"Dear Mr. Congressman: "I appreciate very much your thoughtful inquiry about India's agricultural and family planning programmes because there is such a great need for understanding in depth important developments taking place in this part of the world.

"India is making impressive progress in agriculture, and the prospects for attaining self-sufficiency by the early 1970s are better than when I wrote you in the fall. Because of the record foodgrain harvest, the total available food supply produced will equal or exceed the level that has been available on a per capita basis from production plus imports in recent years.

"This is an important forward step. But with bumper crops also come increased demands, thus keeping India in the market for food. Whether this is concessional or commercial will probably depend to some extent upon the supply and political situation in the exporting countries.

"Your statement that by the mid 70's the U.S. will not have enough excess grain to feed all the poorer nations of the world is I think unduly pessimistic.

"Beginning in 1946, there were numerous statements that population was outrunning food supply and that we were headed downhill toward disaster. Two years ago a surge of such statements was led by officials of the U.S. Department of Agriculture who indicated that we were approaching a danger zone.

"These officials have now modified their predictions by saying that the Malthusian era is some years in the future as a result of developments such as we have seen in India this year.

"I am hopeful that India's dependence on the United States for food imports can be sharply reduced by 1971 and largely eliminated a few years after that.

"I would not like to see our foodgrain policies operate in a legislative strait jacket requiring the provision of 3X, 2X and X million tons of grain specifically for the next three years and then no more. It is conceivable that two or three good crop years would reduce the need for concessional imports of grain to the vanishing point prior to 1971. Poor years might again temporarily increase this need for assistance.

"The following family planning data, put together by the Government of India and U. S. Agency for International Development officials, is in response to your questions. The figures apply to calendar year 1967 unless otherwise indicated.

1. *Question*—How many women of child-bearing age are there in India?

*Answer*—Approximately 100,000,000 (out of a total mid-year population estimate of 507,000,000). Of these, 90,000,000 are married women of child-bearing age.

2. *Question*—How many should be subtracted from that figure because they are currently pregnant?

*Answer*—20,000,000 (est.)

3. *Question*—How many should be subtracted because they have not yet achieved the usually desired number of four children?

*Answer*—48,800,000 (est.) This figure includes pregnant women.

4. *Question*—How many additional women reach child-bearing age each year?

*Answer*—4,500,000 (est.)

5. *Question*—How many are currently receiving the IUD (the "loop" per month?

*Answer*—IUD insertions for 1967 totalled 709,000 or an average of 59,000 a month.

How many are currently being sterilized each month ?

*Answer*—Sterilizations for 1967 totalled 1,501,000 or an average of 125,000 per month.

How many of these are from the upper classes and not in the villages ?

*Answer*—The proportion varies greatly from state to state. The loop tends to be an urban programme. Vasectomies, on the other hand, have proved acceptable so far on an increasing level to both urban and rural men.

6. *Question*—How many retain the IUD after one year?

*Answer*—On the basis of follow-up studies available to date, about 65 per cent retain the IUD after one year, less than 50 per cent retain it for more than two years.

7. *Question*—How many doctors or assistants are there in India now qualified to insert the IUD or perform vasectomies ?

*Answer*—As of 1967, there were approximately 107,000 qualified doctors in active practice in India, 94,000 male and 13,000 female. Of these, 3,797 doctors have received comparatively comprehensive training in family planning, including training in IUD insertions and vasectomies. In addition, 8,913 doctors have received short-term course training.

8. *Question*—How many of these are actually involved in the IUD programme? How many in sterilizations?

*Answer*—As of March 10, 1968, there were 3,699 stationary IUD units (at Public Health Centres and Sub-centres or other clinics offering IUD services), and 364 mobile units. Each of these was staffed with a doctor or an assistant capable of inserting IUD's.

Stationary sterilization units totalled 3,174 and mobile units totalled 328, or a total of 3,502 units each equipped with a doctor capable of performing vasectomies.

(It should be noted that many of these units, and their doctors, provided both types of services.)

9. *Question*—How many additional ones are being trained each month?

*Answer*—Between November 10, 1967, and March 10, 1968, the number of additional doctors trained in long-term courses was 861 and in short-term courses 793 or a monthly average of 287 and 264 respectively.

10. *Question*—To enable the IUD programme to reach all women of child-bearing age and presumably willing to accept it, how many doctors and assistants will be needed?

*Answer*—The size of the programme would depend on whether the target is conceived as being large enough to service the number of women who reach child-bearing age annually (that is, about 4.5 million) or large enough to take care of the full backlog of 90,000,000 married fertile couples.

"A formula for calculating the number of doctors needed which can be applied to any target should assume the following: (a) IUD insertions can be done at the rate of 50 per day per doctor (female) if sufficient candidates are available; (b) Sterilizations can be done at the rate of 20 per day per doctor. (Although more can be done, this is the rate recommended as maximum by a general meeting of State Health secretaries.)

"The critical problem to date appears to be less the availability of doctors in general, than getting doctors, particularly female doctors, out to the rural areas. As an example, only 200 lady doctors, inserting 50 loops a day could insert 3,000,000 IUD's in a year of 300 working days if the women were lined up and ready to be serviced, and if lady doctors were willing to spend full time inserting loops.

"One answer to this which the Government of India has increasingly adopted is the use of mobile vans to bring the doctors, both for IUD insertions and vasectomies, to the rural areas. Even if doctors cannot be found willing to work in mobile vans full time, Government of India experience to date indicates that sufficient numbers could be persuaded to work part-time to enable vans to be staffed adequately to meet anticipated demand.

"A practicable guess is that one fully qualified female practitioner (whether doctor or nurse or even lady health visitor especially trained in vasectomy operation) per rural public health block, or a total of 5400, supplied with transport as needed, to service IUD camps in outlying areas, could take care of any foreseeable IUD insertion demand. Supply of male doctors, given adequate mobility, does not seem to be a problem.

"Loop programmes involve more personnel requirements than those for insertions alone. Decentralization and increased mobility at the block level is needed both for insertion and also for follow ups of cases to provide general reassurance of the patient and substitute means of contraception where the loop is not retained.

11. *Question*—The same foregoing data with respect to sterilization of men.

*Answer*—Data has been provided, where relevant and available, in the answers to questions 5 through 10 above.

12. *Question*—I understand the Government forbids abortions. How many illegal abortions are estimated take place per year?

*Answer*—According to estimates of the Committee on Legalization of Abortion (appointed by the Government of India, Ministry of Health in 1964), as of 1966, approximately 4,000,000 induced abortions are performed annually, most of them illegal.

13. *Question*—I discount the pill as a control method because it has not yet proved effective elsewhere in developing countries. Nevertheless, I hope you will include an "educated guess" as to how many women have maintained use of the pill for, say, one year.

*Answer*—Sales of oral contraceptives through commercial channels is approximately 225,000 cycles monthly. The number of women using oral contraceptives regularly is believed to be about 200,000 at the present time. Government of India distribution of oral contraceptives through public health channels is still in the pilot demonstration phase.

"I agree with your observation that we need a much better family planning method. Perhaps science will, as you suggest, discover such a method, but I wonder if we should be content to let science take its own course and time in the matter? I strongly urge a greatly intensified effort by the United States Government and private industry to put their vast research facilities to work on finding an acceptable, simple, reversible contraceptive for mass consumption.

"While India is making a great deal of progress on coming to grips with their need to control their population growth, a tremendous all-out effort is necessary and success is by no means assured. The U.S. can help India in this crucial programme and help provide an economic base that will permit India to maintain political stability within its own cultural framework.

"My major concern though is that with our primary focus on the frustrating situation in Vietnam at this time, we will fail to provide India with the support it needs to emerge in the next five to eight years as a politically viable, democratic nation offering a better life to its people and capable of providing an effective Asian counterweight to China."

# 11. Confidence: Essential Ingredient of Progress

*At a meeting of the Indian Chamber of Commerce at Baroda, Gujarat, in 1966, Ambassador Bowles challenged the sceptics to see for themselves modern India's progress and urged young businessmen to play a more confident, creative role in making their country economically self-sufficient. Two years later in a series of* American Reporter *columns he noted the progress.*

SEVERAL DAYS ago I had a stimulating discussion with a young European news correspondent who had recently spent eighteen months in China followed by a long stay in India.

Naturally I was interested in his impressions of the comparative economic progress in the world's two largest nations, one operating under a communist dictatorship, the other practising democracy.

Since both countries are vast and complex the correspondent was understandably hesitant to give categorical replies to all my questions. However, it was his impression that the record of the two nations in providing clothing, food and housing for their people is now roughly comparable.

In both India and China he saw appalling slum areas and many thousands of people who suffered from inadequate diets. He also saw the significant progress that each had made in coping with its problems.

Although he had visited several modern factories in both countries, he was reluctant to make a general comparison in regard to industrial development.

Statistics in China are either lacking or hopelessly distorted. Hence it was difficult for him to go beyond the general impression that the economic accomplishments of the two nations are now

roughly equal. However, China's vast nuclear weapons programmes will in the days ahead inevitably hold back the modernization
of China's transport system, the expansion of fertilizer production
and other essential industrial developmental efforts.

Having commented on the similarities, the correspondent
emphasized two major differences which he felt were of the greatest
importance: one positive, the other negative and worrisome.

On the positive side he was impressed with the dramatic contrast
between the atmosphere of freedom which he found everywhere
in India and the police state restraints which faced him in China.

Wherever he travelled in India he felt free to call on Government officials and political leaders; he asked pointed questions
and received frank answers. In China, he said, such freedom
would be unthinkable.

However, on the negative side this observer found a sharp and
disturbing contrast between what he described as the fervent, confidence in the future that impressed him everywhere in China and
the spirit of defeatism which he often found here in India.

"Why", he asked me, "does India, which has progressed at least
as much as China, not take greater pride in its accomplishments?
Why is China so confident. Why is India so insecure ?" These are
crucial questions which deserve thoughtful answers and I am not at
all sure that I can provide them.

Every foreign visitor in India is impressed to find that the public
focus is not what India has done in the relatively brief period since
independence, but on its shortcomings and failures. Everywhere
he hears charges of corruption, confusion, inertia and incompetence
while the accomplishments are either ignored or dismissed as
insignificant.

Let us briefly review Indian economic and social progress since
independence:*

> Malaria has been reduced from 100 million cases in 1952 to
> less than 50,000 in 1966.
>
> India's elementary school system is now providing education
> for more than three times the number of pupils than it
> provided for fifteen years ago. Each year India is turn-
> ing out more than 5,000 doctors and 10,000 engineers.

---

*The following statistics were compiled from 1965-1966 data.

India's steel production has increased six times.

India's electric power capacity is now five times what it was in 1953 and is expected to double again in the next five years.

India's railroads have been largely modernized, the highway system has been expanded and improved, and heavy industry is now growing rapidly.

In regard to agriculture, much has been said and written about India's massive food shortages; rarely do you hear of the equally massive efforts that are now being made to increase food production.

How many Indians know of the five million acres that are being intensively cultivated this year with new seeds, fertilizer, and scientific irrigation, of the rapid expansion of the fertilizer industry, or of the wide scale introduction of pesticides?*

Self-examination that leads to a balanced analysis of the successes and failures and to the correction of past mistakes in programming and administration is a healthy thing. But mass dissatisfaction which ends in a blind national frustration is destructive and self-defeating.

SUCH scepticism, I find, rampant in New Delhi, which reaffirms my belief that national capitals are poor places from which to gain perspective on any nation's progress.

Americans and foreigners who confine themselves to Washington, D.C., become woefully out of touch with what is going on in America.

Similarly, Indians and foreigners who stick too close to New Delhi often fail to grasp the extraordinary changes that are taking place in this vast and complex country.

Recently, on a three-day visit to Palampur in the Kangra Valley, I noted on the back of an envelope more than fifty specific examples of progress and change within a five-mile drive of this lovely mountain town. Here are a few items from my list:

— Six elementary schools, four of them new.

— Two higher secondary schools, both new.

— Two primary health centres with signs promoting family planning services, both new.

---

*For 1968-69 there are 30 million acres.

— A number of Jersey cattle breeding stations, one of which proudly displayed the sign "here we turn grass into milk."
— Four animal husbandry stations, all new.
— Many signs calling for the final eradication of malaria with the dates when the various villages had been last sprayed with DDT.
— Two soil conservation centres.
— Three improved seed stations, all newly constructed.
— Two block development offices.
— Palampur Municipal Library and Reading Room.
— Palampur Leprosy Clinic with signs saying: "now leprosy can be cured" and "help stamp out the false stigma attached to leprosy."
— Three mulberry farms operated by the "Punjab Silkworm Industries."
— Several centres of the Punjab Forestry Department's programme for planting eucalyptus trees.
— A youth Leadership Training Camp organized by the United States Peace Corps.
— An Indo-German collaboration to improve agricultural practices.
— Three reforestation and soil conservation centres.
— More than a dozen impressive enterprises of the Punjab Industries Department.

In each of these centres of activity trained Indian administrators, educators, and technicians were working to open up new visions of progress and opportunity to introduce new techniques, to encourage new efforts, and to create a new sense of participation and personal involvement.

How many of them, I wondered, were there 19 years ago on Independence Day, August 15, 1947. I surmised there were very few.

That evening I was back in Delhi convinced once again that for those who question Indian's future there is a ready-made answer: let them go to the towns and villages where striking signs of change are everywhere evident and see for themselves.

THIS conviction was underscored by a letter I recently received from an outstanding American agricultural expert I had come to know and respect when I served here as Ambassador in the early 'fifties. He too noted the remarkable economic progress which has been achieved in many of India's rural communities since independence.

His comments are helpful in giving us a clearer perspective on these changes. I believe many Indians will be heartened by the observations my friend makes in his letter. Let me share them with you:

"Dear Mr. Bowles: I was very much pleased with my visit to the Etawah district in U.P. a few days back. Having worked there as an employee of the Government of the United Provinces in the late 1940's, and having had a continuing interest in just what has taken place in the years that have followed, my trip was especially meaningful to me.

"My first observation is that crops are generally very good. In fact the crops look much better than I remember the area.

"As we passed through the town of Etawah, and headed down the Kanpur road to the Etawah project area, I noted that the crops looked even better.

"The land along each side of the road was almost completely used and the fields of jowar and other crops were excellent. I found out later that more than 1,000 acres of the new high-yielding hybrid jowar had been planted in the area, and that fertilizer is in great demand.

"I talked to one farmer who showed me his field of jowar that had to be replanted. Since he had no more of the good seed, he transplanted surplus plants from another field. He has an excellent crop.

"I visited one young farmer who harvested more than 100 bushels of wheat per acre last season. I recall that the highest yield we were able to get in 1949 was 67 bushels. This year's was the best wheat that I had ever seen. The new dwarf Mexican wheats together with proper fertilization and management have opened new opportunities to the farmers, and they are making use of these opportunities.

"There were several young farmers who are doing an excellent job—they are the new leaders. They do not want to move to the city. They do not want a job in the Government. They want to stay on the land. I asked one of the young men if he planned to stay on the farm, and he said: 'Now there is no need to leave.' Prosperity lies in farming with modern methods.

"The little villages that I used to know have grown. Many have become towns. The children looked healthier and better dressed. There are many more schools. I did not see any evidence of malaria. Certainly no one was hungry.

"One can't help but be overwhelmed with the increase in people, and concerned with the problems that such increases hold for the future. Family planning is urgently needed.

"However, I am convinced that the people in this area are living better. Certainly production is much higher. None of the children were naked. These villages certainly were cleaner. Almost every farmer had little piles of compost on his field. Most of the villagers that I met had good bicycles, many of them relatively new.

"There is a new power line, and all along this line one can see tube-wells. Farmers are getting water when they need it. There are several hundred of these wells, many of them constructed by private well-drillers.

"I was told by a number of people that the farmers with their own wells are much happier than with cooperative ownership. Good seed, water, access to fertilizer and insecticides and favourable prices have made it possible for the farmers to show what they can do.

"I saw a number of older people whom I remembered and who remembered me.

In one village an old man in answering my question as to what had happened to his people during the past 20 years, had this to say: 'You remember how we lived; we had no hope. Now look at our fields, our cattle. See our children. All who are old enough go to school. They can read and write. My friend, earth has almost met the sky.'

"As the old man talked to me, he held my hands between his. His face beamed and his eyes shone. I was deeply moved. I will never forget him.

"To those who claim that the average Indian villager is slow, dull, not responsive to opportunity; that he does not respond to a decent price; that he somehow has to be made to do those things that are good for him; let them go to Etawah and see for themselves what the villager can and will do when he is given a chance.

"There are no doubt many places where this can be seen. I just visited this one area; an area that I know, and it gives me much hope."

LET ME share two other experiences I have had, again demonstrating the progress India is making.

In the midst of India's record-breaking harvest in October 1967, I visited the East Jumna Canal water-works and irrigation system in Saharanpur District of Uttar Pradesh. It was a delightful and reassuring trip, illustrating at first-hand the agricultural revolution now taking place in India.

In our drives through the countryside, I saw bumper crops—rice, sugarcane, cotton, jowar, bajra—most of them ready for harvesting.

I also visited the magnificent engineering complex, the Tajewala Canal headworks. Here crores of gallons of water from the Jumna is stored, controlled, and distributed to the farmlands of Uttar Pradesh, Haryana and the Punjab.

The massive irrigation system feeds lakhs of acres of potentially fertile fields which need water to become productive.

My observations confirmed to me that rural India is about to harvest a bumper crop. This will come as a shock to those prophets of gloom and doom, both Indian and foreign, who have been telling us that the "backward" Indian farmer can never be persuaded to accept modern agricultural techniques.

While this year's generous monsoon has no doubt contributed to the record harvest, it is not merely a result of adequate rain. An equally important factor is the unprecedented agricultural revolution which is now evident in many parts of India.

The ingredients of this revolution include new, high-yielding seeds—some locally developed, some introduced from Mexico, Taiwan and the Philippines; greatly stepped-up use of fertilizer and pesticides, better use of water, more ample agricultural credit, increased incentives for the cultivators and heavier reliance on free markets. Most important of all, the breakthrough relies on the bold commitment by the Government and people of India to make India self-sufficient in food.

IT ALSO stems from increased self-confidence. For years social anthropologists have been asserting that the hundreds of millions of people who are part of the "traditional cultures" of Asia, Africa and Latin America are uninterested, unwilling and incapable of improving their lot.

A recent conversation in my office underscores the extent to which this old stereotype is now out of touch with today's realities. My visitor was Professor McKim Marriott of the University of Chicago, who in 1951 had spent six months living in and studying a backward, tradition-bound village in Aligarh District in western U.P. Now, seventeen years later, Professor Marriott has returned to this village and found changes which are breathtaking.

In 1951 the inadequate supply of water for the village came from shallow wells. Today there are ten electric tube-wells, assuring most cultivators two crops each year. The new high-yielding hybrid seeds, fertilizer and pesticides are now available to everyone.

Professor Marriott reports that malaria has disappeared, and that cotton gins, bicycles and electric driven mills, virtually unknown in 1951, are evident everywhere.

The villagers now have wool clothing for the cold winter months, where previously only cotton had been available; there are now more substantial houses, very little unemployment, five temples (where previously there had been none) and an impressive new school.

In 1951 education had a low priority and almost no child had gone past the 5th standard. At present more than half of the children are attending school. Some 25 boys have already gone beyond the 5th standard, eight are in inter-college, and one is attending a university. Every land-owning family now has at least one son in high school.

The villagers told the Professor that the changes had come gradually at first, and then with a rush. For example, when the villagers saw how dramatically the new seeds and fertilizers increased output per acre, their demands exceeded the immediate supply.

As a result of these fundamental changes in viewpoint, there has been a marked change in social patterns. Different castes now work and eat side by side; festivals based on caste distinctions are increasingly rare, and many villagers are now showing a new interest in their culture, history and environment.

Most of the villagers are also participating in politics, with the vast majority voting in the current election. The priorities of each village programme are freely and vigorously discussed, and villagers have assumed decisive roles in the decision-making process.

The most striking aspect of all, according to Professor Marriott, is the new sense of confidence. The old fear of government officials, tax collectors, money lenders, police and strangers has almost completely disappeared. And with this new self-confidence has come a determination to direct their own lives, thus depending less on the goodwill of others.

In rural India life is still hard and the problems are still massive. For example, in many villages, including the one Professor Marriott is now restudying, the family planning programme is barely getting underway; some means must be found to provide land for the landless; rural electrification must be speeded up and loans at low interest made available to all cultivators.

However, the tens of thousands of Indian villages, which like this village in U.P. are now coming alive, demonstrate that even the humblest and most isolated human beings, given half a chance, are capable of providing new hope, dignity and opportunities for themselves.


YOUNG men of India are citizens of the second largest nation in the world, a vast nation with a culture reaching back over thousands of years. On all sides they can see evidence of the great civilization which has been built here.

As citizens of the new India they are members of a society which has shown an enormous talent in science and technology and which, when given adequate encouragement, demonstrates a capacity and initiative for hard, effective work.

The defeatists tend to regard the tens of millions of their less fortunate fellow-citizens as apathetic and unthinking literates. Others with a clearer perspective see them as increasingly skilled farmers and workers. Far-seeing businessmen are beginning to recognize them as potential consumers for the goods which India's factories will soon be capable of producing.

Perhaps the professional pessimists are right when they assert that India will fail to draw itself effectively into our modern world. But anyone who knows India simply cannot ignore the talent, the capacity for work and the strong democratic political faith of its people.

The key is to find new ways to release the dynamism of its workers, cultivators and businessmen. A modern, economically viable democracy cannot be built on a foundation of stale ideological slogans. It must adopt and launch development programmes that are pragmatic, hard-headed and realistic.

There is no doubt that in a developing economy such as India's the *government* must be responsible for building the necessary infrastructure. It must provide the capital for building schools, health facilities, communications, power plants and transportation.

However, those developing countries which are now moving forward most rapidly are those providing the maximum opportunities for citizens who are able and eager to produce high quality products at a fair price for an expanding market.

The task of Government is to find ways to encourage the resourcefulness and initiative of its citizens, to stimulate new investment, and to reward those private ventures which are socially productive as well as personally profitable.

The challenge to young business and governmental leaders is to demonstrate that profit does not preclude social responsibility, that they have the courage and imagination to carry India rapidly along the road to self-sufficiency. The fast developing revolution in Indian agriculture, based as it is on unleashing the skill and energy of the Indian farmer, presents tremendous opportunities, not only for the rural people of India, but for urban people as well.

I believe that the young businessmen of India have a special opportunity to play a constructive, creative role in making this great nation economically self-sufficient. If enough of them recognize this opportunity, there is solid ground for confidence. No one expects a new India to be built overnight. It will take time, dedication and a maximum effort.

The obstacles are admittedly great: obstacles of old habits, prejudices and ways of thinking. But there were equal obstacles in the way of other countries and they were overcome.

With confidence and hard work I believe that the new generation of young Indians can enable this enormously promising land to achieve a breakthrough to expanded production, to higher living standards and to increased justice for all of its people.

# Economic Assistance and International Cooperation

*To those peoples in the huts and villages across the globe struggling to break the bonds of mass misery, we pledge our best efforts to help them help themselves, for whatever period is required—not because the communists may be doing it, not because we seek their votes, but because it is right. If a free society cannot help the many who are poor, it cannot save the few who are rich.*

—PRESIDENT JOHN F. KENNEDY

*As the years go by, the only relevant point will be the struggle of the vast number of dispossessed people for a place in the sun. If the richer nations help them, then we can create a relationship of mutual understanding. If they do not, there is bound to be a conflict.*

—PRIME MINISTER INDIRA GANDHI

# 12. What Foreign Aid Can and Cannot Do

*Ambassador Bowles addressed an American audience in New Delhi in December 1963 on the objectives of the United States' economic assistance programme. He also explained in a subsequent* American Reporter *column the dilemma facing the U. S. Government in India in using its large holdings of P. L. 480 rupees.*

THIS SPRING the foreign aid programme is once again undergoing its annual drubbing on Capitol Hill and in certain elements of the American press.

As has become their custom, many frustrated legislators and editorial writers are once again attacking the programme on every possible score while many others who have been among its loyal friends appear to be on the defensive.

Yet there is a paradox in this situation. On the basis of recent Gallup Polls, the programme's popularity in the country as a whole is at the highest level since its inception. According to Dr. Gallup, 58 per cent of the American people are in favour of it, with only 30 per cent opposed.

What is more, most of those who remain opposed to foreign aid grossly over estimated its cost, with the majority of guesses ranging anywhere from 10 to 50 per cent of our budget.

In fact, of course, foreign assistance amounts to less than one-twenty-fifth of our annual federal expenditures, and even this percentage may be reduced further as our national wealth increases and our loans are repaid.*

Now how are we to explain this paradox of a clear contradiction between apparent public approval and vocal political opposition?

---

*In 1968 the U. S. Foreign aid budget was one-sixtieth of the Federal budget.

I believe that the answer lies largely in our inadequate efforts in the last ten years to explain the real objectives of our aid programme to the American people and to their Congress.

The official reasons offered in support of the programme during the 1950's were often contradictory, inaccurate, or irrelevant. The upshot has been widespread public confusion on the programme's real objectives and widespread disillusionment when it fails to achieve the false goals so often proposed.

For instance, the programme has been most widely presented in terms of simple anti-communism. Since a major U.S. objective is to stop communism, this implies that if communism did not exist, there would be little or no reason for the programme itself.

For many years this negative perspective was actually written into the preamble of the enabling foreign aid legislation through language suggesting that the programme would be necessary only as long as the communist conspiracy threatened U.S. interests.

For developing countries seeking aid, such a view also ironically turned communism into a valuable natural resource, such as oil or uranium.

By the logic of the argument, any developing nation devoid of a powerful communist neighbour or a noisy communist minority becomes *per se* a poor candidate for U.S. economic assistance. It has been suggested sardonically that a developing nation which lacked a communist minority should plant and nourish a small but vocal communist movement—and then implore the U.S. to provide the funds to squelch it.

Since even communists are sometimes blessed with a sense of humour, it is not surprising that Soviet spokesmen talking to the people of Asia and Africa have said:

"The Soviet Union offers you loans and technicians to speed your development. For this you are grateful. But you should be equally grateful to Moscow for whatever aid the Americans give you. They are quite frank in saying that if they were not so frightened of us communists, they would give you nothing."

IN 1959, as a member of the House Foreign Affairs Committee, I introduced an amendment to the preamble of the foreign aid bill which outlined the purpose of the aid programme in the affirmative terms of our traditional dedication to freedom and opportunity. Although my amendment was approved overwhelmingly, our thinking on aid is still bound in a major degree by the same narrow, self-limiting anti-communist obsession.

A second fallacy in our past presentation of foreign aid is the claim that the programme will bring us military allies, win us votes in the United Nations, or gain us support against Cuba and the Red Chinese. In other words, it is assumed that the programme's primary objective is to make friends and buy votes.

This argument is equally hollow and futile. It is no more possible to buy the long-term loyalty of a nation than it is to buy the enduring loyalty of a friend. To attempt to do so can lead only to frustration and antagonism.

Suppose a wealthy resident of the town in which you live should offer to build a swimming pool for your children, a new library, and an extension to your town hall—provided only that you and your neighbours agree to support his political views on public questions.

What would you do? You would tell him that your town is not for sale. You would invite him to take his money and go live elsewhere.

Unfortunately, in the past we Americans have inadvertently placed ourselves often in the position of the richest man in the world community, naively trying to buy friends and supporters for our views. Yet common sense and a knowledge of human nature should tell us that foreign aid will not make us love our neighbours, make our neighbours love us, or win international popularity laurels for us—and we should not expect it to do so.

Finally, it has often been wrongly assumed that the success or failure of the aid programme should be judged purely and simply by the rate of economic growth in the recipient country.

Obviously, increased agricultural and industrial production is of the utmost importance. Yet the record shows that when the added production is badly distributed, it only widens the gap between rich and poor—and, in the process, inevitably erodes the political stability which we are striving to create.

There are many examples. Some of the most productive countries of Latin America, for instance, already have per capita incomes greater than several European countries. Yet because the privileged minority at the top may be getting rapidly richer while the impoverished embittered masses at the bottom of the ladder are making little or no progress, these nations can be as politically explosive as the poorest African or Asian country whose per capita income may be no greater than $100 a year.

In view of our past failure adequately to explain the programme, it is a tribute to our national common sense that so many Americans have continued to give tacit support to foreign assistance for basically humanitarian reasons.

This leads us back to the basic question: If the purpose of our aid programme is not simply to combat communism, and if it cannot be expected to buy friends or votes, and if faster economic growth alone is no sure cure-all, what exactly is foreign aid good for? What will it do?

The answer to this question is deceptively simple to state: a wisely administered U.S. aid programme can help build nations that are increasingly prepared to defend their independence against totalitarian enemies—external or internal, overt or covert—and increasingly willing to work with us as partners on common projects which may lead the world a little closer to peace.

In other words, the purpose of our aid programme is to develop independent nations able and willing to stand on their own feet—and thereby to share with us a dedication to peace and freedom.

To put the question more sharply, we have a critical choice: we can help to guide the economic and social upheaval now sweeping Asia, Africa and Latin America into constructive, peaceful channels; or we can sit back nervously and ineffectually, while the revolution of rising expectations in Asia, Africa and Latin America slips into the hands of reckless extremists who despise everything we stand for—and a succession of Red Chinas and Red Cubas comes into being.


WITHIN this more realistic framework of achieveable objectives, let us now consider to what extent our aid programme has thus far succeeded—and to what extent it has failed.

In the years since 1946, the most dramatic success of the foreign aid programme has come, of course, in Western Europe.

Following World War II a political and economic vacuum existed in Europe.    Bombed out industries lay in ruins, and each nation's economy was scarred by inflation, vast unemployment and utter hopelessness.

In the United States, meanwhile, shortsighted political leaders of both parties led a mad scramble to disband our victorious armies and draw back into our isolationist shell.

With most of Eastern Europe already overrun by the Red armies, with large and well-organized communist parties in France, Italy, and elsewhere, and with nearly 200 battle-tested Soviet divisions still under arms, Stalin was confident that communism could quickly fill the entire European vacuum.

Yet his efforts failed.    Soviet pressures toward the Mediterranean through Greece and Turkey were forestalled by the prompt counteraction of a massive military and economic assistance programme under the Truman doctrine.

Within months, Marshall Plan aid was provided to rebuild the war-torn economies of Western Europe, followed by the creation of NATO as an effective military shield between our Allies and the communist world.

Although the communist danger was obviously on our minds, Secretary of State Marshall was careful to present our aid effort within an affirmative framework.    Its objective, he stressed, was not negatively to oppose some other ideology or ism, or to win subservient satellites but positively to create prosperous, independent European nations capable of standing on their own feet and making their own decisions.

It is noteworthy that in the 15 years since the Marshall Plan got under way, and quite contrary to Stalin's confident expectations, there have been no communist territorial gains anywhere on the European continent.    Indeed, Western Europe has achieved a measure of political stability and economic prosperity unparalleled in its history.

There were many of our fellow citizens who charged at the time that the $13 billion we invested in the Marshall Plan was a 'giveaway' — just as there are many today who describe our present aid programme in Asia, Africa and Latin America as a 'giveaway'.

Yet the wisdom of this investment becomes all the more apparent when one compares the dismal Soviet record in Eastern Europe with the blooming economic and political conditions of Western Europe today.

While the Kremlin is still forced to bolster many of its East European satellites with economic loans, U.S. economic aid to Western Europe has ceased and we are now selling well over $6 billion worth of American goods each year to former recipients of Marshall Plan aid. Even the diehards must admit that that is a remarkably good return on our post-war investment in Europe's recovery.

What we have witnessed in Europe—what our foreign assistance programme has helped to create there—is nothing less than a new economic and political renaissance.

To be sure, for the moment some of the symptoms of Europe's new vitality can be irritating to us. Nevertheless, our aid programme to Europe brilliantly accomplished what it set out to do and today we are dealing with prosperous, independent allies. Would any thoughtful man prefer that we deal instead with the chaotic Europe of 1947.

In many other parts of the world foreign aid has also been a major success.

Let us consider, for example, what has happened in less than a generation in India, an underdeveloped country of 450* million people, equalling the combined population of Africa and Latin America.

Since I left India as U.S. Ambassador in 1953 and now ten years later, India's national income has increased by 42 per cent, with foodgrain production up by 56 per cent. In 1947 it was estimated that 100 million cases of malaria developed annually; now this debilitating disease has nearly disappeared. Life expectancy in India in 1947 was twenty-seven years; it is now forty-two.

In a country that was only 10 per cent literate fifteen years ago, 60 per cent of all Indian children under twelve now go to school. Indian industrial production is expanding by 10 per cent annually, one of the highest rates in the world.

In its first years of independence India developed a constitution that combined features of both the U.S. and British experience. Since then India has held three national elections—each the largest

---

*This and subsequent figures which deal with India are based on 1962 data.

exercise of the democratic privilege in the world—in which a higher percentage of people voted than in the U.S.

India has freedom of speech, freedom of religion, freedom of press, and a private enterprise sector that has been chalking up sizeable gains.

India's success has been in large measure due to its own efforts. The Indian people have worked hard, developed able leadership, learned by hard experience, and maintained a sound civil service based on solid British training.

But the Indians would be the first to agree that the outlook for the success of Indian democracy would not be so bright today had it not been for generous assistance from the U.S.

In the last fifteen years we have granted or loaned India $ 3. 9 billion in economic aid. Approximately 55 per cent of this assistance was in the form of "surplus" commodities—wheat, cotton, corn, etc. Another 42 per cent was in dollars for the purchase of materials —steels, railroad transportation equipment and machinery, manufactured mostly in the U.S. and produced by American workers. The remainder went for technical advice and instruction.

India's record of achievement is of great significance to that nation's future and security. Yet this record is also profoundly important to our own security.

Only through a free India, with growing strength and confidence, can we expect to see the development of a political and military balance to Communist China in Asia. What is more, a successful, expanding India demonstrates to all of the doubters and the faint hearted in Asia, Africa and Latin America that democracy is more than an impractical western political luxury; it is a realistic political and economic system that actually works in practice, that produces results.

Within the next 10 years the need for foreign assistance will begin to be reduced; and it foresees its eventual end as India's take-off point of self-sustaining growth is finally reached.

But India is by no means the only dramatic example of successful aid use outside Western Europe. In the same sub-continent, Pakistan is taking equally impressive strides towards national development with U.S. assistance. Together, these two nations hold the key to the future security of South Asia against pressures from Communist China.

These South Asian examples, moreover, are matched in other parts of the world. In Japan, Greece, Formosa, and Israel, our aid programme has either accomplished its purpose and been terminated, or is in the process of being phased out. Indeed, Japan and Israel are already extending such 'assistance to others. In Taiwan, Colombia, Tunisia, and many other countries steady progress is being made.

Therefore, the record shows that foreign aid, when handled wisely, can succeed in doing what it sets out to do—it can help to create viable independent nations.

O N THE other hand, where the programme has not been handled wisely, the results have naturally not been so good. Similarly, where our expectations have been unrealistic and grandiose, we have inevitably met disappointment.

In regard to the wise handling of economic assistance, we have learned some hard lessons from our Latin American experience in recent years; and today we are attempting to apply these lessons through tightened standards for aid distribution through the Alliance for Progress.

The primary lesson that we must learn from Cuba is that the United States cannot afford to support, or even to tolerate, corrupt, oppressive regimes, of whatever ideological base, which deny the basic aspirations of their own people for human dignity and a better life. As President Kennedy himself pointed out on more than one occasion, we wouldn't have had Castro if it had not been for Batista.

Reactionary right wing governments constitute the weakest defence against totalitarianism of the left. They are sitting ducks for the Castro Communists because they deny the dignity and rights of the majority of people—and their eventual overthrow through violence is inevitable as the economic and political pressures intensify.

What is the nature of these pressures? Consider these facts:

In Latin America today one and a half per cent of the people— those with 15,000 or more acres each—are said to own half of all agricultural land. Only a handful of countries have an effective income tax. In several countries local capital is being accumulated in Swiss banks for safekeeping at the same time that U.S. aid is requested, while scarce foreign exchange goes for perfume and Cadillacs instead of for machinery, tools and fertilizer plants.

In many Latin American countries the reforms needed to produce prosperity and stability are dangerously overdue. Yet because the essential economic and social revolution in many cases has not yet taken place, great wealth continues to exist explosively side by side with abject poverty.

The aid programme, therefore, should be used in a sensitive, responsible way to encourage reform. In the broadest political and human sense, we intend to use this programme to prevent situations getting so far out of hand that we are forced to make the impossible choice between the Castros and the Batistas of this world.

Those countries that are unable or unwilling to curb luxury spending, to stop the flight of capital, and to undertake far-reaching social and economic reforms should be dropped as aid recipients; or, in some cases, I believe our assistance should be limited to a modest U.S. presence through the Peace Corps and technical assistance programmes.

There will, of course, be inevitable exceptions in those situations where overwhelming strategic or political considerations make continuance of a dole necessary for our own security.

In such exceptional instances, however, let us at least frankly admit that our purposes are political, and not confuse these exceptions and standards of the rest of the programme.

SO MUCH for the lessons of our fifteen-year aid programme. What must we Americans do here and now, as the annual aid debate begins to rage again?

What we need to do now, as citizens and as a Government, is to strengthen the programme, to support it, and to recognize it as a basic arm of American foreign policy without which we would be sorely, perhaps fatally, handicapped.

In this regard, I believe that we should keep in mind five clear sets of objectives:

First, we have an overriding responsibility to explain to ourselves and to others what the programme can and cannot do. We should never fall prey to the tired old fallacies that have previously distorted our views of aid's possibilities.

Properly administered foreign assistance can do one thing, and one thing only: It can help to build independent nations capable of standing on their own feet and making their own free choices. And if we can do that, we can help create a rational world in which communism is steadily declining in influence—a world that holds some prospect of peace.

Second, we are now establishing and publicizing clear working criteria for the distribution of economic aid. The need for such criteria has been strongly implied in the Act for International Development as passed by Congress and the recent Clay Report has re-emphasized this need.

Let us remember that the Congress has directed us to do precisely what experience has taught us must be done if our overseas assistance effort is to succeed. For instance, the Act says:

> "Assistance will be based upon sound plans and programmes, be directed toward the social as well as economic development; be responsive to the efforts of the recipient countries to mobilize their own resources and help themselves; be cognizant of the external and internal pressures which hamper their growth and should emphasize long-range development assistance as the primary instrument of such growth."

In the spirit of the congressional legislation, we are now posing for ourselves some searching questions in regard to all requests for assistance from abroad.

These questions relate to the applicant's present per capita income and its distribution;

...the competence of the Government, and its sensitivity to the needs of the population;

...the existence of well-conceived, long-range national economic development plan;

...the adequate distribution and collection of the nation's tax burden;

...the priority given to the vast majority of citizens who live in the rural areas; the development of equitable land distribution and the creation of an integrated approach to community development;

...the existence of a favourable climate and adequate incentives for foreign and domestic private investment;

...and the maintenance of effective controls over the expenditure of foreign exchange for luxury imports.

Most important of all, we are asking ourselves whether a government which seeks our assistance exists with at least the general consent of its own population; in other words, is it sufficiently rooted in public support to assure the broad backing of its people necessary for a bold programme of economic and social development?

Although obviously no nation could respond affirmatively on all these counts, these are objectives that we must stress in developing priorities and standards for distribution for assistance.

Now let us consider a third general objective—the need for improvement in the planning and integration of the foreign aid programme, not only within our own Government but in connection with the wide and complex variety of international agencies and other countries that also operate in this field.

The United States Government provides unilateral aid through the Export-Import Bank, which helps the underdeveloped nations to finance the purchase of industrial goods in the United States; the Development Loan Fund, which provides long-term loans on easy terms payable in both dollars and soft currencies; U.S. technical assistance, which offers a wide range of specialists in planning and technology; the Peace Corps, which provides several thousand volunteers trained in teaching, nursing, rural development and the like; and Food for Peace, which distributes U.S. "surplus" farm products, including wheat, rice, powdered milk, and cotton.

But economic assistance for the developing nations is not solely an American enterprise. Loans and technical assistance are available from many international agencies. These include the World Bank, which provides loans payable in "hard currencies;" the International Development Association, which provides "soft loan;" the International Monetary Fund, which helps stabilize currencies; and the so-called specialized agencies of the U.N.—the World Health Organization, Food and Agricultural Organization, and UNESCO.

Finally, West Germany, France, Britain, Canada, Australia, Japan, Switzerland and Israel also provide unilateral economic assistance on a generally similar basis.

The staggering number of sources to which the developing nations can turn for assistance inevitably creates confusion and some over-lapping of effort. This suggests the need for careful planning to make sure that the right kind of aid is made available and that its use is effectively coordinated with the resources of the developing country itself.

COMPLICATIONS do, however, develop. For instance, a major problem which has built up over the years is our use of local currencies. In recent months there have been many inaccurate new stories about the use of rupees which the U.S. Government receives from India in return for American wheat shipments.

These stories have given many Indian citizens a highly distorted view of the size of United States rupee holdings and about the way in which they are distributed and spent. Let us consider the facts.

In the last ten years the United States has shipped to India 50 million (5 crores) tons of foodgrains, plus large quantities of cotton, milk powder, soybean oil and other agricultural products.

Instead of asking the Indian Government to pay for these commodities in dollars or in other hard currencies which are in short supply, we have accepted payment in rupees nearly all of which cannot be converted and spent outside of India.

Over the years an average of 79 per cent of these rupees has been made available by the U.S. Government to the Indian Government to help speed India's economic development. This development assistance has been provided mostly as loans at an interest rate of 2.5 per cent and partly as outright grants.

Of the remaining 21 per cent, about 7 per cent has been set aside as loans to joint American and Indian firms in the private sector which are seeking to expand their factories and hire more workers.

The remaining 14 per cent has been reserved to cover the expenses of the U.S. Mission in India, for educational exchanges, and to support specific developmental projects which are approved by the Indian Government.

In the first category, the U.S. Government has made rupee loans and grants totalling Rs. 1231 crores for a wide variety of projects. These include irrigation, agricultural programmes, industrial development banks, the establishment of 14 regional engineering colleges, malaria eradication, and medical teacher training programmes.

Other projects are the construction of hydro-electric and thermal power plants, improvement to roadways, and the construction of fertilizer plants.

In the second category of loans to private sector firms (the so-called Cooley Fund Loans) some of the recipients include: Otis Elevator of India, Ltd; Hindustan Aluminium Ltd. (Renukoot); Synthetics and Chemicals, Ltd. (Bareilly); Coromandel Fertilizers, Ltd. (Visakhapatnam), Goodyear Tyre and Rubber of India, Ltd.; Bharat Steel Tubes, Ltd. (Ganaur), and Union Carbide (India) Ltd. These loans have helped to provide tens of thousands of jobs for Indian workers.

In the third category is the 14 per cent of our rupee income which goes directly to the U.S. Government and which is used to finance special development projects and to cover some of the American Mission's operating costs in India. Over a period of ten years these expenditures have totalled 122 crores of rupees, or an average of about 12.2 crores of rupees annually.

Roughly 5 per cent of the rupees in this third category has been used to finance U.S. assisted agricultural development programmes and research in India. In addition, the construction and operating costs of seven agricultural universities have been covered by rupee grants to the Government of India. These universities are now making a major contribution to Indian agriculture.

About 25 per cent of the total in this category has been loaned and granted with the consent of the Indian Government to the Nepalese Government for development programmes in that country.

Approximately 60 per cent of the rupees in this same category helps cover the cost maintaining American property, of paying the salaries of our Indian employees, and other expenses connected with the running of the American Mission in India.

The remaining 10 per cent is utilized to finance educational exchange programmes between India and the United States, and to provide scientific textbooks for Indian students.

The U.S. Government, as a matter of policy, obtained the Government of India's agreement for the disbursement of any American owned rupees.

Also as a matter of policy, the U. S. Government seeks to avoid using rupees in a manner that would divert Indian resources from the task of national development.

For instance, because hard currency foreign exchange is the most scarce resource required for national development, we have been careful to keep to a minimum any requests to convert our rupees into dollars. Over the last ten years, only seven-tenths of one per cent of our total rupee earnings, about Rs. 11.5 crores, have been so converted—all with the consent of the Indian Government.

The bulk of reserves of U.S.-owned rupees are invested in Indian Government securities which means that they are available to the Indian Government.

Nevertheless, because of the massive emergency shipments of American wheat in the last two years, U.S.-owned rupees have been accumulating much faster than they have been spent. To help reduce the size of our rupee holdings and to put them to constructive use, I suggested the establishment of the Indo-American Foundation, to which the U.S. Government would assign some Rs. 225 crores as a capital fund. Thus, rupees now owned by the United States would no longer be ours but would belong to the Foundation. The interest from this fund would be used each year to further scientific education, economic research and development for the benefit of the Indian people.

Another possible use of our rupee reserves would be to expand the availability of rural credit, enabling Indian farmers to buy more fertilizer, more foodgrains, and more improved seeds to help speed India towards self-sufficiency.

These and other possibilities are still being explored.

NOW let me emphasize a fourth basic consideration of particular importance; orderly political growth in the developing nations is dependent in large measure upon what happens in the rural areas where 80 per cent of the people live.

When the rural areas are oppressed with poverty, exploitation, and injustice, they are easy targets for communist infiltration. Moreover, it is impossible for any developing nation to increase its industrial output rapidly if four-fifths of its people lack the purchasing power to buy its factory-produced goods.

Our aid programme therefore should be more and more closely related to the improvement of agriculture, the encouragement of land reform, the creation of rural extension services, and the building of rural schools, roads and clinics.

Fifth and last, let us take an imaginative approach to questions of public and private ownership, developing new mixed forms to meet management problems.

This question is one of practicality, not morality. As a matter of pure realism, the overburdened governments of the developing nations have enough to do without taking on the multiplicity of economic problems inherent in Government management of production.

Twenty years of Government service have made me increasingly aware of the limits of Government. As long as the results are satisfactory it is not our responsibility to impose our ideas in regard to public or private ownership on the recipients of our aid. To do so would be to open a Pandora's Box of imperialistic charges and to contribute to a less effective utilization of our own aid.

IN SUMMING up, there is no question but that our foreign aid programme is an absolutely vital instrument of American foreign policy, and that it has already made an enormous contribution to our national security.

The frustration that so many Americans seem to feel with this programme has resulted partly from inevitable mistakes in new areas of effort, partly from the complexities of the Cold War, but more than anything else from the unbalanced presentation in recent years of what the aid programme can and cannot do.

Yet it would be folly to allow our frustrations to thwart our capacity to deal with the present-day world. The fact is the programme in spite of many errors has on the whole been a brilliant success, and its continuance is essential if we are to develop the kind of peaceful world community in which we ourselves can prosper.

As we move to meet this challenge, we may be reminded of the words of Woodrow Wilson who once told a graduating class at Annapolis:

"There have been other nations as rich as we; there have been other nations as powerful; there have been other nations as spirited; but I hope we shall never forget that we created this nation, not to serve ourselves, but to serve mankind.... No other nation was ever born into the world with the purpose of serving the rest of the world just as much as it served itself."

# 13. Partners in Economic Growth

*Ambassador Bowles spoke at the inauguration ceremonies of the large Sharavathy Hydro-electric complex in Mysore in January 1965. Here and in subsequent* American Reporter *columns he outlined the reasons for American assistance to India, citing how foreign aid helped to build the United States and how U.S. voluntary agencies, including the Peace Corps, are contributing to India's process of modernization.*

THE AMERICAN people are proud and pleased to contribute capital and equipment for the building of this great hydro-electric plant. And I am personally grateful for the invitation of your Chief Minister to join with you in this impressive ceremony.

But precisely why should an American Ambassador be taking part in this dedication of an Indian dam, on an Indian river, running entirely through Indian soil, into the Arabian Sea?

I cannot add significantly to the praise which the Indian planners, engineers and workers have earned by their great achievement. Nor can I say anything fresh or new about the momentous contribution the dam will make to the people of Mysore and South India —the thousands of newly lighted villages, the hundreds of new small industrial plants and the scores of larger factories.

But what I *can* do is help answer a basic question on which there is much confusion both in your country and my own: Why have the American people who live on the other side of the world been loaning or giving India each year Rs. 225 crores in dollars plus an equal sum in wheat, rice and other commodities to speed India's ambitious development plans?

In our annual Congressional and public debates over what we

call "foreign economic assistance" a variety of claims are put forward to justify these expenditures to our American taxpayers.

Some advocates, for instance, argue that our contribution to overseas development will win us friends in India and elsewhere in Asia, Africa and Latin America. I sincerely hope that this dam and the other assistance we are giving India will contribute to this end, and I can assure you that there is a deep and genuine spirit of friendship in the United States toward India, her leaders and her people.

Yet if our friendship continues to grow, I do not believe it will be the result of the capital loans, wheat and rice which we send each year to India. In this context I am reminded of Mark Twain's remark to a contentious neighbour: "Why is it that you criticize me so? I cannot for the life of me remember ever having loaned you any money."

Indeed, our own American history should be enough to persuade us that recipient nations are not always grateful for foreign assistance. In the 19th century, for example, the United Kingdom invested literally billions of pounds in the building of American railroads and industry. Yet even today only a minority of Americans are conscious of the massive British contribution to our early economic development.

So, it would be a mistake for us Americans to have any illusions on this score. We earnestly seek the friendship of India, but we know that your friendship is no more for sale now than was our own in the critical early years of our development.

THE first foreign assistance to America came during our war for independence. It is a serious question whether the American colonists could have won their freedom from the British without French troops and financial support and without the efforts of dozens of foreign military advisers.

In the century that followed, the new American Republic made a major effort to attract investment capital from abroad.

This policy was so successful that by the early 1900's foreign investment in the United States had grown to 7 billion dollars (Rs. 525 crores). Since then it has increased to more than 20 billion dollars.

British capital contributed significantly to the rapid expansion of the American railway system, while French money helped build the American chemical industry.

American oil fields were developed by a combination of domestic and foreign capital. Capital from Germany speeded the growth of our chemical and plastic industries.

The Swiss-owned Nestle Chocolate Company presently employs more than 35,000 American workers in ten plants.

Recently, Japanese capital has also begun to move into the United States. A large Japanese-owned paper pulp mill is now being built in Alaska; plans are also under way to develop Alaskan coal resources with Japanese capital assistance.

One reason for the success of America's effort to attract foreign investment is the fact that such investment has been subject only to those restrictions which apply equally to similar American firms.

Thus, foreign investors pay the same corporate taxes, observe the same laws governing labour relations, and are liable to the same strict penalties for monopolistic or other unfair business practices as apply to American investors.

The flow of foreign capital to the United States has been accompanied by the massive influx of foreign technicians, engineers and scientists.

This vast amount of foreign capital has come to America also because foreign capital and foreign technicians are made to feel welcome. And because it helps our economy grow, we have always seen it as a good bargain for both sides.

I might sum up the advantages the United States has derived from foreign assistance as follows:

—additional capital to promote growth in key sectors of our economy (e.g., transport, petro-chemicals, etc.) during our early years of industrial growth.

—influx of new technology into key industrial areas and of the technicians required for rapid industrial expansion.

—creation of lakhs and lakhs of jobs for American workers.

—stimulation of competition with American industry, encouraging higher efficiency and bringing lower prices to the consumers.

The flow of capital and technical skill from abroad has never threatened American sovereignty or undermined American policies. Instead, it has helped build a vigorously expanding economy.

Responsible investment of American technical skills and capital in those developing countries where it is made to feel welcome can have a similar effect.

A SECOND answer to the much discussed question of "Why American aid" is related to the first: By helping India's economic development it is suggested that we may bring you into closer agreement with America's approach to current international questions.

In my opinion this answer is no more valid than the first. Indeed, some nations which we have assisted seem to go out of their way to criticize various aspects of American foreign policy in order to demonstrate to their own people and the world that United States aid money has not undermined their independence. I confess that on more than one occasion in the last ten years this thought has passed through my mind here in India.

We will, of course, continue to seek common ground with India on international questions. But we know that such agreement carries no price tag. So, again we shall have to seek an answer elsewhere.

A third response to the question of "Why American aid" is that our American economic assistance programme is a moral obligation which we, as the richest nation in history, are duty bound to assume. Four years ago, President Kennedy emphasized this point in his Inaugural Address:

"To those peoples," he said, "in the huts and villages of half the globe struggling to break the bonds of mass misery, we pledge our best efforts to help them help themselves, for whatever period—not because the communists may be doing it, not because we seek their votes, but because it is morally right."

Those of you who have visited my country will testify that America's sense of moral commitment runs deep. A recent dramatic demonstration of it is the extraordinary work being done by American voluntary agencies to provide regular nutritious meals for millions of Indian children and to ease suffering and malnutrition in the famine areas. Let us briefly consider those efforts.

United States agricultural legislation, which provides for wheat purchases by the Indian Government payable in rupees, also provides the funds which enable additional food products to be shipped to India as a gift of the American people to help meet critical shortage situations.

From 1951 to the present, more than 112 crores of rupees worth of such commodities from America have been distributed, largely to Indian children and nursing mothers.

The primary American agencies through which these supplies are distributed are CARE, Church World Service and Catholic Relief Services.

The United States and other nations also make funds available through UNICEF (United Nations International Children's Emergency Fund) and Lutheran World Relief.

In the last few years these agencies, working in cooperation with Indian state and local governments, have launched massive child feeding programmes. Operating in every Indian state, largely through the schools, they have been providing mid-day meals for more than one crore children every day.

Last October, when the drought hit Bihar, Uttar Pradesh, Madhya Pradesh and Rajasthan, additional emergency feeding programmes were quickly organized. Today these emergency programmes alone are feeding more than 50 lakh additional children and nursing mothers.

Under the "Food for Peace" legislation, special funds are also made available to the voluntary agencies to help them help India to expand irrigation facilities, to provide well-digging equipment, tools, seeds and the like.

CARE (Cooperative for American Relief Everywhere), the largest voluntary agency in India, was established by American private citizens after World War II to provide food supplies, medical treatment, clothing, farming implements and other necessities to peoples of all nations ravaged by the war.

Like the other agencies it is a non-governmental organization, entirely supported by contributions from millions of American citizens who are concerned with the plight of their fellow human beings.

Catholic Relief Services receives voluntary donations from Catholic organizations in many countries. These funds are used to resettle Tibetan refugees, to rehabilitate fishermen in Madras and Kerala and to assist lepers and refugees from Burma and East Pakistan.

They also aid in the construction of hospitals, the training of nurses, and the construction of technical schools.

Church World Services and Lutheran World Relief are supported by individual contributions from Protestant Church organizations in the United States and other countries. They provide medical and surgical supplies, clothing, soap and bandages to hospitals. They also promote agricultural dvelopment projects.

In India the total paid staff-employed by these volunteer agencies in relief work is in the neighbourhood of 300 people. About ten per cent of these are Americans.

A NOTHER constructive programme is the American Peace Corps which was launched by Prime Minister Jawaharlal Nehru seven years ago. Since 1961 almost 70 teams of volunteers have lived and worked for two or more years in this country. Requests for additional volunteers in India and elsewhere are far greater than our capacity to provide them.

The imaginative concept of the Peace Corps originated during John F. Kennedy's campaign for the Presidency in 1960.

Now volunteer assistance is a two-way street. Sixteen countries are presently sending their own volunteers to America. These dedicated men and women are working in the U.S. to help eliminate poverty in our urban and rural areas, and in turn learning a great deal about American society, people and culture.

For example, five Indian social workers returned to India from America in 1966 after participating in the first stage of this new enterprise. And we hope that this is only the beginning.

American Peace Corps volunteers coming to India, after a strict selection process, receive their training on the area to which they will be assigned. This training is conducted by Indians who are experts in their fields. All volunteers are required to learn the regional or local language.

After an intensive three-month training period, the less effective candidates are weeded out together with any others who are not prepared to face the rigours of a full two-year assignment.

A few days ago I talked with some 25 volunteers who were homeward bound after working in tube-well drilling and irrigation in the villages of Punjab, Haryana and Maharashtra.

They were excited about the miracles which occur when water

and fertilizer are applied. But it was evident that their greatest satisfaction stemmed from what India had done for them.

Through two years of hot sun, dust storms and monsoon rains they had been living and working in the villages with the cultivators and under the direction of local officials—speaking their languages, being introduced to their rich culture, sharing their problems of droughts, scarcities and floods, and rejoicing together over each common accomplishment.

It is not then surprising that many volunteers are taking home with them far more than they had brought to India. Their experiences here have helped make them citizens of the world.

At present Peace Corps volunteers in India are working in the following fourteen states:

Punjab—Agriculture, family planning, secondary education, consumer cooperatives.

Rajasthan—Agriculture, animal husbandry.

Uttar Pradesh—Tube-well construction.

Haryana—Secondary education, tube-well construction, consumer cooperatives.

Maharashtra—Agriculture, rural public health, nutrition, animal husbandry.

Gujarat—Animal husbandry.

Madhya Pradesh—Agriculture, poultry, teacher education, tube-well construction.

Bihar—Water development, family planning.

Orissa—Farm mechanization.

West Bengal—Agriculture.

Andhra Pradesh—Science teacher workshops, minor irrigation, agriculture.

Mysore—Agriculture, poultry.

Madras—Teacher education in nutrition, agriculture.

Kerala—Small industries.

At the request of the various state governments and the Union Government in New Delhi, the Peace Corps effort is now largely concentrated in agriculture and such related fields as tube-well development, irrigation and rural industries.

Next summer a new field will be opened up—the development of inland fisheries in six states. Fish will be cultivated in ponds, lakes, tanks and canals and harvested just like a field crop. The additional inexpensive protein they will provide will help millions of families receive better balanced diets.

In our turbulent, complex and often embittered world it is reassuring to see people from opposite sides of the globe working together towards common goals of universal peace, prosperity and human dignity. However, we must not allow semantics to stand in the way of understanding.

IN INDIA the word "capitalism" suggests the ruthless exploitation of workers by vast monopolistic corporations, while to most Americans it means an efficient, dynamic, free-enterprise system governed by democratic means.

On the other hand for many Americans the word "socialism" brings to mind inefficiency and overpowering fumbling bureaucracy, while many Indians see it as the road to social and economic justice achieved through a democratic framework.

There is, however, at least one word that has a favourable connotation for both Indians and Americans—this is "cooperative". This word reflects our common heritage of self-help and democratic participation.

In both India and the United States cooperatives are now making significant contributions to economic development. In America cooperative organizations have a total of six crores of members and represent investments and sales amounting annually to $18,000 millions (Rs. 13,500 crores).

Let us briefly examine some of the most important:

*Cooperative to Speed the Electrification of Rural Areas*: During the early depression years, the Rural Electrification Administration was created by President Roosevelt. Its purpose was to lower the cost of electric power and thus make this modernization force available to even the most remote farms.

The result was dramatic. In 1933 less than one American farm in ten was electrified; today, more than 97 in 100 have electric power for lighting, heating and refrigeration, for television and telephone, for operating cow-milking machines and even to supply artificial daylight to enable poultry growers to increase their egg production.

The National Rural Electrical Cooperative Association now has approximately 1,000 member cooperative societies serving 50 lakhs of farm families. Through the efforts of these cooperatives there have been almost 700 instances of reduction of electricity rates, saving the members some $20 millions (Rs. 15 crores) annually.

*Cooperative Credit Unions*: There are now 23,000 cooperative credit unions in America with almost two crores of members. These organizations borrow from some members and lend to others a total of $ 1,000 million yearly (Rs. 750 crores).

The United States with 23,000 and India with 15,000 now have three-fourths of the entire world's 53,000 cooperative credit unions.

*Cooperatives on the Farm*: One-sixth of all American farm purchases and one-fourth of all farm products are now marketed through cooperatives. For instance, one-third of all fertilizer is purchased through farmer-owned cooperatives while two-thirds of all dairy products are marketed through cooperatives.

*Housing Cooperatives*: The U.S. Federal Housing Administration has insured the capital requirements of more than 2,000 housing co-ops in forty out of a total of fifty states with a total value of $1,750 millions (more than Rs. 1,300 crores).

*Insurance Cooperatives*: Cooperatives have also been organized available to cover all expenses such as the birth of a new child and health insurance. There are even cooperatives to reduce funeral expenses for bereaved families. Theft insurance and insurance against liability for accident claims are also available on a co-operative basis.

*Educational Cooperatives*: These supply funds to cover the costs for advanced education, and to lower the cost of books and school supplies by operating college book stores.

*Fishery Cooperatives*: These cooperatives operate fishing craft and obtain supplies for fishermen. About one-fourth of all the fish products sold in the United States are marketed by such fishery cooperatives.

*Conservation Cooperatives*: These establish irrigation projects, pay for the construction costs, and deliver water to their members.

*CARE*: This is porbably the best known of all U.S. cooperatives in India. It is now providing a good noon meal for 11.5 million Indian school children daily.

In these American non-profit cooperatives the members elect their own directors, pool their resources to reduce costs, and provide a fair return to the investors. All other "profits" are distributed among the members in proportion to their purchases or the uses made of the services provided.

International cooperation has brought Indian and American co-ops together, chiefly through the activities of the International Cooperative Alliance in conducting exchange of information and personnel.

Dramatic examples are the vast new fertilizer plant which will soon be built in Gujarat with technical  assistance supplied by American cooperatives, and the new rural cooperative electric schemes now planned for five States involving  an investment of 15 crores of rupees for electric distribution systems.

The participation of both of our nations in cooperatives—a marriage of ideals and practicality—serves once more to remind us that working together will meet  economic needs and make firm the structure of our democratic freedom.

YET the American tradition of overseas service provides only part of the answer to our basic question of why American aid.

The rest of the answer grows out of a concept which a hundred years ago or even thirty years ago would have been hard for either you or us to understand, but which in our modern era is overriding.

After two world wars, most Americans have come to see that our own security and prosperity cannot be isolated from that of the rest of the globe.

Whether we all like it or not, whether we always agree with each other or not, we are all members of the human race.   Consequently, our common future depends on our ability to live together rationally on our increasingly crowded and turbulent planet.

As our world grows smaller, each nation, large or small, has a growing stake in the behaviour of everyone else.

In the postwar years, Stalin's intransigence concerned us all. More recently, when an irresponsible China threatened India with a conflict which might have extended throughout Asia, the security of every man, woman and child in America was involved in some degree.

Nor does our mutual interest in a more rational world stop with matters of aggression and military defence.

If we Americans should flounder and fail in our efforts to provide an increasing measure of prosperity, opportunity and dignity for all of our citizens under a free government, the impact would be ultimately felt in every Asian, African and Latin American village.

Similarly, unless the poverty, malnutrition and illiteracy of countries such as India are met and mastered there can be no hope for security and prosperity in the more privileged countries of the world.

Furthermore, because of new technologies the economic interdependence of all nations is rapidly increasing. In today's world the continuing dynamism and growth of the American economy would be impossible without expanding foreign trade. And for India and other developing countries increasing trade with the more highly developed nations is equally essential if an adequate rate of growth is to be achieved and maintained.

In this sense, every living American—indeed, everyone everywhere who believes in peace and human freedom—has a deep personal stake in the success of the unprecedented development effort which has been undertaken by free India.

The Industrial Revolution which in the 19th century laid the basis for the present prosperity of Western Europe and America involved a heavy cost in human suffering which was vividly described by Charles Dickens.

Under different circumstances and through different methods the Soviet Union under Stalin concentrated Russia's energies and resources on building an industrial and military capacity regardless of the consequences to the Russian people.

Today, democratic India seeks what would have been beyond the reach of any developing country not so many years ago: a rapid rate of national economic growth side by side with increasing direct social and material benefits for the individual.

Your success or failure as a nation rests not only on your ability to construct great dams, new factories and more miles of railroad tracks. Equally important is your capacity to build a society which offers a steadily increasing measure of dignity, opportunity and a social justice to each individual.

This calls for higher real incomes and improved living conditions for your urban people, and the right to land ownership and fair crop prices for your cultivators.

This twin objective requires bold pragmatic national planning, the wise use of all available domestic resources, a keen sensitivity to human suffering and enlightened political and economic leadership.

It also requires a substantial amount of capital and technical assistance from the more privileged nations so that the present generation need not be sacrificed for the sake of its grandchildren.

Not only the amount of foreign assistance which you receive but also its nature and the manner in which it is provided are of crucial significance.

In this regard, we Americans have come to see from hard experience that not all developing nations have the will or the ability to do what India is striving to do, and when these qualities are lacking, the effectiveness of our aid is blunted.

For these reasons, we are concentrating our assistance in those countries which are prepared to use their own resources to pursue realistic development practices and where there is a certain degree of mutual respect and understanding.

We consider Sharavathy a prime example of the proper and constructive use of American assistance. It is part of a carefully conceived and well integrated programme for the development of South India. Its planning and engineering were completely Indian.

Sharavathy will promote massive employment; it will encourage rural electrification; and it will permit the establishment of dynamic new industries which will earn foreign exchange to pay for similar projects in the future.

You would have built this great project without American assistance. But with such assistance you were able to build it sooner, and without sacrificing other important projects or unnecessarily suppressing the day-to-day needs of your people.

Thus, the primary purpose of American economic assistance may be summed up in the following terms: To enable competent, socially conscious nations such as India to respond quickly, constructively and responsibly to the forces which are shaping tomorrow's world.

More specifically, it represents an effort by the American Government and citizens to help new nations which are prepared to help themselves to generate increasing national incomes and to ensure political and social stability.

Only on such foundation can any nation contribute effectively to our common objective which is a more peaceful and rational world.

If free India succeeds in reaching her democratic goals, the benefits will be felt in every community in my own country and, indeed, throughout the world. That in a nutshell is why I am here today.

# 14. The Crucial Importance of Foreign Exchange

*In this three-part* American Reporter *column in 1968, the Ambassador described India's need for foreign exchange to speed economic progress. He listed the primary sources from which foreign exchange are available, and explained how tourism and foreign private investment, the most lucrative and practical sources, can be attracted to the subcontinent.*

THE LEVEL of American economic foreign exchange assistance to developing countries such as India will be significantly reduced in the coming years.

These reductions reflect the concern of many Members of the United States Congress about the urgent needs of our own society, the U.S. adverse balance of payments and the costs of the long, drawnout Vietnam war. This is coupled with a sense of frustration over what many Members believe to be the unrealistic economic policies and the consequent slow pace of economic development in some of the countries which the United States has been striving to help.

Why is this foreign exchange so urgently needed to raise India's living standards?

In the building of schools, hospitals, roads, etc., foreign exchange is not a factor. The costs are paid for in rupees which the Indian Government raises through domestic taxation.

However, to speed the pace of economic development, India must also import machinery, certain raw materials, fertilizer and the like, much of which can only be purchased in the more developed nations. The foreign producers from whom these goods and commodities are purchased must be paid in foreign exchange which they can spend in any international market, such as dollars, pounds, sterling, marks, francs and yen.

What are the sources through which India can secure this foreign exchange?

1. *Import Substitutions.* India can develop substitutes for many of the goods and commodities which now must be purchased in foreign countries with foreign exchange.

Last year, for instance, India found it necessary to buy in the international markets over 10 million tons of crude oil products at a cost of Rs. 74. 775 crores ( $99. 7 million); also Rs. 235. 8 crores ($314. 4 million) for non-ferrous metals and rock phosphates. In addition, many spare parts must be purchased from foreign sources for equipment already operating here in India.

India has made substantial progress in "import substitution." Railroad cars, locomotives, heavy structure generators, earth-moving machinery, trucks, jeeps, etc., which formerly were purchased abroad, are now made in India.

Indian experts working with technicians from other countries are also searching urgently for non-ferrous metals and petroleum deposits here in India—with an excellent chance of success.

2. *Exports.* India, like every other country, tries to earn most of the foreign exchange it needs for essential imports by exporting goods it produces to the world market. Traditionally, the major Indian exports have been tea and jute, and more recently some manufactured items such as textiles and pharmaceuticals. In the last two or three years the amount of other products sold abroad has increased sharply. According to present plans, India exports are expected to rise about 7 per cent annually.

3. *Tourism.* India can earn more foreign exchange by encouraging more foreign tourists. The money they spend becomes available as foreign exchange which can be used to pay for additional imports.

The number of tourists now visiting India each year is only a minor fraction of those visiting far smaller countries such as Greece, Portugal, Yugoslavia and Thailand.

Last year Spain with a population of only 31 million earned over $1 million (Rs. 750 crores) in foreign exchange from tourism, or as much foreign exchange as the Consortium nations (World Bank, United States, United Kingdom, Germany, and others) provide

India each year in loans. Greece, a nation of only 8.5 million, earned $100 million (Rs. 75 crores) and Yugoslavia, with a population of 20 million, earned more than $150 million (Rs. 112 crores).

In contrast India, one of the world's most important and fascinating nations, earned in 1966 only $34 million (Rs. 25 crores) in foreign exchange from tourists.

Each year tens of thousands of world travellers with money to spend either overfly India altogether or simply stop off on their way from Teheran to Bangkok for the three or four days necessary to get the traditional glimpse of the Taj Mahal, to see the crowded bazaars of Old Delhi and to take a picture of a snake charmer.

These tens of thousands of tourists who either hurry through India or fail to stop at all represent a wasted opportunity to earn precious foreign exchange and to win friends for India.

If as many as one-third of them could be persuaded to spend a few weeks in India, India's foreign exchange earnings from tourism would soar to many times what they are today.

When we consider why so many nations benefit more than India does from the fantastic expansion of world tourism several points become clear. Tourists go where they are most likely to feel welcome. Quite naturally, being on vacation, they want convenient, comfortable and punctual transportation. They seek new experiences, and they want to enjoy themselves while doing so.

India's tourist potential is relatively untapped for a variety of reasons. Among the most obvious are the lack of enough good hotels, the many uncertainties in air travel, as well as outmoded and frequently annoying government regulations. More important, tourists know few places in India where they can go for longer visits.

WHAT are the steps that will help bring today's well-heeled tourists to India and persuade them to stay for several weeks or more?

First, a world-wide campaign to make foreigners feel that India truly wants tourists and offers them something new and exciting.

Second, a concerted effort to improve the essential services which tourists require, such as food, accommodation and transportation.

Third, a major programme to expand or develop India's many and varied tourist areas. At present the focus is on the splendours of India's past such as Agra, Jaipur, Varanasi, and the caves of Ellora and Ajanta.

Why not advertise the pleasures of winter sports in Kashmir? Why not arrange special tours from Bombay, through Goa, Cochin, Trivandrum and Madurai to Madras? Why not publicize the hill stations, the beaches, the fishing in mountain streams and in the sea off the Malabar coast?

These natural attractions of modern India will draw hundreds of thousands of eager visitors and, properly equipped and organized, will persuade them to prolong their visits.

Moreover, a massive campaign to build India's tourist industry, if well conceived, will do more than simply earn badly needed foreign exchange.

Indian tourist officials can and should introduce foreign visitors to the new India as well as to the old, to the modern India which holds such promise for the future.

For example, IAC flights to Kashmir could fly over Bhakra Dam. Buses to Agra could stop at a school or a family planning clinic on the way to the Taj Mahal. Tourist agencies could be encouraged to take groups to villages where the profound grass roots changes, which are occurring in India today, can be seen at first hand.

In other words, why not enable foreign visitors to see the promise of India's future as well as India's ancient glories and its vast and varied natural beauties?

Why not let India become known for what it really is: a nation both proud of its past and determined to create a new era of opportunity and prosperity for all its citizens?

Thus, in the process of earning many additional crores of foreign exchange, India can earn new world-wide understanding and goodwill.

4. *Loans and Grants.* India can continue to borrow foreign exchange through loans or grants from the more developed nations such as the United States. Since 1951 the United States has either loaned or given the Indian Government Rs. 27,750 crores ($3.7 billion) to help speed India's development.

This represents more than 60 per cent of the foreign aid which India has secured from all sources. Even though U.S. lending, for the reasons I mentioned above, is being reduced, the United States in 1969 will still provide India with far more foreign exchange than any other nation.

5. *World Bank*. India can secure foreign exchange through loans from the World Bank.

The World Bank has thus far loaned to India some Rs. 1425 crores or $1.9 billion. The new Bank President, Mr. Robert McNamara, has announced that he intends to increase, bank loans to developing nations including India in the coming years.

6. *Foreign Private Investment*. A final source of foreign exchange is foreign private investment in India. When foreign businessmen are persuaded to establish factories here they increase Indian employment and provide additional funds for India's domestic use and for export to overseas markets.

India is now receiving only a small fraction of the foreign capital investment that businessmen in the United States, Germany, Italy, United Kingdom, Japan and other industrialized nations have available for investment outside their own countries. The problem for India is to attract this money here so that its benefits accrue to the Indian economy.

According to the latest information (1965), total foreign investment in India from all sources is a nominal Rs. 935.8 crores ($1.25 billion). Only about 25 per cent of this investment is from the United States.

Even on an absolute basis, foreign private investment in India is far below that invested in many developing nations which have only a tiny fraction of India's importance, population, and size.

In Mexico, a country with a population no larger than Madras State, foreign investment is almost five times that in India; in Australia it is almost seven times more. Even in the relatively small Asian nations foreign private investment is playing a far greater role in speeding industrial development and providing more jobs and opportunities than in India.

This situation poses some fundamental questions: Why at a time when more jobs and production are desperately needed is foreign private capital reluctant to come to some developing countries such as India? How can the flow be increased? As an old friend of India, I shall be frank.

Some leaders of developing countries oppose foreign investment on the grounds that it will somehow enable "foreign interests" to control the economy. Although to some extent this opposition is ideological, there is a genuine concern on this point even among anti-communists. Yet these fears are largely a hangover from the colonial era when what we now describe as developing nations were not yet masters in their own house. In today's world these are utterly unrealistic fears.

Although Great Britain and other European nations invested many billions in the development of the United States, it never occurred to them or to us that this could enable them to influence our domestic or foreign policies.

In Canada, our good neighbour to the north, with a population of only 20 million people, the total private foreign capital investment is Rs. 11,250 crores ($15 billion), much of it from the United States. This is sixty times the amount of U.S. capital invested in India. Does anyone seriously think that the Canadians are not their own masters?

Factories in Canada, Japan, India or anywhere else built by private foreign investors employ lakhs and lakhs of people, produce urgently needed goods and in many cases increase exports to earn additional foreign exchange.

These enterprises cannot be bundled up and shipped elsewhere nor can their stockholders make the rules under which they operate. They are fully controlled by the laws of the host country, including laws concerned with taxes, monopolistic practices, labour relations and the like.

Others who oppose foreign capital investment on an ideological basis are convinced that it will somehow be used to "exploit" the workers. In our present-day world of socially conscious governments and privately owned corporations that have learned to think and plan in long-range terms, this fear is also groundless.

WHILE a nation can increase production without increasing economic justice, it cannot achieve even a minimum of economic justice without expanding production. This hard fact is fully recognized by pragmatic leaders in those developing nations in which the most rapid economic expansion is taking place.

Even in the communist countries the advantages of foreign private capital are increasingly recognized. The USSR has been seeking the assistance of foreign investors and technicians from Italy in developing a modern automobile industry. Poland, Hungary, and Rumania as well as Yugoslavia have persistently sought private foreign capital. With private investment they gain more production, then greater export possibilities, then increased investment.

Indeed, it may be argued persuasively that foreign private capital as a source of foreign exchange has some advantage over governmental loans from economically advanced nations or organizations such as the World Bank.

When a developing nation borrows foreign exchange from foreign governments or from the World Bank to build such projects as power plants or fertilizer factories, it must repay this amount plus interest over a period of time regardless of the success of the project. This is true even of so-called "soft" term loans.

In the case of individual plants built by foreign private investors, profits are taken out of the developing country only if the venture succeeds and only after the host government has collected the taxes which are due. As a matter of fact most private foreign investors in India and elsewhere use the bulk of their profits to expand their factories, to purchase more modern machinery and to employ more people.

All developing countries must compete for their share of the relatively scarce foreign capital which is available. Naturally these funds go primarily to those nations which provide not only good potential markets but also a warm welcome and a minimum of bureaucratic red tape. That is why so many American firms are now investing in such fast-developing economies as South Korea, Chile, Mexico and Thailand as well as in the more highly developed markets of Canada, Japan and Australia.

The present rate of American private capital investment in India totals only about Rs. 15 crores ($20 million) annually. Once privately owned corporations in the United States, Japan and Western Europe become convinced that they are really wanted in India, this rate of investment could be increased quickly and massively to speed Indian development and to help assure the prosperity and security of its people.

# The
# Democracies
# of
# India and America

So this is a strange meeting between India, an ancient country and a mixture of old virtues and old failings, and America, a land of new ideas, new vigour and new power. This meeting of the two can benefit both of us.

—PRIME MINISTER JAWAHARLAL NEHRU

# 15. Gandhi's Influence on World Affairs

*Although he never met Gandhi, the Ambassador was greatly affected by the Mahatma's thoughts and deeds. In remarks at the Gandhi Roundtable Conference inaugural in New Delhi on May 5, 1965, Ambassador Bowles described the universality of the Mahatma's message of tolerance, love and peace.*

WHEN I was asked to inaugurate this Conference I was frankly hesitant.

As an American who never had the opportunity to meet Gandhi, what right had I to speak about him before a group of people many of whom knew him well and participated actively in the Indian independence movement that he led ?

Nevertheless, it occurred to me that a foreign perspective might be useful in underscoring to an Indian audience the universal impact of India's greatest statesman, humanist and politician. And that is why I am here this evening.

It has said that there is scarcely an individual on this earth whose life has not been affected in some essential way by Gandhi. This is so because no other public figure of our era so clearly understood, or so confidently welcomed, the implications of the revolutionary age in which we live.

"The cataclysm that is sweeping over the earth today," he said, "is a great sign. As a chaotic force it is pernicious, but it has at its back a noble object;...it desires reform, it seeks the reign of equity and justice."

Among all the revolutionaries who have dominated the political stage in our century—Lenin, Mussolini, Hitler, Stalin and Mao—Gandhi alone offered the prospect of reform without destruction. While his revolutionary contemporaries were feeding the flames of pernicious chaos, he saw in the innate dignity of the individual human being, no matter how humble or downtrodden, the key to orderly political and social progress.

As I see it, there are three distinct revolutionary currents in which Gandhi's practical, earthy ability to apply to new situations what he called "the universal truths" has been instrumental in shaping the history of our times and in moving all of mankind toward a more rational existence.

In each of these three areas no scientist, no statesman, no educator has contributed so much as did the humble Indian lawyer who for nearly fifty years carried a torch for the oppressed peoples of all nations, all races and all creeds.

The first of these is the anti-colonial revolution; the second, the revolution for human dignity; and the third, the revolution for peace.

L ET US first consider Gandhi's influence on the unprecedented anti-colonial revolution which since World War II has freed more than a billion Asians and Africans from foreign rule.

Gandhi was born just six months before Lenin and within two years of Sun Yat-sen, and his career paralleled theirs in many respects.

Lenin, too, was a lawyer, who was to spend years in prison for violating the laws of Czarist Russia. Each of the three was to live and work abroad during his most formative years, and each was to respond in his own way to the powerful revolutionary forces which were generated by the industrial revolution.

While Lenin in Russia was encouraging the abortive armed uprising of 1905 and Sun Yat-sen was organizing the secret Chinese Revolutionary League, Gandhi, in race-conscious South Africa, was conducting his first great so-called "experiment with truth."

When we consider the deeply rooted economic misery and personal humiliation that afflicted millions of Indians both in India and in South Africa in the first decades of the twentieth century, any deeply committed revolutionary might have been tempted to choose the path of violence. Gandhi, however, adopted as his weapon what he described as the "force which is born of truth," *Satyagraha*.

Instead  of exploiting the dissatisfactions of an underprivileged people, he sought to give each individual a sense of personal pride which generated not only patience but an invincible inner strength. Instead of seeking the destruction of his enemies, he taught his followers gradually to persuade them with love and respect.

Within a single generation, we have witnessed an unprecedented transition from a world of empires to a world of free nations and we have yet to see the end of the struggle.  However, a thousand years from now history will record that it was the Indian independence movement under the leadership of Mohandas K. Gandhi that set the standards by which both colonial powers and subject peoples were compelled to judge their actions.

If the Indian revolution, which was the first and greatest of the modern anti-colonial movements, had been led by angry, embittered leaders in a bloody protest against British rule, the history of the last ten years would have been disastrously different.  In that event the frustrated peoples of Asia and Africa would almost certainly have embarked on a similar orgy of violence  and mass destruction against the colonial regimes under which they lived.

But at this crucial moment in history Gandhi demonstrated the effectiveness of the non-violent way of dealing with oppression and aggression.  The result in India was a peaceful transfer of power, the creation of an enduring friendship and respect between the ex-rulers and their ex-subjects, and a politically stable, economically progressive democratic nation.  And because elsewhere in Asia and Africa others followed his lead, independence came to all but a handful of ex-colonial countries with a  large measure of mutual goodwill and respect.

L ET US now turn to Gandhi's contribution to the second great revolution for human dignity.  In this struggle, too, the candle lit by Gandhi in India has grown into a great  light which is giving new confidence and strength to oppressed minorities all over the world.

Gandhi clearly saw that an India divided by communal bitterness and prejudices could never achieve self-respect and independence. His efforts to provide the *Harijans* with equal opportunity and a full measure of dignity, and to awaken the social conscience of all castes and religions are in large measures responsible for the present vitality of Indian democracy.

In his role as a protagonist of equal opportunity and human dignity my own country owes a special debt to Gandhi.

Some 20 million Negro Americans are now pressing their claims to first class citizenship. These demands include the constitutional right to vote, to be fully educated, to have equal employment opportunities and to receive equal treatment in all public accommodations. And it is the Gandhian ideal and Gandhian action techniques with which they are gradually achieving their objectives.

Gandhi once remarked that "It may be through the Negroes that the unadulterated message of non-violence will be delivered to the world." Yet only a decade ago, such a development in America appeared remote and unrealistic.

For instance, shortly after my return to the United States from my first assignment in India, I spoke at a distinguished Negro college in one of our southern states.

In the course of my talk I emphasized that there was no case in history where one race, however well intentioned, had been able to deliver both freedom and dignity to another. Freedom, I said, must be fought for and won; it can never be achieved without struggle.

I then described the role of Gandhi in leading the fight for Indian freedom and how, through a peaceful but relentless programme of action, he and his followers had gradually persuaded the British Raj to grant the Indian people their independence.

I concluded my talk with an appeal to the Negro student audience to help develop and support a comparable programme of cooperative action directed at achieving the full equality of opportunity which was guaranteed to each of them under our own American constitution.

Their response was apathetic. Instead of persuading my Negro audience to protest against their second class citizenship by temperate Gandhian means, I sensed that I was only making them feel uncomfortable.

At luncheon that day, I asked the president of the college for his explanation. "Very few of our students," he lamented, "have ever felt any personal responsibility for group action designed to secure their rights as citizens and they are hesitant to accept such responsibility even now. With a few militant exceptions their primary hope after graduation is to secure a reasonably good job and to be let alone."

It was against this background of inertia and resignation among many of our Negro citizens that Martin Luther King, a brilliant, eloquent young Negro minister, who had been deeply influenced by Gandhi, began to spell out a Gandhian course of action in the churches, meeting halls and public squares of our still segregated South.*

His first success was the organization of a Negro boycott in Montgomery, Alabama that forced the city government to order the desegregation of the bus system.

From this hopeful beginning Dr. King, carefully testing his ideas, techniques and organizations moved steadily into the leadership of a now massive national civil rights movement which in the last ten years has secured more freedom for Negro Americans than all the laborious and sometimes bloody efforts of the previous century.

The spirit and language with which Dr. King lays down the principles of his democratic crusade are pure Gandhian.

"The Negro," he says, "must come to the point that he can say to his white brothers: 'We will match your capacity to inflict suffering with our capacity to endure suffering. We will meet your physical force with our soul force. We will not hate you, but we will not obey your evil laws. We will soon wear you down by our own capacity to suffer.

" 'So, in winning the victory, we will not only win freedom for ourselves but we will so appeal to your heart and conscience that you will be changed also. Thus our victory will be a double victory: we will defeat the evil system and win the hearts and souls of the perpetrators of that system.' "

To provide his followers with the necessary strength that comes of confidence and personal dignity, Martin Luther King has borrowed another basic Gandhian concept—self-improvement.

Sixty years ago in South Africa, Gandhi admonished his followers: "Let us begin by considering the grievances held against us by the

---

*Dr. Martin Luther King was killed in Memphis, Tennessee on April 5, 1968.

white people.  Let us see if the reasons which the whites give for discrimination against us are justified."

"Then," he continued, "let us put our own house in order, even now while fighting for our civil rights, even before they grant the reforms we ask, even as poor as we are.  We can't blame the whites for all our troubles...."

Similarly, throughout America, Martin Luther King is now telling his Negro followers.  "Let us examine the reasons given by white men for segregation.  Let us see which reflect conditions we can do something about, and take action ourselves."

Dr. King then goes on to list the high illegitimacy rate among Negroes, the tendency of many young Negroes towards crime, their frequently low health standards.  He emphasizes that these deficiencies must be recognized as the psychological legacy of second-class citizenship—a legacy that must be removed.

Like Gandhi he calls upon his followers by their own actions to break the vicious cycle of bigotry, submission and resultant squalor which generations of discrimination have helped to create.

The extraordinary effectiveness of the Gandhian civil rights movement in America is reflected in a steady flow of successes, some large and others small.

In August 1963, Dr. King in cooperation with other Negro and white leaders organized the greatest mass demonstration in American history—the so-called March on Washington.

From all parts of the country by trains, buses, airplanes and on foot came an estimated 230,000 men and women, Negro and white, rich and poor.

With no sign of violence or even bitterness they marched peacefully through the streets of our national capital arm-in-arm, singing the deeply moving song of the American Civil Rights revolution "We Shall Overcome."

Last month there was another peaceful march on the segregationist stronghold of Montgomery, Alabama, where Dr. King began his crusade.  And now each night on their television sets tens of millions of Americans watch and applaud the progress of the massive voter registration drive in which Negroes are qualified as voters, the "sit ins" and the "kneel ins", and the long lines of courteous but determined Negroes waiting patiently to be served at segregated lunch counters.

As in India twenty or thirty years ago, a minority of impatient Negro leaders who doubt the effectiveness of non-violent action, have organized militant action groups.

But it is Dr. King's Gandhian philosophy that has captured the imagination of an entire generation of Americans and particularly young Americans who are glad to be rid at long last of their prejudices and inhibitions.

As we move toward a more perfect realization of the democratic vision of equal opportunity under law there are now few who doubt that Gandhism—American style—is the dominant driving force.

When Gandhi suggested many years ago that it may be the Negroes who deliver "the unadulterated message of non-violence to the world," he was demonstrating once again his extraordinary insight into the mind of man.

LET ME finally turn to the third revolution of our times where once again Gandhi emerges as a central figure; I refer to the difficult, frustrating struggle for a world of peace and goodwill.

Although the quest for peace among nations is as old as mankind, we must admit that so far at least it represents one of our least successful efforts. Yet, is there not the basis for a new hope, however fragile, that may gradually be taking hold of us all?

On the eve of World War II, Gandhi wrote, "if the mad race for armaments continues, it is bound to result in a slaughter such as has never occurred in history. If there is a victor left, the very victory will be a living death for the nation that emerges victorious."

The war which Gandhi foresaw came in due course bringing with it the death of some 40 million men, women and children and the development of nuclear weapons which in a future conflict could increase the toll ten times over.

But may not our fantastic new technology also be the instrument that leads us to salvation?

First, the very knowledge that aggression may lead to mass destruction of both aggressor and the victim on an unprecedented scale has a sobering effect on even the most irresponsible of national leaders.

Second, the development of radio, television, communications satellites and supersonic transportation now enables people of different nationalities to see how others think and live. Tourism and student exchanges are helping to re-enforce these gradually growing bonds.

Is it not increasingly possible that average Americans, average Indians, average Russians and some day let us hope even average Chinese may come to see their common stake in development, in understanding, and in peace?

To be sure it is still true, as Gandhi once observed, that "machineries of government stand between and hide the hearts of one people from those of another."

Yet in today's world no political leader however irresponsible can toy with the idea of mass warfare without taking into account the interests of the hundreds of millions whose forebearers were so voicelessly slaughtered in past wars.

In this context I believe that Gandhi's message to the world is of particular importance. It was Gandhi who refreshed the centuries-old concepts of brotherly love and tolerance and gave them meaning in the political framework of the twentieth century.

By thus giving voice at long last to the humble masses of the world, is it not possible that he may have liberated the greatest force for peace? Indeed was it not the spirit of Gandhi which guided the hands of those who provided the mighty vision of the United Nations Charter and who later signed the Nuclear Test Ban Treaty in Moscow?

In mourning the death of Gandhi, General MacArthur summed up the essence of his contribution. "In the evolution of civilization, if it is to survive, all men cannot fail eventually to adopt Gandhi's belief that the process of mass application of force to resolve contentious issues is fundamentally not only wrong but contains within itself the germs of self destruction."

IN CONCLUSION let me briefly sum up reasons why I believe Gandhi's influence on our times surpasses that of any other individual.

We may start with the fact that his philosophy was based on the eternal aspirations of all men for a free and harmonious life.

The universality of his ideas is underscored by the following bit of history.

In the 1820s an English translation of the *Upanishads* found its way into the Harvard library in Cambridge, Massachusetts, where it was read by a young American writer, Henry David Thoreau. In it he found a concept of human dignity and endeavour that he gradually evolved into a theory of non-violent social and political action.

In the 1850s Thoreau, who demonstrated his belief in his own doctrine by going to jail in protest against what he considered an unjust law, spelled out his new concept in a pamphlet which he entitled "Civil Disobedience." Eventually this pamphlet found its way into the hands of Leo Tolstoy in Russia who sent a copy to Gandhi in South Africa.

From Thoreau's presentation, from the writings of Tolstoy and others and from his own so-called "experiments with truth" Gandhi conceived the grand strategy of non-violent action which ultimately freed India and many other countries as well.

From South Africa by way of India these dynamic ideas found their way sixty years later to America where under the guidance of Martin Luther King they have become the driving force of our present great Civil Rights Revolution for individual dignity. And so we see, as Gandhi knew so well, how mankind is bound together by invisible ties of conscience and vision.

Equally important, however, was Gandhi's belief that these eternal aspirations could be realized. "I positively refuse," he said, "to judge man from the scanty material furnished to us by history."

Finally there was his practical capacity to pursue his beliefs in a down-to-earth way, proving his own observation that, "a small body of determined spirits fired by an unquenchable faith in their mission can alter the course of history."

Of the three revolutions which I have discussed—the revolution against colonialism, the revolution for human dignity and the revolution for peace—none is complete and the road ahead is strewn with difficulties.

Yet because Gandhi showed several crores of individual citizens how to speak out for freedom, for peace and for individual dignity, I believe that mankind is on the right path and that our task is an easier one.

# 16. Candid Comments on Indo-American Relations

*During the Indo-Pakistan crisis of 1965 Ambassador Bowles addressed the Laski Institute of Ahmedabad, Gujarat. He reviewed America's support to India, pointed out the differences between the countries, and called for even closer and stronger ties which unite the two great democracies.*

I COME HERE today as a friend of India who has known India's leaders and many thousands of her people since the early days of independence.

I emphasize this long personal relationship because I think it is important that I speak to you today frankly and fully.

It is inevitable that the Pakistan-India crisis would have caused considerable rethinking of old policies and relationships in New Delhi and in Rawalpindi. It is also understandable that major nations such as my own, whose interests and relationships have been affected by this tragic conflict, would wait the results of this re-evaluation to adjust their own policies and commitments to whatever new positions and attitudes may emerge.

During this period of groping for new policies to fit new situations, I believe it behooves the spokesmen of all nations to avoid hasty statements or acts which may jeopardize, in the heat and confusion of the moment, friendships which they have built up in the past and the hopes of still better relations in the future.

Against that background let us briefly consider a few historical facts which affect the relationships of our two countries.

I submit that in the years since independence India has had no better or more consistent friend than the United States. Throughout your long struggle for independence, the great majority of

Americans stood solidly behind India. During World War II successive special representatives whom President Franklin D. Roosevelt sent to India were so outspokenly sympathetic to Gandhi and to the Indian freedom movement that their withdrawal was requested by the Viceroy.

After independence America was the first nation to offer technical assistance to the Indian Government. In 1951, during my earlier service here as U.S. Ambassador, I signed the first capital grant or loan agreement with any Asian or African nation. These particular funds helped to finance India's massive programme to eradicate malaria and to launch the community development programme which now embraces all of India's 550,000 villages.

Since then the United States has loaned or given to India Rs. 1,200 crores ($2.5 billion) worth of capital goods and technical assistance.* These funds have constituted 58 per cent of all the foreign assistance which India has utilized during this period.

More specifically, United States assistance has provided the foreign exchange for 56 per cent of India's electric power development; it has helped to modernize India's transportation, to finance the irrigation of millions of acres of Indian farm land, to establish seven modern agricultural universities, to cut roads through the mountains, and to equip the Indian Army and the Air Force.

In addition to these capital loans and grants, the United States in the past 14 years has delivered to India 35 million tons of foodgrains; right now these shipments amount to about 7 per cent of your total annual foodgrain supply, which is roughly 18 per cent of all the wheat produced in America. Milk from America is now being drunk each day by 10 million Indian school children.

Having mentioned America's massive commitments to Indian economic development, let us consider with total frankness some of the political questions which have divided us and also those which have helped pull us together.

In 1950, in collaboration with Joseph Stalin, the Chinese mounted a major attack on the U.N. forces which were defending South Korea. The ultimate target of this aggression was unarmed Japan which, as the most advanced industrial nation in Asia, was a tempting target for Chinese ambitions. In the crucial struggle which

---

*This and subsequent figures are based on 1964-1965 data.

followed, India assumed a neutral position, as it did in the periods when free Berlin had been under heavy pressure.

On numerous occasions during the following years the United States Government warned India and our other Asian friends that the Chinese Communist leadership had massive expansionist ambitions. However, war-weary Japan held itself aloof, as did the other three major Asian nations—India, Indonesia, and Pakistan.

Five years after Tibet fell to China's aggressiveness, many Indians were still chanting "Hindi-Chini Bhai-Bhai" in the vain, although understandable hope, that China might somehow be persuaded to live in peace.

During this long, difficult period the responsibility of containing Chinese aggression and pinning down some 100 tough, well-trained Chinese army divisions rested almost entirely on the United States. Although our efforts to contain China were not particularly popular in India, I wonder what kind of Asia we would have today if the United States had decided during those crucial years to sacrifice its convictions for your approval.

In the late 1950s, as we had predicted, China began to build its case against India as an "aggressor" along the Himalayan borders. Because these claims were blatant falsehoods, India under Jawaharlal Nehru courageously rejected them, at the same time working patiently for a peaceful settlement.

In October 1962, when the Chinese forces suddenly attacked along your northern frontier, the United States responded firmly and promptly to your call for assistance. Within two days giant U.S. Air Force C-130 cargo planes were disgorging massive quantities of machine guns, rifles, mountain artillery, radios, ammunition, and other military supplies on Indian airfields for the support of the jawans who were defending India's borders against the Chinese onslaught.

B UT, you may ask, what about America's military relationship with Pakistan?

In early 1954 the United States offered both Pakistan and India military equipment and support for the defence of South Asia and the Middle East, which were then under increasingly heavy political pressure from the communist forces.

Although Pakistan accepted the offer, India refused in the hope that your Government could be a more effective force for peace by attempting to moderate Chinese aggressiveness—admittedly a worthy objective.

When the U.S. arms and equipment which we gave Pakistan were used against you, there was inevitable resentment. Under the circumstances, we felt that the most effective contribution we could make toward a cease-fire was to cut off all American military aid to both nations. This we promptly did.

Since August we have worked patiently within the Security Council to end the conflict between your two countries, which together contain one-fifth of the world's population. Although we have proposed no specific plan, we deeply believe that some basis for better relations must be found. We also believe that the final achievement of peace must eventually come from the two nations themselves; it cannot be imposed by an outside power, however well intentioned.

Speaking for the United States, let me say that we intend to make the same sincere attempt to bridge the differences between Pakistan and India that India has made over the years to bridge the gap between the Soviet Union and the United States.

Millions of Americans, and I am sure millions of Russians as well, wish you well in your own bridge-building effort. I am equally confident that in their hearts millions of Indians are equally hopeful for the success of our efforts to create more neighbourly relationships here on the subcontinent.

The primary concern which all of us share is whether or not India and Pakistan can solve their individual problems of more rapid economic development.

Here in India it is not a question of survival. India has survived for thousands of years and, come what may, will survive for many thousands more to come. The key question is: can India expand her economy fast enough and by democratic methods to permit the maximum freedom and dignity to each citizen?

You know that you can achieve this objective and so do we. More specifically, we believe that you can grow enough food to free yourself of foreign imports within five or six years.

Within ten years, through your own determined efforts and with the help of your friends, we believe India can generate the necessary capital savings to do without foreign economic assistance together.

We Americans not only believe these things; we have been betting on them and betting heavily with the economic assistance which has been steadily flowing into Indian ports from the United States for many years.

Now what is the purpose of this American aid?

Certainly our objective, as some here have charged, has not been to exert political pressure on the Indian Government. On some of the key questions which most directly affect American interests, India has on occasion taken a position quite different from our own.

For instance, on the question of Vietnam, I have yet to meet an Indian leader who was not concerned over the Chinese threat to overrun Southeast Asia. Yet some have criticized our efforts to cut Hanoi's supply lines to the North Vietnamese-directed forces in South Vietnam. It is ironic that North Vietnam was one of the first nations to support the Chinese ultimatum against India last September.

I have also read in some Indian newspapers that the United States has been using our PL-480 foodgrains to somehow shape Indian political thinking. Let me say with great emphasis that this charge is utter, unadulterated nonsense.

In September, when the fighting between Pakistan and India reached its peak, 34 ships with 537,300 metric tons of grain arrived in Indian ports. In October, 35 ships brought 586,000 metric tons. In November, the wheat imports from the United States are running at the same rate. And so they will continue in the months to come.

To be sure, we have placed our foodgrain agreements on a 30-day basis. But this has nothing whatsoever to do with the Pakistan-India conflict.

This policy was put into effect months before the fighting began, for one simple reason: because rightly or wrongly, many of our agricultural experts were not persuaded that India had been doing all that it should and could to raise its foodgrain output.

In regard to the development loans, grants, and technical assistance on which we have previously reached agreement, there has been no interruption. India is now scheduled to receive Rs. 256.2 crores ($528 million) of assistance under such agreements.

What we have held up is agreements in regard to future loans both to India and Pakistan. We have taken this position because we have no desire directly or indirectly to finance a continuing conflict on the subcontinent. We deeply believe that the primary problem which must be tackled is economic development.

Living standards must be rapidly increased and the basis laid for expanding agricultural production and the development of modern self-sufficient industrial establishments. Future assistance can only be effective when the public focus returns decisively to development.

NOW LET me emphasize one additional point. Although there have been no political strings on U.S. aid to India, my country has gained considerable experience in some 60 developing countries in regard to the developmental policies which are likely to be most effective.

The American people and the American Congress need to be convinced that our aid money is well used. It is our responsibility to continue carefully to examine developmental plans on which American money is spent.

India's economic performance in the last ten years has been generally good and in some areas outstanding. But in all frankness, we agree with those Indian economists and political leaders who think it can and must be better.

For instance, we agree that agriculture must be given the very highest priority and India's efforts to control the growth of her population intensified and expanded so that each Indian citizen can be assured the improved living standard which modern technology now makes possible.

We also agree with those Indian experts who believe that it is essential to facilitate the import of spare parts and raw materials, the lack of which are now causing thousands of plants in India to run far below their capacity.

Finally, we are convinced that the Indian economy will grow faster if India borrows from the experience of Japan, Italy, and other fast-growing democratic countries which give greater encouragement to private industries, large and small, domestic and foreign.

As India and America consider the interrelated question of mutual objectives, self-sufficiency, and assistance, it is useful to remember that almost every prosperous nation has relied in large measure on foreign capital and foreign technicians for its own development.

NOW, IN closing, let me stress what I believe to be a basic truth. Although we cannot expect to agree on all the many complex problems which now confront Indians and Americans throughout the world, we should never underestimate the strong ties which unite our two peoples, citizens of the two largest democracies in the world.

In the last 15 years thousands of Americans have come to India to teach at your universities, to help build your dams, to work in your hospitals, and to assist in your rural development.

For instance, these include some 542 U.S. Peace Corps volunteers, most of whom right now are working side-by-side with Indian cultivators in the rural areas raising poultry, teaching school, and working in health clinics.

Almost all of these thousands of Americans return to the U.S. with a deep feeling of respect and friendship for the Indian people.

During the same period more than 68,000 Indian citizens have travelled to the United States for technical training or education. At this moment there are some 8,000 Indian students in American universities—far more than the number who are studying in any other foreign country. Moreover, more than 4,000 Indian professors are now teaching in our universities.

At the same time, in America, Gandhi's concepts of non-violent action serve as an inspiration for the massive peaceful revolutionary effort by American whites and Negroes to provide the American Negro with increased opportunity and dignity.

Yet even with all the goodwill in the world, a truly sympathetic relationship between great nations is not easily achieved. Different cultural backgrounds, different languages, experience and view-points often create barriers which can be broken down only by a vigorous effort at understanding and occasionally by some frank talk on both sides.

This is especially true of democratic societies like those of India and the United States where everyone speaks his mind, not always with full regard for the consequences. In totalitarian nations, where governments are able to stifle criticism and public expression and thereby cover up differences, a facade of agreement can often be created which masks rather than solves the basic differences.

Although there will always be some differences between India and America, the goals we have in common are vastly more important. Here in India I feel a deep realization of this fact; and it is rare that you meet an Indian visitor to the United States who does not sense in my own country a similar warmth of feeling among Americans for India.

We deeply believe that a free, prosperous, and peaceful India is a primary requirement for a stable and free Asia and that a democratic India will constitute a long step forward toward a democratic and free world society. We also believe that the basic goodwill and mutual interest exist to achieve this objective.

That is why we Americans have been helping India over the last 15 years; that is why we expect to continue our assistance.

We are facing troubled times when all nations are dealing with complex and unfamiliar problem. Inevitably, we shall sometimes see this turbulent new world from somewhat different perspectives.

But as we seek common ground, let us never forget that America and India are working for precisely the same objectives: The right to live in a free society, the right of each individual to a full measure of dignity and economic justice and the opportunity for all people to live in a peaceful world.

# 17. America's New Focus on India

*Ambassador Bowles reported on the deepening interest of the American people about Indian culture and society, which was further stimulated by Mrs. Gandhi's visit to Washington D.C. and New York City in March 1966.*

WHEN THE history of the Indian and American relationship is written, Prime Minister Gandhi's visit to the United States in early April 1966 may be marked as a turning point.

From the moment an assured and beaming Mrs. Gandhi stepped from the helicopter onto the White House lawn to be warmly welcomed by President Johnson, until she waved farewell five days later from the ramp of the President's plane as it prepared to leave for London, her visit was a spectacular success.

Mrs. Gandhi and President Johnson discussed the differences of judgment and perspective between America and India with what President Johnson termed that "frankness and candour and detail that always mark conversations between good friends."

Because each is the elected leader of a great democracy, they had from the very beginning a mutual understanding of each other's problems, opportunities and concerns. This led to a meeting of the minds on essential issues.

At the same time, within a brief five days, Mrs. Gandhi became known to every American family through the miracle of television.

With a television set in almost every American home most Americans were able to see her four or five times a day speaking before large audiences, meeting the President, talking with Indian employees at the Indian Embassy and meeting with high officials at the United Nations. Out of this public exposure Mrs. Gandhi emerged in the minds of Americans as a person of dignity, courage and intellect who is willing and able to speak her mind frankly and to the point.

Mrs. Gandhi's visit is one important part of the rapidly increasing interest in India among many Americans.

Fifty years ago all that most Americans knew about India was a residue of distant school-day memories.

Succeeding generations of young Americans learned of Christopher Columbus, who in seeking a new trade route to India, had quite accidentally discovered North America and had mistakenly named the inhabitants of the newly discovered continent, "Indians".

In the late nineteenth century Swami Vivekananda established Ramakrishna Missions in the United States and won a large American following. In the twentieth century Mahatma Gandhi's Freedom Movement drew an enthusiastic response from Americans conscious of our own tradition of revolution and self-determination.

The open intervention of President Franklin D. Roosevelt on behalf of Indian freedom led to a further quickening of Indian interest in America, which created a strong reciprocal response in the increased study of America in Indian universities and colleges.

In the last twenty years this mutual interest has been greatly expanded by a revolution of education, resulting in Indian scholars studying American subjects and American scholars delving into Indian culture on a level unimaginable before 1947.

The development of American studies in India is rapidly increasing. The subjects of American history and American literature are now each taught at 49 Indian universities, while 14 offer courses in American Government.

The establishment of the American Studies Research Centre at Osmania University, Hyderabad, in 1964 marked the end of the first phase of the development of a rather broad-based study of American history, government and literature, which was followed by more intensive and specialized study at selected centres.

The development of integrated programmes of American area studies at three or four selected Indian universities is now encouraged and assisted both by the University Grants Commission and the United States Educational Foundation in India (USEFI). The prestigious Indian School of International Studies in New Delhi also has a department of American studies.

Meanwhile, the interest of American scholars in India has grown rapidly. The first development was sparked by Dr. Norman Brown's founding of a department of South Asia Regional Studies at the University of Pennsylvania in 1947.

Since then many hundreds of American research scholars have pursued their interests in various aspects of Indian studies.

As I have noted in the previous chapter, more than 68,000 Indians have studied in the United States while several thousand young Americans have travelled to India. Today there are 8,000 Indian students in American universities, 3,000 Indian medical doctors, and about 4,000 Indian members of university faculties. There is also a sizable farming community of Sikhs in California.

In 1967 alone more Americans earned doctorate degrees in Indian studies than in the entire first half of the twentieth century.

Indian area studies programmes have been established at 25 American universities and at scores of colleges. American interest in India is also typified by the changing curricula in many American high schools.

Summer Science Institute programmes have been held in India with American college professors and high school teachers by the Educational Resources Centre, the Fulbright Foundation and the U.S. foreign assistance programme. These institutes have led to the establishment of even more programmes of Indian studies in the United States.

In addition to senior and junior research scholars who come to India under the auspices of one organization or another, groups of young Americans, undergraduates or new graduates, have visited India and spent many months in this fascinating land, either studying at Indian universities or working as interns with the American Government. Syracuse University, the University of California at Berkeley, and Wisconsin University, all offer their students opportunities for a firsthand study of India.

From among former Peace Corps volunteers already trained in a regional language, a sizable number have returned from India to take up India-related subjects for master's and doctor's degrees.

The founding of the American Institute of Indian studies in Poona in 1962 enabled American universities with established Indian area studies programmes to provide for American professors and research scholars to refresh their knowledge of India and to keep abreast of the rapidly changing scene in India.

The Library of Congress project, based in New Delhi, is a great source of strength to American universities interested in India.

This organization acquires 20 copies of every book, journal and pamphlet published in India in any language. Each of 19 American universities who share in this project receive one copy each of the new publication, enabling these universities to build a complete current collection of Indian publications.

India has also contributed to American culture and society, a composite of many nationalities, races, languages, religions and ideas.

In recent years American interest in Indian handicrafts, music, dress, dance, drama, and philosophy has been growing spectacularly.

More recently, U.S. Negro leaders, in particular the late Martin Luther King, borrowed Gandhi's tactics of non-violent political action to help secure equal rights for our Negro citizens.

Many young Americans are also finding in Hindu culture an answer to their own quest for new patterns of life, new values, a new sense of personal identity. Hinduism, as they see it, places the highest priority on finding the "still centre" within oneself.

Next to the concept of non-violent resistance and Indian philosophy the most influential Indian export to America is music. American young people in particular like the extemporaneous elements of Indian music, which they believe helps to liberate their minds from the routine of their own technological society.

Ravi Shankar has become Guru to a large and growing sub-culture of Americans fascinated by the "new sounds" from India. Ali Akbar Khan, Bismilla Khan, Nikhil Banerjee have also been enthusiastically received by American music lovers.

The sale of records of Indian music in America is second only to those of Greece in foreign record sales. The recording of American violinist Yehudi Menuhin playing morning and evening ragas with sitarist Ravi Shankar in "West Meets East" is a best seller. The sitar is now widely used by rock-and-roll groups, while jazz musicians are making increased use of Indian rhythms.

Indian handicrafts, which are effective interpreters of the sub-continent's arts and crafts are another aspect of America's new interest in India. With increased travel to Asia, many more Americans have become aware of the beauty and unique design of

Indian products, such as brass, teak, sandalwood and papier mache objects.

The export of Indian cloth to the United States has grown within eight years from half a million dollars to nearly twenty million dollars.

America's leading dressmakers are using these fabrics in designing suits, gowns, dresses, and evening coats. Many of these such as saris, cholies, kurtas, pyjama type pants and sandals worn with Indian gold and silver jewellery follow Indian styles. "Nehru jackets" have become fashionable among American men for evening wear.

Indian classical and folk dance has also become enormously popular. American students of the dance are intrigued with the ancient and beautiful art that involves the use of the face and eyes, which are slighted in Western dance.

Indrani Rahman and Balasaraswati, two of India's most magnificent dancers, have had several successful tours in the United States. Large audiences have been thrilled by their personal beauty, dynamic presence and spectacular dance interpretations.

An art exhibit now touring American museums, "The Unknown India; Ritual Art in Tribe and Village", is also drawing large crowds of Americans.

Thus millions of Americans are being introduced to India's rich cultural heritage and tradition, and their response is enthusiastic. While neither *nirvana* nor instant *karma* is likely to come from this new enthusiasm for things Indian, there is no doubt that it is opening minds and building bridges between the world's two greatest democracies.

# 18. Recent Trends in Indian-American Relations

*The successful Indo-American talks, which took place in New Delhi in late July 1968, affirmed Ambassador Bowles' belief in the benefits of frank and full discussions between officials of the two governments. When Mr. Richard M. Nixon was elected President of the United States, the Ambassador outlined the important forces in the world today with which Mr. Nixon will be required to deal, including the growth of understanding and co-operation between India and America. Both discussions appeared in his* American Reporter *columns.*

RECENT informal discussions in New Delhi between representatives of the Indian and United States Governments established wide areas of agreement and understanding between our two countries.

The Indian delegation, ably led by Minister of State for External Affairs B.R. Bhagat, and an American team headed by Under Secretary of State Nicholas Katzenbach, discussed in a relaxed atmosphere the forces—both old and new—which are now shaping international affairs, and the likely effects of these forces in the years ahead.

In addition, Under Secretary Katzenbach and his associates took a two-day trip to Ludhiana Agricultural University, Bhakra Nangal Dam and Chandigarh, where they saw at first hand the revolution in Indian agricultural life. They also visited family planning centres at Agra and Delhi.

As Mr. Katzenbach said before he departed: "I had expected to see a lot of good things and to find a very friendly and vital and growing country . . . India has exceeded my expectations in every respect . . . ."

Under traditional diplomatic procedures governmental representatives normally meet only when some crisis disturbs the relationship between their respective governments. Consequently, the meetings are often conducted by harassed and ill-prepared individuals who must deal with both the current issue and an aroused domestic public opinion.

As a result, every government faces the danger of becoming tied to outworn concepts of national interest and, thus, to rigid attitudes which create distrust and further misunderstanding.

The United Nations and its specialized agencies provide an important forum for discussions between nations. However, since these meetings are open, the participants often feel inhibited from the kind of frank exchange that is essential to better understanding.

That is why I have been trying to bring about annual private bilateral meetings between representatives of the Indian and United States Governments to discuss and hopefully to develop wide area of understanding of the general trend of world affairs before crises develop.

Precedents had already been set by the annual meetings that the United States has with Canada, Great Britain, Japan and Brazil; in similar fashion India confers regularly with the USSR, Japan, France, Malaysia and Australia.

The purpose of the various bilateral meetings in which the United States is involved is not to settle current issues but to establish mutual respect, familiarity and understanding between the participants.

Face-to-face contacts among government heads of international organizations and private citizens can also play an important role in furthering broader understanding.

For instance, the great majority of American officials, educators and tourists who visit India for any length of time come away with the clear impression that India is a vital, democratic nation in which great progress is now being made in agriculture, family planning, industrial development, education and science.

They also come to know Indians as friendly, hospitable people who welcome strangers to their homes, towns and villages and who respect the same principles of freedom, human dignity and economic justice as does the United States.

At the same time the thousands of Indian visitors, students, businessmen and officials who visit the U.S. each year see both the dynamic progress of American society and also the many problems and tensions which this progress has helped to create.

Almost invariably they return to India with the knowledge that all Americans are not rich, that our streets are not filled with cowboys on white horses exchanging gunfire, that essentially Americans want a better, more secure and prosperous world for themselves and for the tens of millions throughout the world whose standard of living is not as high.

In addition, there are thousands of international non-governmental meetings held each year among students, trade union groups, industrialists, scientists, educators and others.

At the informal "Pugwash Conferences," nuclear scientists from the Soviet Union, Europe and the United States, speaking as private citizens, discuss frankly the dangers which are involved in the possible misuse of nuclear energy. Already these exchanges have led to the Nuclear Test Ban Treaty of 1963 and the Non-Proliferation Treaty which is now under consideration.

This experience indicates that a direct exchange of views across international boundaries between individuals and government officials, where opinions can be expressed frankly and freely, can play a constructive role in creating better world understanding. The recent talks between America and India in New Delhi confirm me in this belief.

A LONG these lines, another important question arises: What effect will the recent American election have on U.S. foreign policy, and particularly on relations between the democracies of India and the United States?

Although I have no crystal ball to assist me in my analysis, there are certain basic points which every observer of the American scene should take into account.

Any American President, whether he is a Republican or a Democrat, will be called upon in the years ahead to cope with world forces which neither he nor anyone else can control. His task will be to design policies which will cushion or shape these forces in a way that serves not only U.S. national interests but also the cause of world peace.

What are the most important forces?

1. *The Danger of nuclear conflict.* The nuclear powers now have the capacity to destroy each other and much of mankind. This puts strict limits on the adventuresome, reckless policies which in the past have led to major wars. Moreover, mankind is entitled to more than a fragile peace based on terror; and pressure for control of this destructive force will mount.

2. *The arms race.* A closely related problem is the heavy burden of military arms most nations are carrying in the name of self-defence.

If these arms build-ups provided genuine security, they could be considered worthwhile. However, after a decade or more of steadily increasing military expenditures, most people in the world feel far less secure than they did in the first place.

The new President of the United States and the top leaders of the Soviet Union know that if their respective nations are to provide adequate housing, schools, doctors, roads, consumer goods and recreation facilities for their people, and finance the process of development elsewhere, the heavy cost of military defence must be sharply reduced.

3. *The limits of power.* Any American President has to face the fact that, regardless of wealth and power, no nation, including the United States, is able to solve all of the problems which encircle this complex and turbulent globe.

In Vietnam the new President of the United States will be faced with the same problems which face President Johnson. Consequently he is likely to come up with much the same answers, *i.e.*, the negotiation of some kind of cease-fire, the phased withdrawal of troops, insistence on the right of the South Vietnamese people to elect freely their own government, and the right of people of both South and North Vietnam to decide to remain separate or to join into one nation.

4. *The rich nations and the poor nations.* Abraham Lincoln once said: "This government cannot endure permanently half slave and half free." In a similar view the world cannot prosper while half of its citizens live in luxury and the other half in squalor.

The maldistribution of income throughout the world is a hard fact of our times. However, if our world is to have political stability along with improved living standards and better opportunities for the multitudes, the income gap must be steadily reduced.

5. *The United Nations.* The United Nations is often criticized for its "failure" to come up with tidy answers to deeply rooted international conflicts.

The criticism is grossly unfair. The United Nations provides a vitally important forum in which the leaders of the world can exchange views and seek solutions to their differences. No American President can ignore its importance in our quest for peace.

6. *What about India?* Democratic India, with a population greater than Africa and Latin America combined, is a vitally important key to the stability and progress of Asia and a potentially decisive force in world affairs. India's independence, unity and well-being are crucial.

The newly-elected President of the United States has visited India on several occasions. Less than two years ago he had a fruitful talk with Mrs. Gandhi in New Delhi. I am confident that he will continue to give high priority to Indo-American understanding and cooperation.

As President, Mr. Nixon's style, tactics and methods of working will reflect his own experience and personality. But the forces to which I have referred will, for the most part, shape his administration's policies.

Consequently we may expect the United States Government to continue to work not only for greater opportunities and freedom for its own citizens but also, within the limit of its resources, for rising standards of living and a higher measure of human dignity for people throughout the world.

# The Political Dynamics of the New Asia

*If India fails, Asia dies. It has been aptly called the nursery of many blended cultures and civilizations. Let India be and remain the hope of all the races of the earth, whether in Asia, Africa or any part of the world.*

—MAHATMA GANDHI

# 19. Let Us Keep the Cold War Out of India

*Chester Bowles advocated a thaw in the cold war on the
subcontinent so that the U.S. and the USSR could work
together for an independent and strong India. This and
other articles on U.S.-Soviet cooperation appeared in
the* American Reporter *in 1967 and 1968.*

ONE OF THE most critical factors in determining world stability
in the years immediately ahead will be the relationship between the
Soviet Union and the United States.

This has become a fundamental fact of our time, much as the
French historian Alexis de Tocqueville predicted in 1835 when
he said:

> "There are two great nations in the world which started
> from different points, but seem to tend towards the
> same ends. I allude to the Russians and Americans.
> Although their courses are not the same, each seems
> marked out by history to sway the destinies of the
> world."

In the last thirty years the relations between these "two great
nations" have fluctuated between friendliness and conflict.

In June 1941, when Hitler's armies launched their invasion of the
Soviet Union, a great wave of sympathy and support swept across
the United States. In the days that followed the courage of the
Red Army and the Russian people in the defence of their country
won the admiration of us all.

Within weeks a massive flow of United States military supplies
and equipment, eventually amounting to $11 billion, was under
way and by mid-December of that year American soldiers, sailors
and airmen were fighting as allies of the Russian people.

When the war was over substantial amounts of American food and medical supplies were promptly provided to help the Russian people through the critical post-war period.

In 1946 we came forward with a proposal to give up our monopoly of nuclear power and turn the future of atomic development over to the United Nations. A year later the United States offered the Soviet Union economic assistance through the Marshall Plan: an offer that unhappily was rejected.

Then suddenly came the Cold War.

Stalin turned down our offer of nuclear cooperation on behalf of world peace, and confronted the countries of Central and Western Europe with an open military threat. This plunged the people of the United States and Soviet Union into a prolonged, bitter, wasteful and wholly needless confrontation.

With the death of Stalin and the emergence of more moderate leaders such as Khrushchev, Kosygin, and Brezhnev, confrontation has eased and taken on a different, less militant aspect.

Cultural exchanges have been established on a broad scale.

In 1963 the Nuclear Test-Ban Treaty was signed and the two nations, with the United Kingdom, took the lead in banning nuclear experiments in the atmosphere.

Plans to initiate a regular air service between New York and Moscow have been completed and an agreement has been reached to restrict the use of outer space to peaceful purposes.

Unhappily, Soviet-U.S. relations are still clouded by serious differences over the conflict in Vietnam. But, even here, I believe, there is a basis for understanding and, eventually, for cooperation.

Neither nation wants to see the war in Vietnam broadened; both countries desire a peaceful and stable Southeast Asia; each would welcome the opportunity of decreasing its own military budget once such stability is assured.

In regard to the Indian subcontinent, certain fundamental interests of the U.S. and USSR appear to coincide, although the USSR undoubtedly wants India to adopt an economic and political system similar to its own while the United States hopes that India will maintain a free, open democratic society.

Both the United States and the USSR have a stake in a politically stable, economically viable India and each is ready to help. Although American aid to India in the last ten years has been more than five times that of the USSR, the Soviets have made an important contribution in steel production and in heavy industry. With this year's huge wheat harvest, there is hope that the USSR can continue to help India to meet its critical food shortage.

Above all, the United States and the USSR should be able to agree on the basic need for an independent and strong India. Consequently, the people of India, and, indeed of the whole world, have an important stake in the ability of American and Soviet leaders to work out a continuing constructive relationship with each other and the other nations of the world.

UNFORTUNATELY in the last few months it has become apparent that a carefully calculated, massively financed campaign by the communists has been launched to undercut American efforts to speed the rate of India's development. Here are a few examples:

For more than two years an average of two ships a day, loaded with American wheat, have docked at Indian ports. To save India's scarce foreign exchange the United States has agreed to sell this wheat for rupees which can be spent only in India.

By a whole series of vicious editorials and concocted 'news' stories the communists have sought to transform the shipments of American wheat designed to prevent famine or malnutrition in India into a nefarious plot to undermine Indian self-reliance.

Among other things, it has been charged that the rupees the United States receives for this wheat have been used to finance the campaigns of various Indian politicians. These charges are utterly false, and the communist newspapers which print them week after week know they are false.

In the fifteen years $ 1.7 billion (Rs. 1,280 crores) of the funds earned from the sales of American agricultural commodities have been used to print lakhs and lakhs of Indian textbooks for Indian students, to finance our American libraries which 37,000 Indians visit each week and to finance exchanges of Indian and American students and professors.

In addition to these rupees earned from the sale of foodgrains, the United States has loaned or given India $ 3.3 billion (Rs. 2,500 crores) in foreign exchange to help ease the cost of India's economic development.

This money is spent by the Indian Government, which has used it for equipment to speed the modernization of India's railway system, machinery and raw materials for industrial growth, the expansion of India's electric power supply, the improvement of health and educational facilities and similar projects.

This vast effort to assist India is also under heavy fire from the communist propaganda apparatus, which charges that the United States is plotting to turn this country over to the "Wall Street Imperialists", "Neo-Colonialists" and even "Neo-cultural pene-trationists."

Let us consider another example. In the last three years Peace Corps Volunteers have worked—and are still working—in Indian villages helping their Indian hosts to improve poultry, to boost foodgrain production, to start rural industries, to assist in health clinics, to teach school, and the like.

Each of these dedicated young men and women has come to India in response to a request by one of the state governments with the approval of the Central Government. Yet they, too, have now become targets of communist propaganda, which falsely describes them as "spies and saboteurs."

Finally, in the last few weeks a series of forgeries have been launched, each of which was carefully calculated to harm the U.S. efforts to assist Indian development. The Indian Government has the full facts on all of these matters.

Why do the communists attempt to undermine American efforts to help India? Why do they seek to stop the flow of wheat for India's hungry millions? Why do they strive to cut off the dollars needed to build dams and power plants, and to import pharma-ceuticals, agricultural equipment, and fertilizers?

Obviously, their aim is to create distrust and antagonism between the world's two largest democracies, the United States and India, and to undermine the entire American economic assistance programme.

The United States deeply believes that a free and independent India, politically strong and economically viable, with a vigorous and independent foreign policy, has a major role to play in Asia. Indeed, it is difficult to visualise a stable Asia without a stable India.

An individual in a democratic country who is falsely charged can bring suit for libel and collect damages in the courts. When a nation has been similarly libelled there is no recourse except a bold airing of the facts, so that the public can know and judge the full story.

We Americans are here to participate in the task of helping India to become self-sufficient in the next ten years. We are eager to cooperate with any nation, regardless of its ideology, which genuinely seeks to assist India through this difficult period.

Let us therefore put an end to this international character assassination. Let us work together for a peaceful, prosperous, independent India that is free to choose its own future.

A S THIS slander continued, however, I wrote the following letter in mid-December 1967:

"Editor, Radio Peace and Progress
"Moscow, U.S.S.R.

"Dear Mr. Editor:
"For many years I have been convinced that the peace and progress of our world depends in large measure on the ability of your country and mine to work together in a constructive manner.

"Obviously, we cannot expect agreement on all of the complex questions of our present-day world. Our political and economic philosophies are different and, inevitably we see some issues from a different perspective.

"In regard to India, however, there is every reason why our legitimate national interests should closely coincide, *i.e.*, to support India's own massive drive to achieve political stability and economic progress, with an increasing measure of social justice.

"To help India achieve these objectives, the United States has shipped more than 52 million tons of foodgrains to India to ease the acute food shortage. We have also helped to modernize Indian railroads, to increase electric power production, to eliminate malaria, to build new fertilizer plants and agricultural universities, and generally to promote higher living standards for all the people.

"The Soviet Union has also provided India with economic assistance. Moreover, your Government made a major contribution to peace in South Asia in 1966 when it sponsored the Tashkent

Conference which created the basis for peace between Pakistan and India.

"However, our ability to work together in helping to speed Indian economic development is being undermined by the series of hostile broadcasts now being beamed into India over Radio Peace and Progress which contain slanders against my Government and my people.

"According to your broadcasts, virtually every American now living in India is a secret agent working to block India's economic progress, to create internal strife and to bribe public officials. I have even been personally accused of attempting to merge East Pakistan and West Bengal into an independent nation.

"On several occasions members of our American Embassy staff in New Delhi have informally discussed these broadcasts with Soviet representatives here in New Delhi. On each occasion your Embassy here has stated that it is not aware of the content of your broadcasts.

"I am writing to ask you to consider whether such broadcasts are serving the best interests of your own country and of the people of India.

"Do you really believe that what should be our common objectives in India are served by the falsehoods which you are directing against the people of the United States who more than any other foreign nation are contributing to help assure India's success?

"Why not forego these bitter attacks and join in a common effort to establish closer understanding among the peoples of India, Russia, and the United States, who together constitute nearly one-third of mankind?

"Working together, the U.S.S.R. and the United States can play a crucially important role in helping India to achieve a greatly improved standard of living and broader opportunities for all its people. However, if we slip back into the cold war atmosphere, which I believe your broadcasts are promoting, we shall all be the losers—Russians, Americans, and Indians—and a historic opportunity will have been lost.

"I can assure you that the American Mission in New Delhi will cooperate in every possible way to further what we believe should be our common objectives in this great country."

**P**EOPLE throughout the world—in Asia, Africa, Europe and the Americas—have been profoundly shocked by the invasion of Czechoslovakia by the armies of five communist nations.

This global revulsion has cut across ideological, racial, religious and national lines. Communists, capitalists, socialists and advocates of the welfare state have condemned this invasion as a ruthless intervention in the internal affairs of a hardworking and peaceloving people, who wanted only to be left alone to develop their own nation in their own way.

Czechoslovakia has always had a special place in the hearts of American people. The dogged persistence of President Woodrow Wilson in the negotiations at Versailles following World War I in 1919 helped Czechoslovakia to become an independent nation.

Since then, the Czech borders have been violated by foreign armies on three occasions. In 1938, Nazi troops occupied a sizable area of the Czechoslovak Republic and later took over the whole country.

After liberation from Nazi rule in 1945, the Czechoslovak people resumed their task of creating a free society based on democratic rule with a free press. But in the winter of 1948 foreign pressures were again brought to bear—this time from Stalin's Russia.

In late February 1948, while on a United Nations assignment in Prague, I had dinner with Jan Masyrk, the Czech Prime Minister. A few days later, due to political pressures, he jumped or was pushed from a window of his official residence following the Stalin-organized communist coup.

Now in August 1968 comes a third shocking violation of Czech independence.

This most recent aggression is particularly tragic since it occurs at a moment when governments and people throughout the world, regardless of their ideology, are beginning to recognize the need for mutual tolerance, patience, and respect for the rights of others as the essential basis for world peace.

The efforts of the United States and the Soviet Union to reach a common understanding on the issues that led originally to the old war have been a reflection of this hopeful trend.

Patient negotiations by representatives of these two great powers have already resulted in agreements to ban nuclear testing in the atmosphere and the more recent Non-Proliferation Treaty. In addition, cultural exchanges have been established, passenger flights agreed to between Moscow and New York, and the rules governing tourist visas relaxed to encourage the people of America and Russia to see each other's qualities, accomplishments and problems at first hand.

According to recent newspaper reports, at the very moment when the invading forces crossed the Czech frontier, plans were being completed for a meeting between President Lyndon Johnson and Soviet leaders. Had they met, the objective would have been to discuss not only roads to peace in West Asia and Vietnam, but also plans to divert a greater share of the resources of the two nations from the escalation of military strength to a massive effort to end worldwide poverty, ignorance and disease.

Will this steady progress towards mutual understanding and accommodation now be reversed? Will we again slip into a nonproductive and dangerous cold war atmosphere?

War and aggression have been the lot of mankind since the beginning of history. Power, Mao Tse-tung once remarked, comes from the barrel of the gun. Recent events in Czechoslovakia would seem, unfortunately, to prove his point.

Yet, in our age of long-range missiles and nuclear power, such thinking, with the implications of eternal conflict and utter destruction, represents sheer lunacy.

If modern civilization is to survive, hundreds of millions of ordinary people of all nations must reject such cynicism and reaffirm their faith in the capacity of the human race to work out peaceful solutions to their differences.

Is there not evidence that something akin to a world conscience committed to this objective is already evolving? Does not the very magnitude of the protest against the invasion of Czechoslovakia reflect a worldwide consensus for the peaceful solution of international problems?

No amount of rationalization or wishful thinking can hide the fact that a serious blow has been struck at world peace and understanding. But this is no time to retreat into the negative acceptance of "inevitable" conflict and bloodshed.

It is the responsibility of men of goodwill everywhere to intensify their efforts to create, step by step, a world society in which all nations, large and small, and regardless of their ideology, can live in peace and freedom.

# 20. China and India: Problems and Prospects

*In a Delhi University lecture in 1963 and an* American Reporter *column in 1966 Ambassador Bowles compared the neighbouring Asian giants—Democratic India and Communist China.*

IN ANY discussion of national development a comparison of India and China is inevitable because of their political importance, because of the striking parallels in their needs, and because of the vast contrast in their approaches to development.

Together these two countries contain two-fifths of the world's people and cover one-fifth of the inhabited area of the globe. Both have been dominated by foreign powers, although, as an Indian history professor pointed out, India had only one colonial overlord while China was exploited by almost everybody. Both have recently passed through revolutionary periods, although India's was far less violent and disruptive than China's.

India and China launched their development programmes from comparable economic bases. Both countries were under-developed relative to their needs and their potentials with 80 per cent of their populations largely dependent on agriculture. In 1947 the per capita income in China was about $45 per year; in India it was $52.

India gained her independence in 1947 and started her first Five Year Plan in 1951. The Communist Chinese Government established control over the mainland in 1949. Both countries have completed two Five Year Plans and are now involved in their third plans.*

---

*The statistics used here are based on 1961-62 data.

Although these similarities are striking, their respective approaches to their common problems differ greatly. China based its programmes on a doctrinaire interpretation in Marx while India leaned pragmatically toward a democratic welfare state. India emphasized agriculture in her first plan, while China placed top priority on heavy industry. China stressed capital goods, while India tried to achieve a balance between capital goods and consumer goods and services which would provide incentives to greater production.

It is in the area of politics and human relationships, however, that the differences are most significant. Whereas India sought to foster and encourage democratic discussion and participation, the Chinese communists, as the first step toward a minutely regulated dictatorship, weeded out the embryonic democratic institutions that were beginning to take root in China.

Whereas India tried to dignify the individual as part of the process of development, China regarded him as an instrument of the state. While India sought benefits for the present generation, China chose to squeeze the present generation to the limit of human endurance for the presumed benefit of their grandchildren.

In cultural affairs the differences are equally striking. Whereas India sought to preserve and enrich her ancient culture and to modernize her society within the context of her traditions, Communist China attempted to replace the traditional Chinese culture and institutions with a completely new and alien social system. While India tried to minimize the amount of social dislocation caused by the development process, China sought to maximize it.

Finally, China from the beginning was determined to assert her influence as a radical and militant element in international politics, while India chose the more constructive path of mediation, non-alignment and peaceful accommodation.

Any comparison between these two great nations that fails to take these differences of priorities and approach into account will prove misleading. All aspects of the development process must be considered in perspective. Each nation must be judged by its own standards as well as ours, and by the relationship of its achievements to the world society in which it is striving to find its place.

THE fundamental characteristic of the Chinese communist programme, as we have seen, has been a determination to transform,
as quickly as possible, a weak, underdeveloped and predominantly
agrarian society into a strong, industrialized totalitarian state.

Through the decades of intense revolutionary activity, through
the suffering of the Long March, through the final bloody struggle
for national control, Mao and his followers developed a deep-seated
commitment to this task.   The theories of Marxism-Leninism, which
are essentially political and not economic, were their  guiding
principles.

From this perspective the Chinese leaders saw their task as a vast
project of human engineering as well as economic engineering.
They wanted not only economic growth; they wanted a new and
radically different society.

Following the collapse of Chiang Kai-shek's armies, the Chinese
communist leaders moved  ruthlessly to consolidate their control
and eliminate present or potential opposition.   They hoped to do
this by destroying old centres of loyalty, creating new ones which
would serve the state with a single-minded commitment.

To break the authority of the rural landlords, tens of thousands
were executed.   A massive programme was launched to undermine
family loyalties, to destroy ancient religious beliefs, and to discredit
the Chinese cultural tradition.   At the same time, Mao and his
associates moved to consolidate power at the centre by substituting
new institutions, each tailored to special political or economic
objectives, for the old loyalties.   The Communist Party, its youth
organizations, para-military establishments, innumerable mass
organizations and total command over all means of communication
provided Peking with an extensive and pervasive system of control
over the  Chinese  people.

The Government then moved to the second stage: the task of
focusing its newly-organized mass of human energies on the overriding problems of economic development.

According to official Chinese claims the share of the national
income allocated to capital investment during the first Five Year
Plan was three times as great as the share invested by India at this
same stage of development.   As a result, by the mid-1950s the
Chinese were able plausibly to claim a rate of growth three times that
of  India.

Although Chinese communist statistics have proved to be notoriously inaccurate, a high level of investment was undoubtedly achieved. For a brief period, at least, the totalitarian control apparatus was able to compel individuals to work their hardest without concrete rewards such as consumer goods.

Part of the Chinese investment went into a crash programme for the education of technicians and scientists to support the industrial growth which was presumed to be forthcoming. School building and teacher training were vastly expanded. Highly specialized courses were provided to enable individuals to operate efficiently in a limited capacity. The brave beginnings of Chinese liberal education, which had been designed to encourage independent thinking, were abandoned as wasteful and dangerous. As long as the Communist Party leaders knew the truth, why should others be taught to think?

With Soviet and Eastern European assistance, the Chinese proceeded first to restore and then rapidly to expand their prewar industrial capacity. Manchurian installations, dismantled by the Soviets in 1945, were replaced or rebuilt; new factory complexes were added.

According to highly questionable official figures, electrical power capacity rated at 7.3 billion KWH in 1951 on the eve of the first Five Year Plan rose to 55 billion KWH by 1960. Equally extravagant claims were made for steel, coal, and other basic industries. Nevertheless, bridges were in fact built over the Yangtze, which had never been bridged before. Chinese shipyards did begin to produce ocean-going commercial and naval craft. Railway mileage was substantially increased.

Whatever the exaggerations, there is no doubt that by 1955 the combination of ruthless human and economic engineering had begun to pay off in terms of industrial progress. The first and hardest stage of industrialization, the creation of basic industries and power, seemed to be well under way.

Meanwhile, the population of the Chinese mainland had been growing at between 2 per cent and 3 per cent a year. Although a large population is looked upon by most Marxists as a source of economic strength regardless of circumstance, the dangers of unchecked population growth had become so obvious by the summer of 1955 that the voices behind the loudspeakers began to announce a hastily devised birth control programme.

In the spring of 1958 this brief effort at population control was just as suddenly terminated; henceforth, it was said, all efforts were to be focused on the "Great Leap Forward" programme. The massive projects which the Leap would bring into being would soon make population control unnecessary and even create a labour shortage. Sixty million people were to be put to work producing steel in backyard furnaces. One hundred million more were to be employed in irrigation projects. Throughout Asia the political impact of this vast outpouring of plans, projects and propaganda was substantial. The Chinese, now supremely confident, called upon representatives from all developing countries to come to China to note their progress and adopt their methods.

On my visit to India in 1955 I found many people deeply impressed with the dramatic developments in Communist China. Even those who believed most fervently in a free society were beginning to question the capacity of developing nations to meet their essential economic goals through democratic methods.

By the late 1950s, however, the Chinese plans rapidly outran the available resources and the Great Leap Forward began to peter out. In 1960 came the slowdown of Soviet aid and the downward economic spiral was intensified. As part of what the Peking *Peoples Daily* described as a "perfidious action," the USSR "tore up 343 contracts and supplementary provisions" and then "heavily slashed the supply of whole sets of equipment."

Although Peking has published no further economic statistics, the industrial gains made between 1957 and 1960 appear largely to have been lost. Electric power output, which had reached about 55 billion KWH in 1960, is believed to have dropped to 30-35 billion KWH; steel has fallen from 18 million tons per year in 1960 to 8 million tons in 1962. Similar decreases have occurred in coal, cement and other industrial products.

Work on many railroads and dams has been interrupted for want of equipment and technical skills. Scores of factories are shut down or running part time because of raw material shortages and unavailability of spare parts. China has become the only country in the world in which total production has actually decreased.

THE failure of the industrial phase of the Great Leap Forward was duplicated in agriculture, which has always been the Achilles' heel of Communist nations. Between 1952 and 1960 the output of foodgrains remained virtually stagnant as China's population continued to mount at the rate of 12 to 15 million people annually. By 1962, the food deficit in terms of the per capita consumption of 1958 had grown to 15 million tons. With the population expanding at its present rate, the deficit will continue to increase by about 5 million tons of grain each year.

These grim statistics suggest that in a favourable year China's food supply will be barely adequate to feed her people. In a normal year there will be serious shortages. In a bad year there will be widespread malnutrition.

There is a little promise moreover, in remedies which are available to the present Government. Although only about 14 per cent of China's total land area is now cultivated, the possibilities for expansion are strictly limited. For generations, China's farmers have been striving to bring more acreage under cultivation with only marginal success. Under the most favourable circumstances it is unlikely that the present arable areas can be increased by more than 20 per cent; since most of the additional acreage will be substandard, the resulting increase in output would be substantially less than that.

Nor can China expect major gains in agricultural production from more intensive cultivation of existing acreage. Chinese farmers are among the best in the world; in Asia their rice yields are surpassed only in Japan and Taiwan, where, in addition to greater personal incentives, there is a far greater use of chemical fertilizers. Because of its key importance this latter factor deserves more detailed analysis.

China now produces nearly three million tons of chemical fertilizer annually. It is estimated that under extremely favourable circumstances a crash programme of fertilizer production might add another five million tons in the next six to ten years, at a cost of roughly $600 million. Even if the skilled personnel, electric power and physical resources were available to launch and manage such an effort, an industry of this magnitude could be built only by foregoing other essential projects. Moreover, even if the goal were fully achieved, it could not begin to meet China's future agricultural requirements.

One pound of chemical fertilizer produces about three extra pounds of food. The added five million tons of fertilizer would therefore produce about fifteen million additional tons of food—enough to feed forty-five million more people at the present inadequate levels. But by 1970, which is the earliest that the new fertilizer plants could be completed, there will be 100 million more people to feed, assuming the present rate of population increases.

On the other side of China's agricultural ledger, however, are several factors, in addition to the cultivation of some marginal land, which are potentially favourable. Increased irrigation can provide an extra crop in many areas and increase production in others. Seeds may be improved. Through a determined effort population pressure may gradually be reduced.

Yet even under the most favourable circumstances it seems unlikely that the Chinese Government can produce an adequate supply of food for its people from the land now within the boundaries. If this judgment is correct it may prove to be one of the most decisive political facts of our time.

PART of Peking's failure in agriculture, like its failure in many areas of industry, must be attributed to defects in its ambitious efforts at human engineering which became evident in the late 1950s. In an effort to secure total political control of the Chinese people, the Chinese Communist leaders embarked on restrictive measures which undercut the popular support they had successfully cultivated during the long civil war.

At the moment of their revolutionary triumph there is no doubt that the Chinese people, who were tired of war and saw Mainland China unified for the first time in many decades, were willing and eager to give the new regime a chance.

In the early stages this popular support was strengthened by the massive redistribution of land which the new regime initiated. When the dust settled, however, each Chinese farmer owned an average of less than an acre, which he soon found was inadeqate to support his family.

Some observers believe that the revolutionary promise of "land to the tiller" was in itself a calculated fraud; in other words the communist leaders never had any intention of respecting the independent position of 100 million farm families, each with the pride, dignity and security that goes with land ownership. But whether the Government failed to take the political realities into account or whether they planned it that way at the outset, Mao and his associates, in the Stalinist tradition, soon proceeded to break the political promise which had persuaded millions of young Chinese peasants to volunteer for service in the Red Armies. As the new programme of total regimentation was instituted, the disenchantment of rural China mounted rapidly.

The first stage was the establishment of hundreds of thousands of mutual aid teams which shared their privately-owned animals and equipment for harvesting and planting. Second came Agricultural Producer Cooperatives in which land was also pooled on a permanent basis. Each member received shares which, he was assured, entitled him to an annual dividend according to the size of the land he originally contributed.

The third stage was the establishment in 1955 of collective farms in which all vestiges of private land ownership, which had been the traditional dream of the Chinese cultivator, were eliminated and land dividends abolished. Payments were now made out of the profits of the enterprise in proportion to the working hours contributed. The Marxist-Leninist slogan, "To each according to his work," was revived as the ideological explanation of this step.

In 1958 the first commune, the ultimate device of collectivization, was launched in Hunan Province. These enforced cooperatives with an average of some 50,000 people each were to become the agricultural instruments of the Great Leap Forward. Their purpose was the total mobilization of some 550 million Chinese villagers into a massive human work force under the ruthless control of the central government.

To meet the new situation another slogan was quickly substituted: "From each according to his ability; to each according to his need." A Peking interview, lauding the new communes, carried the headline, "Oh, Commune ! Everything I have is yours except my toothbrush!"

The communes were the final disastrous step in Mao's experiment in human engineering. They were an effort to assure the central regime a vast reservoir of mindless and soul-less human energy which could be used for construction projects as well as for food production.

Overnight, students became agricultural supervisors, farmers became dam builders, housewives became smelter operators. The net result was the greatest dislocation of manpower in human history, followed by pervasive public frustration and the nearly complete collapse of the Chinese economy.

ALTHOUGH Communist China's economic mistakes have been devastating, their political repercussions may be even more far-reaching. Because the government totally disregarded the wishes of the people and because it set out to destroy the old basis of Chinese culture, it became separated from the people.

Today, Communist Party literature refers to non-party people as "the masses" and "the masses" call party members "they." In a pamphlet entitled "How to Be A Good Communist," party members are warned that even the labouring class—the proletariat, the backbone of traditional Marxism—shall be treated with suspicion.

The lesson is an old one which, it appears, must constantly be relearned by modern totalitarians who seek to manipulate people for narrow and self-seeking purposes. When the people fail to identify their interests with the rulers, and vice versa, and when each group comes to fear the other, the political stability upon which economic progress depends is undermined and ultimately will be destroyed.

China's agricultural crisis also served further to undermine her sagging industrial development. The low level of agricultural production forced a diversion of scarce investment funds and foreign exchange totalling $450 to $500 million annually for the import of grain from Australia and Canada. In addition, land was diverted from industrial supply crops to foodgrain production with the result that many factories which relied on agricultural raw materials such as cotton closed down, expensive equipment and skilled workers were idled, and exports were curtailed.

A Chinese leader recently observed that in a country as large as China, if the leaders make even a small mistake and this mistake is compounded by 700 million people, it becomes a national disaster. Although Communist China's mistakes cannot properly be discounted as "small," this comment may serve as a fitting epitaph for the "Great Leap Forward."

A GAINST this background of China's dilemma let us consider the problems and prospects of India. It is difficult to imagine a more radically different economic, social and political environment.

In any democratic country people must be persuaded to see for themselves the advantages of working together. This takes time and is seldom fully realized.

Since false slogans are quickly debunked by a free press, they have only a passing effect. Consequently, the peasants, workers and managers must be offered tangible rewards for greater efforts. This means that capital investment must be limited to allow for additional food, clothing and consumer goods.

Nor can anyone deny that democratic development in any nation has a disorderly appearance. The government can seldom get everyone to pull together. Most individuals work primarily for their personal benefit and only indirectly for the good of a society. Newspapers and opposition parties constantly criticize the government and its planning—and not always responsibly.

Yet, out of this apparent disorder come many advantages: the release of human energies, the encouragement of new ideas and new techniques, and the knowledge that no one mistake or even a series of mistakes is likely to be disastrous.

Consequently, the cycle of quick forward spurts followed by catastrophic relapses which characterizes the development of Communist China is rarely found in a democratic environment. Although development may appear more haphazard, it proceeds at a more certain pace.

When India's recent experience is contrasted with that of China, the strengths and weaknesses of democratic development come sharply into focus. There have been mistakes in Indian planning. Performance has lagged in agriculture and industry. Population growth has exceeded the early estimates and, as a result, per capita progress has been slower than anticipated.

But India began with a concept of balanced growth whereby agricultural goods and manufactured consumer goods were included as an integral part of the growth pattern; therefore, shortfalls in some sectors have not had a magnified impact on the rest of the economy. Her more flexible planning has been the product of countless discussions and compromises. While India's statistical progress has not been spectacular, it has been relatively steady, with successes in some areas more than offsetting the setbacks in others.

The differences are particularly noteworthy in regard to social change. While India has made a determined effort to reshape her traditional social system, the approach has been respectful of old values. Pressures to modify the caste system and to outlaw child marriage were designed not to control the individual but to release him from the constraints of customs where such customs have prevented him from reaching his full potential. There has been no effort to destroy the past or to impose new cultural values; the objective has been to revitalize old concepts and to fit them to new conditions.

Although the Chinese heroes of the Long March were able to communicate some of their ideological fervour to their people, their dogmatism has prevented them from pragmatically altering their programme when changes have been urgently needed. While the Chinese were sure they could interpret the future, the Indian Government has remained sensibly agnostic. Where the Chinese system has cracked under adversity, the Indian has simply bent.

THE future in both countries is unpredictable. Yet certain trends are evident.

In seventeen years India has created a stable base for future growth. It is moving ahead, even though slowly, and it has been doing so since the first year of her first Five Year Plan.

The rewards for the Indian people are increasing, not decreasing. A recent public opinion survey indicated that three out of every four Indians feel that they are somewhat better off than five years ago.

Ways of limiting population growth are being developed and introduced.

The people are gradually absorbing the techniques of democracy and as they do so their sense of dignity is expanded and assured.

The political and social systems of India have both reached a point where they seem not to be subject to radical change or collapse.

Furthermore, because India's political and economic growth within the framework of a free society has earned her the confidence of much of the world, her Government and people are receiving substantial assistance from many of the more developed nations. This continuing flow of assistance from foreign governments and private foreign capital, which at present is denied to China, will continue to have a vitally important ·bearing on the pace of Indian development.

China, on the other hand, is currently at a low point in her development. The price of her extremism, of her abortive effort to play a dominant role in world affairs, and of her embroilment in ideological squabbles, has been her isolation from the rest of the world.

THERE is mounting evidence of deep-seated differences between those Chinese on the one hand, who favour a more rational approach to the problems of economic development and to questions of foreign policy, and on the other, the hard-line reactionaries who are determined to move relentlessly toward world domination under the Maoist formula of revolutionary conquest.

The turbulent situation which has grown out of this conflict underscores a problem which affects all dictatorships, both fascist and communist: the problem of succession.

Once the contest begins, there is no room for old loyalties, there is no sanctuary except in victory, there are no constitutional safe-guards or recourse to the people's will.

Invariably the men who fight their way to the top are those who are most successful in eliminating or buying off their rivals.

In the case of China the struggle among the potential successors of the aging and headstrong Mao Tse-tung is clearly under way. Mao and his chosen heir appear to have launched a systematic campaign of terror and coercion to insure the continuation of his policies after his death.

To carry out Mao's objectives large numbers of young people have been organized into units of the so-called "Red Guards" and given licence to intimidate, terrorize and even to murder men and women whom they arbitrarily label as "enemies of Maoist thought." The excesses of the "Red Guards" rival those perpetrated on the Chinese people by the Communist in the 1949-53 period.

What does this mean in terms of the future of Chinese policy and the stability of the Government?

We can assume that many top communist leaders who have

been pushed aside are resentful and anxious to regain their former position of power.

The Communist Party apparatus which has been the primary target of the "Red Guards" must be profoundly shaken.

The Army must be wondering whether China's irresponsible policies are leading it to a war for which it is not prepared.

In the meantime the long-suffering, exploited Chinese peasants and workers must be wondering how long this horror can go on, while they hope for the day when at long last they can be free of the shifting whims of a communist dictatorship.

While we cannot deny the possibility that Mao's successors may be even more extreme than he, we may still hope that he will be followed by men who are more concerned with the welfare of the Chinese people, better attuned to the realities of our contemporary world, and more willing to accept the right of neighbouring peoples to determine their own destinies.

TODAY it is difficult to anticipate a satisfactory course for China. Her present government cannot go back and start again because too much dislocation has occurred. Yet it is highly unlikely that her present erratic course can produce a substantial overall advance.

Still, China remains a country to be reckoned with. A nation of 700 million, however weakened by inept leaders and a sterile ideology, cannot be expected to disappear. Ultimately some solution will be found. Sooner or later, the attractive, capable Chinese people will again become a useful member of the world community.

One final word. Perhaps the most important conclusion that can be drawn from our comparison of China and India is that totalitarian "efficiency" is a myth. A few years ago it was widely believed, even by those who hated its methods, that a dictatorship provided the most efficient administrative tools for economic development. In the mid-fifties responsible people were beginning to assert that sooner or later the less developed world would have to make a choice between iron-fisted regimentation on the one hand and a grim future of poverty for their people on the other. Now it appears that those nations which have had the courage to under-take development democratically may have the better prospect of success.

Brazil, Japan, Mexico, Taiwan, and many other developing countries have developed far faster than China. Moreover, the rate of economic growth in all communist countries averaged only 3. 6 per cent in 1962, a figure which was bettered by every democratic nation in Western Europe and North America.

This does not mean that authoritarian systems cannot bring about development; the Soviet Union, through an agony of effort, has become the world's second industrial power. But it does suggest that nations which have chosen a democratic path to development may move ahead with confidence.

They can proceed now with the knowledge that the dignity of the individual can be secured side by side with economic progress. Indeed, the contrast between India and China suggests that the strength of a free people and the diversity and vitality of a pluralistic society are the greatest assets any nation can have.

Not so long ago the leaders of Communist China proclaimed that all developing nations must ultimately choose between bread and freedom. After ten years of frantic effort, they themselves have secured neither. There is solid reason for hope that democratic India may achieve both.

Yet there is no room for complacency. India's problems are awesome in their magnitude and complexity. With all of her brave efforts India is only now barely starting down the long road of orderly political, social, and economic growth.

In the years to come the eyes of the world will continue to focus on these two ancient lands—India and China—each in its own way seeking a new life for its people. Although no one can foresee the outcome, every person who believes not only in material progress but in the dignity of the individuals who create that progress has a personal stake in India's success.

# 21. Nuclear Power: Danger or Opportunity?

*With violence occurring throughout the world in 1968 and 1969—Czechoslovakia, Southeast Asia, Western Asia— Chester Bowles, in a speech to the Bombay Rotary Club and in several* American Reporter *columns, discussed the need to curb the spread of nuclear weapons and the hope for a cooperative effort to assure a peaceful, constructive use of outer space.*

OUR GALLOPING scientific technology has now brought us to a political crossroad which is dramatized by the extraordinary development of nuclear energy. The way we take in the use of atomic energy will hold profound significance not only for us who inhabit the earth but also for our children of many generations.

One road leads at its worst to the destruction of the best in our imperfect civilization in a manner more gruesome than our minds can conceive.

The other road runs through way stations of hope into a new era of applied nuclear science. This new era promises within decades more progress in easing human burdens than any of the previous centuries of struggle.

Here in India, the choice has been made. At the Tarapur nuclear power project work is already under way in India's biggest step so far in the development of nuclear energy to serve its people. May I add that I am particularly glad that my Government is associated with yours in this important undertaking.

To understand the meaning of the choice that has been taken we should glimpse briefly into the promise of the new nuclear era. The existence of atoms has been suspected for many centuries, but it has been only in relatively recent years that anyone has done much about them.

About 400 B.C. Democritus in Greece believed that everything was made of atoms and that they could not be divided into anything smaller. He said that "in truth, nothing exists but atoms and the void." Warmth and cold and colour, sweetness and bitterness, were only appearances.

Aristotle in the next century concluded that everything was made of four elements—earth, water, fire and air. Some three hundred years later a Roman, Lucretius, revived Democritus' beliefs, but the concept of Aristotle continued to discredit the whole idea of atoms.

In the 17th century the search for the atom was renewed but progress was slow until the 20th. The modern genius Albert Einstein showed that mass can be changed into energy and vice versa. And the Italian, Enrico Fermi, at the University of Chicago in 1942 started and maintained a controlled chain reaction of nuclear fission in the world's first nuclear reactor.

Since then nuclear science has been applied to our lives in hundreds of ways, and we are only beginning.

One of our greatest needs is for power, and atomic energy is becoming an important source of it.

In Europe, for example, the gap between what the continent needs in energy and what is available is expected to increase sharply in the years ahead. Through a European atomic community— Euratom—Western European nations have pooled their skills and resources to close this gap with atomic energy.

Foreseeing a shortage of coal for the production of electricity in the years ahead, Britain built the first full-scale nuclear power station which began operating at Calder Hall in 1956. Within a few years nuclear power in Britain will provide electricity equal to that generated by 40 million tons of coal annually.

In the United States, the first full-scale nuclear power plant began to produce electricity in Pennsylvania in 1957, and we have built a variety of reactors to test relative efficiency.

Tarapur, the plant to be constructed through Indian and American cooperation, has been rated as potentially one of the world's most efficient. Even as a pioneering station in India, this largest plant of its kind in Asia will compare favourably in costs with the more conventional sources of power.    Of equal importance is the contribution it will make to the development of nuclear technology in India.

For we are only beginning to learn the ways that atomic power can be used.    We do not yet know what the full results will be in transportation let alone the full prospects for space research.

Perhaps radioactive isotopes or forms of elements which are unstable, may become as important as atomic power to human society of the future.    Already they have proven their value in industry, agriculture and medicine.

To cite only one example, scientists at the Brookhaven National Laboratory on Long Island, New York, have shot neutrons at oat seeds to develop a rust resistant variety.    The discovery will save American farmers approximately $100 million a year.

Some of our greatest hopes are in the application of nuclear science to medical research and treatment.

We have much to learn.    None of our youth need fear that they arrived on the scene too late, or that all the great discoveries had been made.

Nuclear fission today is a reality.    However, nuclear fusion, which might produce energy in cheap, almost inexhaustible amounts is not yet controllable because such high temperatures are required. Some day, perhaps, we shall be able to control the release of energy from nuclear fusion, and that will catapult us into an entirely new prospect for a better life.

MEANWHILE, what about the threatening nuclear arms race? The prospects for the human race are closely tied to the question of whether we can devote the energies that presently are absorbed by the production of weapons to peaceful uses of atomic energy.

The history of mankind is marred by a long succession of bloody encounters.    With the help of a computer, a Norwegian professor recently calculated that in the 5,560 years of recorded history, there have been 14,531 wars.    This adds up to more than two and a half wars per year.

Since the end of World War II in 1945, we have done a little better, *i.e.*, only thirty wars in twenty-three years, many of which have been modestly described as "police actions"—too violent to be called peace, too constrained to be declared as war.

At the same time, most nations of the world in their quest for "national security" have been devoting an increasing proportion of their scientific talents and a major share of their gross national incomes to a frantic effort to devise even more efficient ways of destroying those with whom they disagree.

In the early stages of history men fought each other with rocks and clubs, then with spears and crossbows, and finally, with the discovery of gunpowder by the Chinese, with muskets which have evolved into machine guns, bazookas, grenades, artillery, and bombs.

With the splitting of the atom came the horror of Hiroshima. This was followed by a competition between the nuclear powers which has resulted in a shocking increase in our capacity of mutual destruction.

Today, nuclear armed missiles can be launched with deadly accuracy against cities 5,000 miles away. Nuclear bombs can be dropped from airplanes one-half lakh feet above the earth. Nuclear missiles can even be fired from submerged submarines.

In the years ahead the fast growing weaponry technology will no doubt provide us with even more fantastic instruments of destruction.

For instance, scientists are now studying ways to flood coastal cities with artificially produced tidal waves and even to create destructive hurricanes and earthquakes.

Also in the foreseeable future scientists may be able to puncture the earth's zone shield, thereby providing ultraviolet rays that could kill all exposed life over a targeted area.

Then there are newly discovered weapons of chemical and biological warfare. Gases such as MACE can incapacitate an opponent temporarily, or a few pounds of poison in a city water supply can destroy life on a major scale.

In many nations laboratories are working overtime to develop fiendish new viruses or bacteria that reproduce with great rapidity and can threaten an entire "enemy" population.

Scientists are also working frantically to develop defences against these new weapons. But their new air filter systems, gas masks, shelters and early warning devices are woefully inadequate to contain these deadly forces.

Nor have we made much progress through international negotiations and agreements. In 1963 the United States, the Soviet Union and Great Britain agreed to eliminate nuclear explosions in the atmosphere and to conduct all future testing underground.

As President Kennedy pointed out shortly before his death in 1963:

"It is an ironical but accurate fact that the two strongest powers are the two in the most danger of devastation. All we have built, all we have worked for, would be destroyed in the first 24 hours. And even in the cold war, which brings burdens and dangers to so many countries—including this nation's closest allies—our two coun'ries bear the heaviest burdens. We are both devoting massive sums of money to weapons that could be better devoted to combating ignorance, poverty and disease. We are both caught up in a vicious and dangerous cycle in which suspicion on one side breeds suspicion on the other and new weapons beget counter-weapons.

"In short, both the United States and its allies, and the Soviet Union and its allies, have a mutually deep interest in a just and genuine peace and in halting the arms race."

Early this year, after long negotiations, the Governments of the United States and the Soviet Union agreed on a programme to combat nuclear proliferation, making available to every nation the use of nuclear energy for peaceful purposes while barring the production of nuclear bombs except by those who already have them.

Before the recent Czechoslovak crisis, the United States and the U.S.S.R. were prepared to take a much more important step: the negotiation of an agreement actually to reduce their stockpiles of nuclear weapons.

Yet the horrible cold fact remains: while the weapons of total destruction steadily grow more awesome, our capacity to control these weapons lags far behind. Are we travelling along a road which will lead to our own destruction?

Now there is every evidence that this important cooperative effort will move forward. The new American President, Mr. Richard M. Nixon, recently asked the U.S. Senate to "act promptly" on the Nuclear Non-Proliferation Treaty. The Treaty, Mr. Nixon said, "can be an important step in our endeavour to curb the spread of nuclear weapons and it advances the purpose of our Atom-for-Peace Programme."

President Nixon has also indicated his desire to hold talks with the Soviet Union on the limitation of military armaments.

Faced with this fateful dilemma, let us pray that men of goodwill everywhere, regardless of ideology and nationality, will join in the mighty effort to break through the barriers of fear and mistrust which now cloud our vision and distort our perspective.

ONE of the more reassuring elements in this direction is the great promise which the recent Apollo 8 space flight around the moon provides for the exploration of outer space by the United States and other nations.

The implications of this breathtaking flight transcend national boundaries, and were the subject of comment by leaders the world over.

The Secretary General of the United Nations wrote: "I warmly congratulate the astronauts. . .and all those planning and backing up this first manned translunar expedition, for its magnificent success."

President Podgorny of the U.S.S.R. cabled the White House: "Accept, Mr. President, our congratulations. . .Apollo 8. . .is a new accomplishment in mastering the outer space by man."

Mrs. Gandhi said: "We have followed with anxious suspense the celestial journey of Borman, Lovell and Anders. I congratulate the U.S. Government and its people on this occasion."

U.K. Prime Minister Harold Wilson said that the voyage had "added a new dimension to our appreciation that ours is indeed one world."

The challenge of space exploration was accepted by the United States in 1958. Our concept then is still valid today: (1) that space should be devoted to peaceful purposes; (2) that our U.S. space programme should not be a secret endeavour, but should be open and subject to scrutiny by anyone; and (3) that all we learn should freely be made available to the scientists of all nations.

Already some of the practical benefits of this great effort are beginning to emerge. For example, we now have weather satellites which detect major storms and provide advance warning for those who may be affected.

We have communications satellites which speed the flow of information throughout the world and may soon bring educational television to developing nations such as India. New metals produced by space research are making an increasing contribution to medicine and industry. Photography from outer space has helped us to discover new ore and petroleum deposits.

The implications of the moon flight are incalculable. We now know that individual genius and dedication can combine with twentieth-century technology to accomplish what was thought to be impossible.

This leads me to three fundamental questions:

1. If we can develop monstrous weapons to destroy whole nations in a matter of hours, why are we unable to find the means to develop a world society based on coexistence, cooperation, and peace?

2. Why cannot space exploration and research become a cooperative *international* enterprise? Joint efforts in space exploration will not only bring the participating nations closer together but will enable us to avoid duplicating activities and hence to accomplish more at less cost.

3. If the physical scientists can take us to the moon, why cannot the social scientists, supported by their governments and by new technology, work comparable miracles for the benefit of all mankind ?

I have in mind such objectives as an adequate balanced diet for people everywhere, control of the world's burgeoning population, solving the world's water shortage by taking the salt out of sea water, making modern medical care available to everyone and education available to each individual in accordance with his capabilities, regardless of his income.

In short, if we can create a technology to probe the heavens, why are we unable to develop the mechanism to establish world peace and at the same time provide more comfortable, satisfying and secure lives for the 3.5 billion human beings who share our own planet ?

## SECTION FIVE

# Interpreting America

*Now the trumpet summons us again—not as a call to bear arms, though arms we need; not as a call to battle, though embattled we are; but a call to bear the burden of a long twilight struggle, year in and year out, 'rejoicing in hope, patient in tribulation'—a struggle against the common enemies of man; tyranny, poverty, disease, and war itself.*

—President John F. Kennedy

# 22. The Unfinished American Revolution

*In his Feroze Gandhi Memorial lecture on September 8, 1963 Chester Bowles outlined the three periods of crisis in American history, describing how old alignments and familiar slogans had proved inadequate to solve new problems of the day. Presidents Jefferson, Lincoln, and Franklin D. Roosevelt each ushered in a creative period of reorientation. The Ambassador believed the U.S. to be on the verge of a fourth great political revolution, enabling the nation to take another long step forward toward its ideals and objectives.*

THOUGHTFUL men everywhere are deeply conscious of the fact that we are living in a period of world revolution when extraordinary technological developments are colliding with old habits of mind. But the dimensions of the world revolution which now challenge us extend far beyond our exploding technology. Equally important, it is a revolution in the attitude of man toward man and in the relationship of the individual and the society of which he is a part.

For the first time in history the words "freedom, justice, dignity" are on the lips of millions of men and women in every corner of the globe. In each country the challenge to men of goodwill is how best to marshal the new techniques of medical care, of farming, of education, of industrial production and marketing in a fashion that will fulfil the material aspirations of their fellow citizens and also provide an increasing sense of spiritual harmony and well-being.

I would like to discuss the nature of this effort in my own country and suggest some of its effects on our political structure.

In America as elsewhere the impact of new issues on established political alignments is causing heavy strain and many observers believe that new alignments to meet new conditions may now be in the making. Because the situation is fluid, analysis is difficult and prediction dangerous. However, a short review of American political history may help us to understand what may be in the wind.

Since our Revolutionary War of 1776 we see a certain rhythm of political thought and action which has been repeated several times. The first phase of this cycle has been characterized by the impact on our society of new forces and circumstances which inevitably give rise to new political issues. Eventually and sometimes very reluctantly, the political dialogue comes to focus on and be oriented around these new issues.

The second phase of the cycle occurs when a political party which has assumed power seeks to respond to these new issues and attempts to resolve them. In the final phase we see the digestion and gradual acceptance of the new concepts by all major political factions and their integration into our evolving political philosophy.

In the course of this continuing rhythm of political change, the issues between the older and the newer views are sometimes debated fully, and the voters given a clearly stated choice between alternatives. More frequently, however, we have backed into a new political era under pressure from a national crisis while clinging to a political folklore and to political slogans that had already lost their relevance.

From the birth of our American political parties 160 years ago to the present, three such cycles are evident, each characterized by a clearly defined political consensus.

It is interesting that in each of these three periods the dominant consensus developed in response to public insistence on a broader interpretation of human freedom to meet new conditions.

Each was introduced by a period of political imagination and creativeness in an atmosphere of bitter debate. This was followed in each case by a period of consolidation and eventually by an era of "good feeling" during which partisan ardours were restrained and the American people recharged their political batteries for the next forward move.

The first era of this kind, largely dominated by the Democratic party, extended from Thomas Jefferson's election as President of the United States in 1800 to the outbreak of our Civil War in 1861.

It was characterized by a broad public reaffirmation of the basic principle of the American Revolution, *i.e.*, that our system of government must be responsive to the majority will—to the wishes of artisans in towns and villages and farmers out on the frontier as well as of the gentlemen landowners or businessmen.

Jefferson's basic philosophy was expressed in the following quotation from his writings: "All eyes are opening to the rights of man. The general spread of science has already laid open to every view the palpable truth that the mass of mankind has *not* been born with saddles on their backs, nor a favoured few booted and spurred, ready to ride them legitimately, by the grace of God."

On another occasion Jefferson wrote: "Men are naturally divided into two parties. (1) Those who fear and distrust the people, and wish to draw all powers from them into the hands of the higher classes;

(2) Those who identify themselves with the people, have confidence in them, cherish and consider them as the most honest and safe, although not the most wise depositary of the public interest."

The opposition to Jefferson's concept of a free and expanding society was led by Alexander Hamilton, our brilliant first Secretary of the Treasury. Hamilton's contrary view of society was expressed in the following words:

"All communities divide themselves into the few and the many. The first are rich and well born, the other the mass of the people..... The people are turbulent and changing; they seldom judge or determine right....Give, therefore, to the first class a distinct share in government. They will check the unsteadiness of the second."

By the 1850's Jefferson's concept of human dignity, dedicated in his words to the "Rights of Man" had been fully accepted in our American society. Hence, the issue of slavery, which had been sidestepped in the Jefferson era, was now steadily pressing to the centre of the political stage.

The members of both of our two major political parties at that time—the Whigs who were conservative on the Jeffersonian issues and the more liberal Democrats—were each keenly aware that this embittering new question would split their political organizations up the middle. At first, therefore, both attempted to ignore and submerge it.

Yet because slavery had become the central question in the public mind, it persisted in forcing itself into the arena of political discussion and action. Because members of the established parties were unwilling to accept the challenge, public demand grew for a new and more effective political party which would be willing to fight and remove this evil.

THE national election of 1860 saw the emergence of the Republican Party as a major factor in American politics, the election of Abraham Lincoln as our first Republican President and the creation of a new national consensus which continued to dominate American public affairs for seventy years.

In addition to its position in opposition to slavery this new consensus introduced by Lincoln imposed on the democratic inheritance of the Jeffersonian-Jacksonian consensus a fresh American response to the Industrial Revolution.

By important amendments to our Constitution it expanded our concepts of civil rights; it opened the door for the immigration of over 35 million people from foreign countries within 50 years; it settled the American West with the help of our land reform "Homestead Act" that provided 160 acres of free land for each farm family; it supported high tariffs to protect our spreading infant industries; and it encouraged the development on a large scale of an old economic instrument—the corporation—to assemble money, materials, machines and men for the accelerated economic development of the nation.

This consensus which was largely dominated by the Republican Party, lasted until 1932. In that year, following the stock market collapse of 1929, the Great Depression reached its height with more than one-third of all American wage earners unemployed. Because the Republican Party did not appear responsive to the economic disaster which nearly overwhelmed us, it suffered a devastating defeat at the polls.

And so it was Franklin Roosevelt who ushered in the third political consensus in American history. At its core was the conviction that our national government had a direct responsibility to promote the full use of our human and material resources and to provide for a minimum of security for our older people, for better housing, for medical care, and for full employment for all Americans.

Under President Roosevelt's successor, Harry Truman, this consensus in regard to our domestic affairs was widened to include vigorous U.S. participation in world affairs through building efforts such as the Marshall Plan and Point Four backed by a system of alliances to counteract armed aggression.

Between 1932 and 1952 the American people demonstrated the strength of this consensus by electing a Democratic President in five successive elections. Nevertheless it was a period marked by bitter partisan debates over employment policy, budgetary policy, labour-relations policy, price policy and, from the beginning of World War II to the Korean conflict, of foreign policy.

Inevitably, after 20 such years of exhausting innovation and often bitter debate, most Americans were eager for an opportunity to catch their political breath and to turn away from divisive domestic and international questions. As a result since 1952 we have been moving through a period of relative political balance in which the President's proposals for action have often been effectively countered by those who are determined to maintain the status quo.

So much for our brief historical review. What about the future? Can America solve its most serious problems? Will the spirit of the unfinished American Revolution re-emerge?

In the last year there have been indications of a new political churning and ferment as new issues are beginning to take shape. Indeed some observers believe that the United States may now be on the verge of a fourth great consensus.

Already debates on limiting nuclear weapons and the pressures by our Negro citizens for full democratic rights now represent strong new currents in American political life.

If a fourth consensus is in fact in the making, it will be stimulatingly different in at least one characteristic: Whereas in the past the party in power, faced with new and important issues, has traditionally *resisted* change, the Kennedy and Johnson Administrations have shown the initiative to lead on controversial issues, the courage to face up to the new challenges, and the imagination to offer its own affirmative response.

# 23. Holidays and Heroes

*Ambassador Bowles in several* American Reporter *columns from 1967 to 1969 and an address over All India Radio suggested that the test of a modern democratic society is to make available to the people as many liberties as possible.*

IN RECOUNTING the progressive liberal tradition upon which America was founded and has developed, the following highlights of America's ideals—its holidays and heroes—may be of some interest:

On July 4 the United States will celebrate the 192nd anniversary of the Declaration of Independence by the American colonies from British rule.

Against the background of this historic effort to secure for the American people their full rights to individual freedom and liberty, it is fitting, I believe, to pose the question: What do we really mean by "liberty"?

In the midst of our costly and tragic Civil War, Abraham Lincoln, whom I consider the greatest of all American Presidents, said: "The world has never had a good definition of liberty, and the American people, just now, are much in need of one. We all declare for liberty: but in using the same word we do not all mean the same thing."

We still do not all mean the same thing, yet what each individual thinks about liberty and, even more important, what he and his nation does about liberty, affects the policies of every government and the people of every nation.

Consequently, intelligent citizens throughout the world cannot allow themselves to become confused about what liberty means and how they may secure it.

"Liberty" is a many-faceted word; liberty itself is of many kinds. To call liberty indivisible is neither honest nor realistic.

First, there is *political liberty*: the liberty to go to the polls to choose our own representatives, prime ministers, presidents, and many local officials; and to approve or to disapprove government policies.

Then there are *civil liberties*: the liberty to speak our minds freely; to assemble in peaceful groups; to have equal access to public service; to move freely about in our own countries; the right to a fair trial by law; freedom from illegal search, seizure or exile.

There are *personal liberties*: the liberty to practise our own religion; to marry and to raise a family according to our own concepts.

There are certain *human liberties*: the liberty for every one of us, regardless of race, religion, national origin or economic status, to develop freely and consistently with human dignity and to the full extent of our abilities.

Then there are *economic liberties*: the liberty to work where we will; to choose our job or start a business; to invent or market a new product; to take a job or quit; to own and sell property with our capacity, intelligence and willingness to work.

Most civilizations have granted some of these liberties. None until our day has even pretended to grant them all. Most frequently, in past civilizations, all or most of these liberties were granted to a favoured ruling class and denied for the most part to all other classes.

The test of a modern democratic society is not only how many of these separate liberties exist in actual practice, but how many are available to the people at large.

The goal of a people dedicated to liberty in this broad sense is not equality of material wealth—although it is a welcome by-product—but equality of opportunity to live and to work and to move ahead in line with our capacity and interests; the right to a good education and good health for ourselves and our children; the right to a basic minimum of security; these in addition to the growing political and civil liberties which have always been the basis of our liberal tradition.

Within this framework of liberty the least that the less timid among us can do is to stand for the essential truths of our time:

—That man's future on earth need not be cancelled;

—That we need not resign ourselves to catastrophe;

—That our political ingenuity still may rescue us from ruin;

—That some things, like war and injustice, may seem everlasting, but that these things are everlastingly wrong, must be everlastingly wrong, must be everlastingly fought and must some day be conquered.

THE revolutionary objectives which are now stirring the peoples of Asia and Africa are much the same as those which in 1776 gave birth to the American Revolution.

Today the struggle against the last vestiges of colonialism and imperialism in Africa and the world-wide demand for human dignity for more rapid economic progress and for peace echo the objectives of the American revolutionaries of two centuries ago. In our Declaration these objectives were described as equal opportunity for all men and the universal right and I quote to "life, liberty and the pursuit of happiness."

The American Revolution was the first instance in our present historic era of a colony achieving independence from its mother country. It established a pattern of legitimate revolution which has had a massive impact on the aspirations of hundreds of millions of subject people.

Because the American Declaration of Independence was based on the legitimacy of revolution against foreign rule Americans have always had a particularly deep and abiding sympathy for people seeking to win their freedom.

Indeed it was the express intention of the leaders of the American Revolution that their revolution should encourage subject peoples throughout the world to free themselves from colonial bondage.

Thomas Jefferson, who as a young man of 32 wrote the Declaration of Independence, expressly stated and I quote, "I join in the hope and belief that the inquiry which has been excited among the mass of mankind by our American revolution and its consequences will ease the condition of man over a great portion of the globe."

The American Declaration of Independence and the revolution which followed also marked America's acceptance of the principle of economic change. Freedom from foreign rule, we saw, was not only by an end in itself, it was a measure to a still greater end.

Thus as America prospered it became evident that we could remain true to the principles of our revolution only if we were sure that the fruits of our rapid development were made available to all members of American society.

To this end successive generations of Americans, often in the face of the most bitter political opposition from supporters of the status quo, have fought to establish new systems and institutions which better serve the economic and political needs of our people while eliminating or altering old ones which no longer fully met these needs.

In this long continuing process, President Roosevelt's so-called New Deal was perhaps the most radical programme of economic and social reform. The primary elements of the New Deal were designed to achieve faster economic growth, to increase personal security for farmers, factory workers and small businessmen and to assure a steady improvement in the quality of American life.

Today, in the wake of the world-wide drive for independence from colonial rule which followed the war and which was led by India, the concept of more rapid economic and social progress is being rapidly spread throughout the world.

ON this fourth day in November Americans throughout the world will celebrate a special day of Thanksgiving. The custom of setting aside the fourth Thursday in November as a day of thanks for the bounties of nature dates back to 1620, when the first settlers from England celebrated, with their American Indian neighbours, a plentiful harvest in their newly adopted land.

These men and women came as refugees from religious persecution. To assure all members of their new community full rights as citizens, they created the historic Mayflower Compact, one of the world's first democratic charters guaranteeing self-government and individual freedom under law.

These Pilgrim settlers were followed by successive waves of immigrants from Europe who, in the face of great hardships, established a series of new colonies along the eastern seaboard of what is now the United States.

It was inevitable that sooner or later the liberty loving descendants of these early refugees from political oppression would come into conflict with the old order, finding their dependent relationship to the English crown intolerable.

Their petitions ignored and their discontent at the breaking point, the American colonies declared their independence from England in 1776, and successfully defended it in a long and bitter war.

With the establishment of a free and independent United States, the flow of immigrants from Europe sharply increased. In the early stages most of them came from England, Scotland and Wales and, following the potato famine, from Ireland.

After the failure of the 1848 uprisings against the reactionary governments of Central Europe, their numbers were swelled by tens of thousands of Germans. They, like their predecessors, were determined to create a new life in a free and open society where a man's worth was calculated not by his wealth or antecedents but by his abilities and will to work.

Toward the end of the nineteenth century, they were joined by more newcomers, largely from Italy, Poland, Hungary, Greece and Russia.

By the end of the first World War in 1918, more than forty million men, women and children had left behind the economic injustices and religious intolerance of their European homelands to make a fresh start in the new world of America. In the early years of this century these immigrants averaged two million annually.

One common characteristic of these new Americans was their courage, inquisitiveness and sense of purpose. As philosopher George Santayana, himself an immigrant, pointed out, it was "the fortunate, the deeply-rooted, and the lazy who remained at home."

These uprooted people represented a massive challenge to America's democratic faith, and the challenge was eagerly accepted. As the immigrant ships sailed up New York harbour, one of their first sights was a huge statue dedicated to liberty and inscribed with a poem that concluded:

> "Give me your tired, your poor,
> Your huddled masses yearning to breathe free,
> The wretched refuse of your teeming shore.
> Send these, the homeless, tempest-tost to me,
> I lift my lamp beside the golden door!"

It is these "huddled masses," these dedicated working-men, artisans, engineers, merchants, teachers and doctors, who enabled the United States to develop so rapidly, to build its extensive network of railroads, its hundreds of miles of canals, and to open up vast virgin lands for cultivation.

This unprecedented migration of peoples from the old world to the new was not accomplished without suffering and strife. For instance, there were often bitter conflicts between the older, established immigrants and more recent arrivals.

Yet the vast undeveloped American West provided a ready escape from the conflicts of the industrialized urban areas. To encourage this westward movement, the federal government provided free grants of virgin farmland to families who would agree to establish and to cultivate their own farms.

The greatest single factor in welding together these millions with their disparate backgrounds was the American public school system, which guaranteed all citizens and prospective citizens equal rights to a free education. It was largely through our public schools that these new comers were "melted into a new race of men."

On Thanksgiving Day 1967, we may hope that some day the diverse peoples of our modern world may capture the spirit and sense of common purpose that moved these crores of immigrant Americans to join hands in building an integrated, secular and prosperous America and that a peaceful, interdependent world will some day become a reality.

THIS week the American community in New Delhi is celebrating National Day by commemorating the democratic ideals of Thomas Jefferson.

Jefferson, philosopher and politician, democrat and diplomat, agriculturist and architect, has been reverred throughout the annals of the history of the United States; his is the voice of imperishable political freedom and human rights.

The achievements listed on his tombstone highlight the essential facets of his humanistic creed: "Here was Buried Thomas Jefferson, Author of the Declaration of Independence, of the States of Virginia for Religious Freedom, and Father of the University of Virginia." He was also the third President of the United States.

In the 150 years since his death, the mind of Thomas Jefferson has remained unsurpassed in its erudition and flexibility. James Madison, a contemporary statesman and scholar, considered Jefferson "the most learned man" ever to hold public office.

One hundred and fifty years later, President John F. Kennedy, addressing a large group of distinguished American scholars, artists, and scientists in the White House, remarked wryly that sitting before him was the greatest collection of talent "since Jefferson dined here alone."

Jefferson's contributions to America—and the world—were numerous, varied and enduring, but perhaps foremost was his lifelong championship of the democratic process.

"All men," Jefferson asserted, "are created equal". This conviction has influenced the thinking, the attitudes, the expectations, and the institutions of many generations of Americans and hundreds of millions of people in all parts of the world.

In his masterpiece, the Declaration of Independence, Jefferson proclaimed his theory of natural rights.

Each individual citizen, he asserted, had a natural right to life, liberty and the pursuit of happiness.

"To secure these rights," the Declaration proclaimed, "Governments are instituted among men, deriving their just powers from the consent of the governed. That whenever any form of Government becomes destructive of these ends, it is the right of the people to alter or to abolish it, and to institute a new Government, laying its foundation on such principles and organizing its powers in such form, as to them shall seem most likely to effect their safety and happiness."

Jefferson's assertion of universal human rights was not mere political rhetoric uttered by a young idealist in a moment of historic crisis. Ten days before his death at the age of 83, Jefferson affirmed in a letter to a friend his belief that man's equal rights were on the way to realization, all over the world. The spread of the light of science, he wrote, has already made clear the "palpable truth" that the mass of mankind was "not born with saddles on their backs, nor a favoured few, booted and spurred, ready to ride them."

Jefferson was well versed in the arts of government and diplomacy. After spending several years in Europe, he came home in 1789 to become America's first Secretary of State under our first President, George Washington.

Jefferson and his most bitter political opponent, Alexander Hamilton, the Secretary of the Treasury, soon clashed over Washington's domestic policies. Jefferson believed in rule by the majority, which was then largely made up of small land-owning farmers and artisans. Hamilton was convinced the best government was that of an elite, made up of the "rich and well-born."

However, when Jefferson and his party won the crucial, bitterly fought election of 1800, and the dust of political conflict had settled, the new President admitted that the areas of agreement were greater than the political oratory might indicate.

In an effort to bring harmony to a nation torn by party strife, he observed in his inaugural address: "Every difference of opinion is not a difference of principle.... We are all Republicans, we are all Federalists."

Americans, seeking to personify their nation and the ideals on which it rests, have found their most important unifying symbols in the life and principles of Thomas Jefferson. His democratic ideals are still alive for the whole world to cherish; as the historian Allen Nevins wrote, "He was one of the greatest liberators of the human spirit."


A NOTHER great American President was Woodrow Wilson, scholar and political leader, who in 1912 became our 28th President.

His first four years in office were characterized by a vigorous effort to improve the lot of American workers and small farmers, to curb the great monopolies and to provide increasing measures of justice and opportunities for each citizen.

In November 1916, when President Wilson was re-elected for a second term, his public career entered a new phase; the United Kingdom, France and Russia were dead-locked in a bloody war with Germany, and Wilson sensed that the United States ultimately would be drawn into the struggle.

His concern was compounded by the conviction that American participation could be justified only if the war were transformed from a classic balance of power conflict into a crusade for a new world organization that would create a more stable Europe, establish the right of self determination for all colonial peoples, and guarantee the peace.

In his Fourteen Point Peace Programme Mr. Wilson spelled out these objectives.

In April 1917 when he asked the United States Congress to declare war against Germany the President stressed that "We have no selfish needs to serve.   We desire no conquest.   We seek no material compensation for the sacrifices which we shall freely make."

An American army of over three million men was transported across the Atlantic Ocean and after heavy fighting, the German Government in November 1918 asked for an armistice on the basis of Mr. Wilson's Fourteen Points.

A few weeks later when Wilson arrived in Paris to negotiate the final terms of the peace, an adoring population hailed him as the champion of a new world order.

On June 28, 1919 with glittering ceremony, a peace treaty including a new world-wide organization, the League of Nations, was signed at Versailles.  The President then returned to America to seek the approval of the United States Senate as required by our Constitution.

In the meantime, isolationists had combined with  his most embittered political opponents to prevent America from joining the League or of accepting the role in world affairs which President Wilson envisaged.

In a nation-wide speaking tour he placed the issue squarely before the American people.  The League of Nations, he said, was not only the most important part of the treaty, but was inseparable from it.

In his opening speech in St. Louis, Mr. Wilson said that if he should lose his fight for the new world organization he would call together the young soldiers whom he had sent to France and say to them, "I told you before you went across the seas that this was a war to end all wars.  Although I did my best to fulfil this promise, I am now obliged to come to you in mortification and shame to say that I am not able to fulfil this promise.  You have been betrayed.  You have fought for something you did not get."

"If this struggle is lost," he prophesied, "there will come sometime in the future another struggle in which many million more young men will die to accomplish the final freedom of the people of the world."

A few days later when the President walked onto the stage of a crowded auditorium in Pueblo, Colorado, he was cheered to the rafters with a ten-minute ovation.  Drawing on his last nervous and physical resources, the President poured all of his eloquent conviction and passion into a final plea for a world organization to assure world peace. "Our boys," he said, "died for something that far transcends the immediate objects of war."

After Mr. Wilson finished, the hall was hushed. Then there burst forth a deafening roar of applause, the greatest ovation of his tour.

Later that night the weary President suffered a nervous and physical collapse from which he never recovered, and so died the hope for an effective League of Nations which alone could assure a lasting peace. America retreated once more into isolationism and twenty years later, as he had prophesied, the world was plunged into a second World War even more costly than the first.

President Wilson's critics assert that he compromised too much in the peace negotiations in Paris and too little in dealing with the isolationist United States Senate. Yet it was his vision and leadership which created a shining new goal for all mankind—an effective world organization dedicated to peace, freedom, justice and increasing opportunities for all men.

THE anniversary of the birth of a more recent American President—Franklin Delano Roosevelt—occurs on January 30th. He was the first President whom I knew personally.

In the early summer of 1943 when the war was at its peak, President Roosevelt asked me to take charge of the Office of Price Administration. The job included responsibility for rationing, the regulation of rents and prices and later, control over wages and the production of consumer goods.

In the following months our frequent and lengthy conversations gave me a deep insight into his unique personal qualities, his breadth of vision, his courage and above all, his dedication to human rights not only for Americans, but for all men everywhere.

The world remembers Franklin Delano Roosevelt as the inspired leader who came to embody the democratic ideals for which millions were fighting and dying during the troubled years of the Second World War.

To India, he had special meaning; for he was the outspoken foe of colonialism, and friend of Gandhi and the Independence Movement.

I remember him best as the architect of a far-reaching social revolution, as the man whose ideals shaped the destiny of post-war America.

As the war drew to a close, it became increasingly apparent to the President's friends that his interests were focused on the world that would follow the peace.

Out of his deep concern for the welfare of the people in the post-war world came his famous Economic Bill of Rights, which he presented to Congress in January, 1944.

This remarkable document spelled out for every worker the right to a good job and decent wage, for every farmer the right to own his own farm, for every businessman the right to compete in the market place free of the pressure of monopolies, for every family the right to a decent home, for every girl and boy the right to a good education, and for every citizen the right to medical care and a secure old age.

Later in the same year, during Roosevelt's fourth campaign for the Presidency, he followed up his earlier plea for a larger measure of social justice for all Americans with a call for an economy that would give regular employment and good wages to a labour force of sixty million men and women.

His political opponents dismissed the figure as fantastic and unrealizable; they said it was nothing more than political demagoguery. But a few years later his goal was reached and then quickly surpassed.

Indeed, all of the targets President Roosevelt set for post-war America have largely been met. Like all great men with the courage of their convictions, he stirred endless controversy and made many enemies. However, even those Americans who opposed his policies have come to accept his vision of a just society as a fundamental concept of our national life.

The last time I saw Mr. Roosevelt was in late March 1945. He had recently returned from the Yalta Conference where he had caught a severe cold.

On April 12, 1945, at his winter home in Warm Springs, Georgia, he died suddenly while working on a speech that was to have been delivered at the Jefferson-Jackson Day dinner in Washington.

In the closing words of this speech, he said:

"The only limit to our realization of tomorrow will be our doubts of today. Let us move forward with strong and active faith."

To me, these words are as revealing of Franklin Delano Roosevelt as any he had ever written.

He was a man deeply committed to the cause of human rights and economic justice; a man dedicated not only to the abstract concept of world peace, but to those ideals and institutions that would make world peace a reality.

# 24. The United States Has Problems, Too

*All nations face economic and social difficulties. The Ambassador pointed out in several* American Reporter *columns the serious problems presently besetting the United States, especially civil rights, and how the Government and the people are seeking to solve them.*

AGAINST America's background of achievement remains much unfinished business.

Yet somehow the idea has taken hold that only under-developed countries like India have problems, while it is assumed that economically more advanced countries like the United States are largely free of divisions and concerns.

I would like to correct this impression.

The United States, like every major nation, is beset with difficulties, many of which are formidable and deeply worrisome to our government and our people.

Let me give you a few examples:

1. In the last several years we have undertaken a massive campaign to eliminate racial discrimination which in some ways is similar to caste discrimination in India.

Although extraordinary progress has already been achieved, emotional attitudes accumulated over many generations cannot be changed overnight. Consequently in many parts of the United States, including many of our northern cities, deep differences persist.

2. The Cold War, a result of Stalin's expansionist policy following the war, created the need for a massive U.S. defensive establishment, not only to protect ourselves, but to discourage attacks on other nations.

Although the cost of this effort has been great, our efforts to negotiate a disarmament agreement, to reduce our defensive burden and that of other nations, have thus far been frustrated.

3.  The war in Vietnam makes it difficult for us to concentrate on the primary business at hand, that is, the development of our own nation and the building of a stable world society.

4.  The profusion of technological advances which have occurred in the last few years have had an awesome effect on the American economy and our society in general.  Millions of unskilled and semiskilled workers are steadily being replaced by incredibly complex machines which are products of the new scientific advances.

A massive expansion of our educational and technical training facilities is required to enable our workers to adjust to this economic revolution.  Already more than one-third of all American boys and girls of college age attend universities.  This number must be sharply increased with special emphasis on engineering, science and the professions.

5.  The American people and their Government have embarked on an effort to rebuild our cities, and provide better opportunities for those American families (estimated at one-fifth of the population) which still lack modern housing, and recreational, health and educational facilities comparable to those available to their neighbours.

Democracy calls for an equal measure of economic and social justice for evey citizen.  Until each American is assured of these rights we will not have fully met the challenge.

Thus America's problems, although different from those of India, are real.  And, as in the case of democratic India, we shall continue to strive vigorously to solve them.  Let us consider some of the most challenging questions with which we are required to deal.


ON JANUARY 1, 1968 President Johnson announced that the U. S. had a serious balance of payment problem and was taking drastic measures to regain a stable monetary position.

What is behind this American dollar dilemma?

Why is the United States, the world's most productive nation, cutting back some of its overseas spending?  Why, at the time of unprecedented prosperity, should Americans be asked to postpone

their plans to travel to Asia and Europe, and to curb their investments in the developed countries?

The problem occurs because Americans have persistently been
spending more abroad for imports, investments, tourism and other
items than foreigners have been spending in the United States.

This excess American spending results in an increasing amount of
dollars being held by non-Americans, including foreign governments,
financial institutions and individuals. Since many of them insist on
exchanging their dollars for gold, which the United States is firmly
committed to provide, our gold reserves have steadily declined.

The United States still has about twelve thousand million dollars
in gold, nearly one-third of the world supply. Moreover, total
American-owned assets abroad are overwhelmingly greater than
total foreign-owned assets in America.

Our dilemma stems from the fact that United States-owned assets
are mainly tied up in long-term investments, for example in factories,
while most of the foreign assets in the U.S. are in cash, securities,
bonds, etc., which can be quickly withdrawn or exchanged for U.S.-
owned gold.

Since there is no other readily available alternative to the present
international monetary arrangement, the United States will continue
to support the present system, with all its inadequacies, until a better
one is created to take its place.

This support can best be provided by bringing the dollars Americans spend abroad into balance with the money foreigners spend
in the United States. We are going about it in two ways:

First, by cutting down non-essential U.S. Government spending
abroad, by curbing some new private industrial investments overseas, and by encouraging Americans to travel only in the Western
Hemisphere.

Secondly, by increasing our earnings from U.S. exports sold abroad
and also by increasing the number of foreign tourists coming to the
United States.

A major effort has been made to keep the recently announced
programme from working to the detriment of developing countries
such as India. This is made easier in respect to India because dollar
expenditures of American economic assistance to India are almost
totally spent in the United States.

Developing countries, such as India, will also be favoured under the new programme in respect to U.S. private investments. While the amount permitted for such investments will be stopped totally in Western Europe and cut to 65 per cent of the 1965-66 average in other developed countries, similar investments in the developing countries can be increased by 10 per cent over the base period.

One of the main objectives of the present UNCTAD II meeting in Delhi is to stimulate world trade rapidly. To achieve this, the world urgently needs a new international currency that can be expanded at a sufficient rate to meet the growing needs of expanding world trade, but not so rapidly as to breed inflation and economic chaos.

At the same time such a currency could provide an unchanging yardstick against which the relative value of other national currencies can be measured.

Since World War II, all nations have relied on the American dollar as the primary monetary instrument for world commerce and trade. No other currency has had sufficient strength to assume these responsibilities and functions.

Backed by massive U.S. gold reserves, the American dollar has fulfilled in a reasonably effective way the role of an international currency. However, if world development and trade are to expand as rapidly as they must, other nations, in view of our dwindling gold reserves, will have to share this responsibility with the United States on a cooperative, equal basis.

An important start in that direction was taken last September when the Board of Governors of the International Monetary Fund, meeting at Rio de Janeiro, approved a new system of Special Drawing Rights (SDRs). These SDRs will be eventually held by the paticipating countries as part of their reserves along with gold and dollars.

Meanwhile, it is essential that the United States maintain as stable dollar as the basic unit of international trade and finance. This is why President Johnson is reluctantly cutting back overseas spending by Americans.

It is our hope that these restrictions are temporary. Once the present imbalance has been adjusted, the United States is committed to continue to participate fully in the expansion of world investment, trade and travel.

I OFTEN hear the United States referred to as a "free enterprise nation" where presumably the Government has only a marginal interest in people as individuals. In fact, nothing could be further from the truth.

It occurred to me that Indian readers might be interested in the extent to which our Government participates in the day-to-day operation of the American economy to promote and, as far as possible, assure the security and welfare of all Americans.

I.     If you are an industrial worker, you are guaranteed:

* a minimum wage, now $ 1. 60 (Rs. 12) per hour, although it was as low as $.30 (Rs. 2. 25) per hour when the law was first enacted 30 years ago.

* the right to join a labour union whose honesty is assured by the uniform application of the law; 1.8 crore American workers are now union members with many more working under union contracts.

* insurance benefits, if for any reason you are unemployed, up to $ 65 (Rs. 488) per week as long as 9 months, depending upon the individual's work history and residence.

* total Government health insurance for older workers as well as sick leave and medical payments for employed workers.

* vacations with pay, as much as four weeks for many workers; most agreements provide ten days or more of paid holidays.

* regular Government inspection of all work places, including factories to assure safe working conditions.

* retirement plans, with many union agreements often providing benefits over and above Government social security payments.

* strictly enforced laws forbidding child labour.

* compensation if you are injured on the job for as long as you are unable to work and rehabilitation if your future employability is affected.

II.     When you reach the retirement age, you will receive:

* regular social security payments each month from a fund to which you and your employer contributed during your working years.

* free medical care.
* similar benefits if disabled before reaching retirement age.
* when you die, your family are entitled to pensions for widows and orphans, as well as funeral grants.

III. If you are a farmer, you are guaranteed:
* minimum prices for your crops.
* subsidized tools and machinery.
* loans to buy additional land.
* access to the most extensive agricultural research programme in the world to guide you selection of crops and your use of seeds, fertilizer, etc.

IV. If you are a businessman, you are guaranteed:
* protection against price rigging by monopolies.
* government loans to start small businesses, tax incentives to expand your business.
* technical assistance on production methods and machine utilization.
* government subsidies to key industries such as shipping, airlines, railroads.
* laws that prevent dishonest advertising by your competitors.
* laws that require all food and drugs to be carefully tested before being sold with the contents and ingredients clearly printed on every container.

V. If you are in the armed forces, you are assured:
* lifetime free health care for yourself and your family.
* subsidized higher education.
* access to subsidized food, clothing and household essentials.

VI. If you are a student, you have:
* access to a free education from primary school through high school and in several states through the university.
* low-interest loans to finance a university education.
* free or low-cost books and supplies.
* highly subsidized libraries and scientific laboratories.

VII. If you are unable to earn an adequate wage, you are entitled to:

* relief payments.
* special maternity care.
* job training.
* low-cost subsidized housing.

In spite of this massive effort, involving millions of people and billions of dollars in tax revenues, almost one-sixth of America's population is still unable to secure enough income to participate fully in the nation's prosperity. Often this is due to the lack of technical education and other reasons. Although the income of these underprivileged families would appear extremely high to Indians, it must be remembered that the cost of living in the United States is also high.

To help meet this challenge several political leaders—both Democrats and Republicans—are now pushing for a guaranteed minimum annual income to all families. If a sufficiently high guaranteed wage is established, some of our present direct welfare programmes could be eliminated.

OUR most explosive problem is the struggle for equal opportunity by America's Negroes. Civil rights have always been a matter of deep concern for thoughtful Americans conscious of our own shortcomings. Since the Civil War enormous gains have been made in behalf of Negro Americans. Private organizations have been developed to carry on an unrelenting effort. Many states have established Civil Rights Commissions to create equal opportunities, employment, eating and hotel accommodations and so on. The Federal Government has led the way through administrative guarantees of equality of opportunity.

However, this great demonstration has introduced a *new* dimension in the struggle. Now, for the first time since the Civil War the question of equal rights for the Negroes in all spheres of their lives—in housing and employment as well as in schools and voting booths—has become a pressing national issue in which *every* American citizen is involved and on which each must take his stand.

The present concern in the U.S. centres around the extreme tensions in our cities. These tensions have resulted from three factors: (1) the traditional conflict between those at the bottom of the economic ladder and those a few rungs above, (2) the rapid progress of automation, and (3) racial antagonisms.

America has often been described as a nation of immigrants. In the hundred years before World War I more than 40 million people (largely Europeans) crossed the Atlantic to find a new life and new opportunities in the United States.

As each new wave of immigrants arrived, they inevitably challenged those who had preceded them by offering to work for less money and to hold more menial tasks. As a result there were frequent conflicts.

This process is continuing but within a different framework. The present "newcomers" are not immigrants from Europe, but millions of Negro families who are moving from our southern states to seek better jobs in the northern industrial centres such as Chicago, Cleveland and Detroit.

The tensions created by this vast migration have been made increasingly explosive because the new automatic machinery, with which most American industries are now equipped, has been creating more demand for well-educated and highly skilled workers and less demand for those unskilled and under-educated.

As a result, in the last several years there have been serious riots in many American cities and there are likely to be more in the future.

To analyze the causes and to stress the urgency of this crisis, the President's Commission on Civil Disorder was established with eleven members from business, trade unions, churches, civil rights organizations and elected officials. The Commission has just issued a comprehensive, courageous and, I believe, historic report.

The facts set forth in this report abundantly document and validate the problems of life in the Negro slum areas.

With commendable candour the Commission lays the blame where it belongs—on white racism. It charges that many generations of white Americans have created and enforced an inferior status on Negroes; consequently the non-Negroes cannot now avoid responsibility for evil consequences.

The positive recommendations stressing the critical areas of employment, education, housing and welfare are highlighted by the following:

—Create as rapidly as possible ten lakhs of new Government jobs, plus another ten lakhs in the private sector.

—Consolidate federal, state and city manpower programmes, emphasizing on-the-job training with the extra cost to private employers being borne by the Government.

—Extension of early-childhood programmes to every needy child and expanded opportunities to higher education.

—Enactment of a law that forbids discrimination in the sale and rental of housing.

—Provision of 60 lakhs units of decent housing for low and moderate income families by providing Government loans at low interest rates.

—Revisions in the present welfare system to help provide a greater measure of security and welfare to all who need it with the Federal Government bearing at least 90 per cent of the total payments.

Since even the U.S. Federal Government lacks the resources fully to rebuild and modernize our cities—and that is what is called for—many business corporations, previously reluctant participants, are now playing a major part in the common struggle against urban decay and civil disorder.

For example, Job Opportunities in the Business Sector (JOBS), the National Alliance of Businessmen, and the Urban Coalition are new schemes committed to produce 10 lakhs of new jobs for the hard-core unemployed and urban Negroes.

It is too early to predict the extent to which these far-reaching programmes will meet their objectives. Nevertheless, it is reassuring to know that a massive effort is now under way to provide every American citizen, regardless of race, creed or colour, not only with a good education and a decent home but with a sense of dignity and personal involvement in creating a better society.

D URING my recent visit to the United States, I was impressed once again with the breadth and vigour of the American Negroes' own efforts to achieve, in fact, the freedom of opportunity which the American Constitution guarantees to its citizens.

Although some Negroes in a spirit of bitter frustration have resorted to violence, the majority remain committed to the non-violent techniques advocated by the late Dr. Martin Luther King, and other moderate leaders who have already broken down many solid economic and political barriers in all parts of America.

Martin Luther King was one of the greatest leaders of our times. He is the first private American citizen for whom a national day of mourning was observed throughout the United States.

I met Dr. King in 1956 when he was engaged in the initial non-violent attempt to achieve equal opportunity, justice and freedom for Negro Americans. This movement started from a local incident—a bus boycott in Montgomery, Alabama—and grew into a national crusade.

A quiet Negro seamstress, Mrs. Rosa Parks, had been forced many times to give her bus seat to a non-Negro. But one day she suddenly decided not to move. When the driver threatened to call the police, she said, "Then you just call them."

Mrs. Parks was arrested. Martin Luther King, then a 25-year-old clergyman, called for a one-day city-wide boycott of all buses. When white extremists reacted vigorously, the protest grew until it covered the entire city bus system and involved almost every Negro family in Montgomery.

The Gandhian movement which ultimately freed India from foreign rule started in much the same way; in this case the spark which set it off was struck on a train in remote, race-conscious South Africa in 1893.

The night of his train ride in South Africa, Gandhi was ordered to leave the compartment reserved for whites. When he refused to do so, he was pushed off the train at the next station stop.

As he stood shivering there in the dark, his overcoat and baggage still on the train now fast disappearing down the tracks, Gandhi asked himself a fateful question, "Should I fight for my rights here or go back to India?"

"I came to the conclusion," he recounts, "that to run back to India would be cowardly". The "golden rule," he decided, "is to dare to do the right at any cost."

During his short life Martin Luther King dared the same thing and with similar non-violent techniques.

Dr. King's programme had its spiritual roots not only in Christianity but in the ancient religions of Asia; he was frank in saying that his programme had been largely borrowed from Gandhi who used this appeal so brilliantly to bring freedom to the Indian people.

In fact, one Civil Rights organizer recently said: "There is a foreign influence present . . . that of Mahatma Gandhi. It is the Gandhi of non-violence, non-injury, and a willingness to accept suffering. This Gandhi has given us."

Thus, the political techniques of boycott and non-violence which freed India from British rule and are now opening up new opportunities for American Negroes, have travelled from India to America, then from America to India via South Africa and now back again from India to America.

Mahatma Gandhi's followers, including Jawaharlal Nehru, and Martin Luther King often stressed that the principal condition for the success of Gandhi's way of fighting injustice was that it take place within a legal system administered by people who believe in a democratic creed and who permit a large measure of free speech and free press.

These conditions exist in America where all but a minority of racial extremists know that discrimination against any man based on his race, creed or colour is morally wrong.

Although the concept of the inherent dignity of man is deeply embedded in our American Bill of Rights, experience in even the most law-abiding nations suggests that laws which touch deep prejudices and emotions are obeyed only when the great majority of people come to accept them as morally right.

Abraham Lincoln once said, "Public sentiment is everything. With public sentiment nothing can fail, and without it nothing can succeed. Consequently, he who moulds public sentiment goes deeper than the who enacts statutes or pronounces decisions. He makes statutes and decisions possible or impossible to be executed."

The non-violent way of persuasion and change in India, America, or elsewhere, is designed to stir the conscience of the vast majority of decent, law-abiding people, and to persuade that majority to bring its actions into line with its beliefs.

The spirit of tolerance, faith and brotherhood—which mankind is desperately in need of—will go forward because of the courage and leadership of men like Mahatma Gandhi and Martin Luther King.

Gandhi still lives; so does Dr. King, and their thoughts and deeds have helped to bring equal opportunity to all of America's citizens.

# 25. The Evolution of America's Foreign Policy

*After tracing the historical development of America's foreign policy, Chester Bowles analyzed the role of the United States in the post-World War II era. In particular Ambassador Bowles believed America's policy in Asia should be to work with non-Communist indigenous political consensuses which would provide an effective counterweight to China. This in turn would allow for the emergence of politically stable and economically viable nations such as India. This material appeared in the* Yale Review *of March 1965 and in an essay in* To Heal and to Build: The Programs of President Lyndon B. Johnson, *Edited by James MacGregor Burns, New York 1968, the latter being serialized in* The Indian Express.

SINCE THE surrender of the Nazi armies and the collapse of the Co-Prosperity Sphere in 1945, America has committed its resources and its energies on an unprecedented scale to the task of creating a stable world order.

We have largely financed the rebuilding of Europe and Japan, created a powerful military shield against Communist aggression that extends from Berlin to the Aleutians, and poured money, technicians, and goodwill into the development of the emerging nations of Africa, Asia and Latin America.

Yet, as we take stock of our efforts, many Americans feel a sense of frustration. Although Western Europe and Japan have emerged from the destruction of war to become prosperous allies and trading partners, much of the world has stubbornly refused to behave the way we think it should.

Instead of gratitude for our economic assistance, we have often faced criticism, insults, and even the destruction of our property. Instead of appreciation for the protective shield of American charged military power, we often find ourselves charged with imperialism and interference. It is not surprising that influential voices should be raised in Congress and the press to demand that we punish the recipients of our help and protection by withdrawing into our old isolationism, by letting them go their way while we go ours.

Although these impatient reactions are understandable in human terms, they make no sense whatever in terms of our national interests. We cannot withdraw from the human race. With our far-flung interests of trade and security we are irrevocably committed to a policy of world involvement. What happens or fails to happen in the most remote areas of the world will inevitably affect our lives as Californians, Dakotans, Kansans, or Vermonters.

Our task, therefore, is not to run away from the realities of our increasingly interdependent world but to re-examine our policies objectively, learn from our mistakes, and gear ourselves for a better performance. As a great power, rich, privileged, and strong, we carry widespread responsibilities to help assure the peace and to provide the conditions under which new nations can develop the political stability and economic capacity that will eventually enable them to make their own effective contribution to a more rational world.

When we become impatient with our role in today's world it is both sobering and reassuring to look again at our own history during the period when we were ourselves a new nation, as reluctant to play a constructive role in world affairs as most of today's new nations are, and at least as ungracious in regard to the efforts of those who made our progress possible.

In the period before our Revolutionary War the course of events on the new world side of the Atlantic was strongly influenced by nationalistic forces in Europe. From the outbreak of the War of the League of Augsburg in 1689 until the Peace of Vienna in 1815, Europe was torn by an almost continuous conflict that fluctuated between cold wars and hot wars and in which the principal antagonists were France and Britain. Each of the four major wars fought during this period was reflected on our side of the Atlantic in blockades, troop movements, guerrilla raids, massacres, and other classic manifestations of a worldwide power struggle not unlike those we face in many parts of the world today.

When the American colonies finally came to a parting of the ways with the mother country, it was not surprising that the King of France should grasp the opportunity to embarrass his British adversary. In March 1776, Silas Deane, accredited by the Continental Congress as its "Commercial Agent", arrived in Paris to inquire about the prospects of French political and military assistance for the rebellious American colonies.

After a few weeks of negotiation, Louis XVI, a most unlikely supporter of upstart colonial revolutionaries, agreed to provide the Continental Congress with credits amounting to one million livres ($200,000). Only when the revolutionary leaders in Philadelphia heard that this French military and economic assistance was firmly in hand did they decide on the final break with Britain. On July 4th, four months after Deane's arrival in France, came our Declaration of Independence.

Following the surrender of General Burgoyne's British Army at the battle of Saratoga in October 1777, George III and his advisers decided that the time had come to cut their losses in America in order to free themselves for the decisive struggle against France. When news reached Paris that the British had offered the American colonies home rule with the Empire, the French monarchy took immediate steps to prevent what it considered a "premature" peace.

In early 1778 a treaty was hurriedly signed between the French and American Governments. Under the terms of this "defensive alliance," the French recognized the independence of the United States, granted generous privileges to our shipping, and promised massive military assistance in return for a pledge that neither nation would make peace with Britain without the other's consent. The greatly expanded flow of French military equipment which soon followed, in addition to the active support of a French army and fleet, assured the decisive victory of the Continental Army two years later at Yorktown.

Although our Founding Fathers had had almost no previous experience in world affairs, they demonstrated a capacity, no less shrewd than that of many new nations in our own era, to manipulate the great power rivalries of Europe to assure our national independence.

From this early experience came the American commitment to non-alignment which President Washington reflected in his Farewell Address in 1796: "It is our true policy," Washington said, "to steer clear of permanent alliances with any portion of the foreign world." For the next 121 years, American foreign policy remained rooted in this neutralist concept.

The commitment of the new republic to a non-aligned approach to international problems was soon put to the test. Once we had signed a peace treaty with the British, the relations between the revolutionary new American republic and the doddering French monarchy which had helped us to secure our independence began to cool rapidly. Nor did the overthrow of Louis XVI in 1789 serve to clear the air.

Indeed, nine years later Congress reacted against French interference with United States shipping by authorizing the capture of French warships, suspending commercial intercourse with France, and declaring the treaties of 1778 void on the grounds that they had already been violated by the French Government. A few years later when Citizen Genet, the first minister to the United States from the new French Republic, sought by direct personal appeal to persuade the American Government and people of the follies of neutralism, he was accused of indiscreet conduct and asked to leave the country.

Although the French were resentful, they could hardly charge the nationalistic young Republic with favouritism. In 1812 when the long struggle between democratic Britain and the Napoleonic French police state was moving toward a climax, the United States declared war on Britian. Although the official reason given by our Government was to insure "freedom of the seas" for American shipping, this was a freedom which, as a belligerent, we have never before or since accepted as a right for other belligerents in time of war.

In the words of the eminent historian Samuel Flagg Bemis, "The War of 1812 was caused by a western expansionist urge rather than solely by the just grievances of neutral rights and impressment." The western "war hawks" led by Henry Clay hoped for the quick conquest of Canada, while their southern counterparts looked eagerly toward Florida, which was then in the wobbly grip of Britain's ally, Ferdinand VII of Spain.

Three years later, the Peace of Vienna, which confirmed the British Navy's command of the seas, ushered in a century of relative peace in Europe, while the Peace of Ghent laid the basis for a relationship between the United States and Great Britain which has evolved from indifference, through a grudging interdependence, to the firm alliance which exists today. By the time of the Peace of Ghent the United States had been an independent nation for 39 years, three times as long as most of the emerging nations of Asia and Africa have enjoyed such a status. Living in a far simpler world, we had achieved a high degree of political stability, our economy was booming, and our national objectives, although limited, were clearly defined.

The unspoken nineteenth-century relationship between America and Britain was destined to shape the economic and political development of our country in many critically important ways. Its origins may be traced to the decision of the British Government to prevent the four Holy Alliance powers (France, Russia, Prussia, and Spain) from restoring Spanish sovereignty over its former Latin American colonies after they had won their independence during the Napoleonic Wars.

In August 1823 Foreign Minister George Canning proposed to our Minister in London that the United States and England should jointly declare that they would not be indifferent to any attack on the newly independent states of Latin America. In response to Canning's proposal, Secretary of State John Quincy Adams, reflecting our traditional "neutralist" conviction that the American and European systems should be kept as separate and distinct from each other as possible, recommended to President Monroe an independent stand in which we would oppose European intervention in the New World without becoming a "cockboat in the wake of the British man-of-war."

Therefore, in December 1823 Monroe, while rejecting Britain's proposal for a common position in opposing the Holy Alliance, declared that the United States would not only continue to avoid involvement in the politics or wars of Europe, but also would oppose any effort on the part of the European powers to acquire new territory in the New World or to interfere with the political system in the American continents. Several months later Canning privately informed the French that this was British policy, which henceforth would be enforced by the British fleet.

In his history of the Monroe Doctrine, Dexter Perkins underscores the significance of the British naval barrier which made our brash unilateral pronouncement meaningful. "The Government of the United States," he writes, "spoke out boldly and independently with regard to the colonial question, with the knowledge that in a pinch it would be supported by the mistress of the seas."

There were, of course, occasions when Britain failed to support our closed door position in regard to Latin America, notably when it occupied the Falkland Islands, when it approved Emperor Maximilian's involvement in Mexico during our Civil War, and in 1895 when the British themselves intervened in Venezuela. But these were the exceptions.

Through much of the nineteenth century it is fair to say that the effectiveness of our Monroe Doctrine in maintaining the integrity of Latin America against European expansionism was in large measure due to the fact that the British Navy provided a protective shield and that British diplomacy, anxious to maintain a political balance in Europe, found it expedient to underwrite Monroe's unilateral pronouncement that the Old World Powers had no business on our side of the Atlantic.

It is interesting to consider how different our economic and political development might have been if this British shield had not existed and Prussia, Russia, France, and Spain had been free to move at will into the New World. In order to hold the expansionist minded Europeans on the other side of the Atlantic, we would have been forced to become deeply involved in European political machinations and to create an expensive army and navy capable of defeating whatever military challenge might be thrown at us. Inevitably our dynamic surge westward to the Pacific and our unprecedented industrial development would have been drastically curtailed and the shape of modern America affected in many unpredictable ways.

IF OUR nineteenth-century commitment to non-alignment and our manipulations of the European power balance to serve our short-range national interests are reminiscent of what some of us believe to be the "unrealistic" attitudes of many non-aligned nations today, the same may be said for much of our early economic development.

Immediately after the American Revolution our Government and its people turned to Europe for capital assistance to finance our social and industrial development. The prospect of profits and political influence in the rapidly expanding new America soon served to attract large amounts of capital from Britain and lesser amounts from other European countries. Of the $ 11.2 million raised to finance the purchase of Louisiana from France, $ 9 million came from Britain. The $ 7 million bond issue which financed the Erie Canal passed largely into British hands. In 1805 Samuel Blodget estimated that one-half of all American securities were foreign-owned. By 1838 the British investment alone had grown to $ 175 million—a sum larger than all United States private investment in India today. By 1899 this figure had increased to $ 2.5 billion. On the eve of the First World War it had reached a fantastic $ 4.5 billion. Indeed, in terms of present-day purchasing power, this is substantially more than our total present capital investment in any country in the world with the exception of Canada.

During this same period, thousands of able European scientists, engineers, and craftsmen crossed the Atlantic to contribute their skills and experience to building the new American nation.

On August 3, 1914, when the Kaiser launched his grey-clad infantry divisions westward toward Brussels, Paris, and the English Channel, there were few Americans who grasped the political significance of the event.

Having taken for granted the protective shield of British diplomacy and naval power for nearly a century, we, like many non-aligned nations today, had lost contact with international realities. We still could see no reason to question the continuing wisdom of our century-old policy of neutralism in what we believed to be no more war in the never-ending struggles of Europe. Indeed when British purchasing agents sought military equipment for their hard-pressed armies from American manufacturers they were forced to liquidate three-fourths of Britain's massive investments in the United States to pay for it.

America's awakening to her profound stake in the victory of the Western powers came with painful slowness. Perhaps the turning point was the bleak afternoon of May 31, 1916 when the British high seas fleet was very nearly destroyed in the Battle of Jutland. Only when we saw Britain actually pressed to the wall did we begin to understand the vital importance of the British naval and diplomatic shield which had stood between us and Europe for more than a century but which we had taken for granted.

With massive help from an awakened America the Germans were ultimately forced to surrender and we embarked on the historic debates over Woodrow Wilson's proposals for a League of Nations which in his words would "lead the world into pastures of quietness and peace such as never have been dreamed of before."

The destruction of the Wilsonian vision at the hands of the "little group of wilful men" in the United States Senate who had learned nothing from the near-defeat of our Western Allies need not be reviewed here. It is sufficient briefly to record two tragi-comic incidents in the 1920's that reflect the effort of million of Americans to return to a neutralist approach to world affairs.

In 1923, the Illinois legislature passed a resolution declaring that the official language of the State of Illinois would henceforth be known as the "American" language, not as "English". Three years later, "Big Bill" Thompson, running for re-election as Mayor of Chicago, boldly vowed to keep the British Navy out of Lake Michigan; indeed if King George should attempt to visit Chicago itself he would personally hit him on the "snoot". When asked which King George, III or V, His Honour is reported to have exclaimed, "My God, don't tell me there are two of them!"

Not only did we remain manifestly unappreciative of Britain's decisive contribution to our own security and development throughout the nineteenth century, we also continued resolutely in the face of overriding evidence to reject any future share of responsibility for maintaining world peace.

In 1935, when Mussolini, in violation of the mandate of the League of Nations (a mandate which our own refusal to become a member had rendered ineffective) invaded Ethiopia, Congress responded by passing the Neutrality Act which embargoed arms shipments to all belligerents in the event of war. In 1939 when the Germans launched their second attempt within a single generation to conquer Europe, Congress agreed to lift the embargo on arms but only when a "cash and carry" stipulation had been added as well as a provision that denied the right of United States ships to enter declared war zones (a "right" for which we had presumably fought the war in 1812).

With all our unprecedented wealth and power, it is fair to say that the United States did not come of age in regard to foreign affairs until we had been literally dragged into two world wars, each of which we might have prevented.

Only in the midst of the second grave and costly struggle did we as a people recognize that we could no longer protect and promote our national welfare and security through the often irresponsible posture of international non-involvement which marked our isolationist years. With massive public support, the leaders of both political parties introduced the principle that henceforth America's security and prosperity depended not only on the avoidance of war but on the encouragement of orderly economic and political growth throughout the world.

A MERICAN foreign policy in the post-war era can be divided into four periods or phases.

The first covers the critically important period between the end of the war and the early 1950's; the second extends until 1960; the third from 1960 until the present; the fourth, and probably most decisive period, lies just ahead.

I do not suggest that the beginnings and ends of these periods can be determined with any degree of precision. Each flows into the other with significant overlaps. Nevertheless, they provide a convenient framework to consider the evolving world forces with which we have had to contend in the last 23 years, the adequacy of our response to these forces, and the challenges we are likely to face in the years ahead.

V-J Day, August 1945, ushered in the first of these four phases as a confident America faced a new kind of world. We had fought in Asia against an imperialist Japan and in Europe against the Nazis. Our democratic institutions were the model for a dozen newly independent governments.

After a hundred years of isolationism, the United States emerged into the new post-war world with unchallenged power and influence, determined to carry its share of responsibilities.

The first challenge came in Europe where we responded promptly and vigorously. When Stalin's Russia, in the tradition of Czarist expansionism, launched its push toward the Mediterranean we threw our support behind Turkey and Greece and the pressure was relieved.

When the Soviet Union sought to engulf Berlin by cutting all rail and road access to the Western sectors we again acted firmly. Within 48 hours American and British cargo planes were landing every 90 seconds at Tempelhof airfield to supply the embattled city. A few months later the Berlin blockade was lifted.

In June 1947, Secretary of State Marshall announced America's willingness to support a massive European economic recovery programme, a plan "not directed against anyone, but against hunger, chaos and poverty." In 1948 the Organization of European Economic Cooperation was established joining seventeen European partners in the unprecedented and imaginative Marshall Plan.

At the same time, we organized a defence programme to assure the military security of Western Europe. In 1949, the North Atlantic Treaty was signed by fourteen nations and NATO came into being.

In this first post-war phase our record was one of imaginative concepts carried through vigorously and effectively. Yet in retrospect certain miscalculations are now evident.

It was logical and proper, for instance, that our immediate post-war concerns were focused on Europe. Europe represented a vast concentration of industrial resources; it controlled the approaches to the Atlantic and stood astride the most important routes of world commerce. Even more important, it was in Europe that our Western ideals of liberty and humanism were born.

Consequently it was not surprising that U.S. foreign policy during this critical period was in large measure an extension of the British policies which had helped maintain the peace of Europe between the Congress of Vienna in 1815 and World War I.

This called for a power balance in Europe which the British had skilfully maintained by opposing any power or combination of powers that sought to dominate the continent.

There was, however, a fundamental difference: in the nineteenth century a peaceful Europe was the primary requirement for a peaceful world. The economic, political and strategic decisions concerning Asia and Africa were not made in New Delhi, Hanoi, Leopoldville or Batavia, but in the imperial capitals of London, Paris, Brussels and The Hague.

What we failed adequately to take into account in this first post-war phase was the revolutionary surge which was rapidly demolishing the old colonial ties and enabling the new nations of Asia, Africa and Latin America to begin to shape their own destinies.

We also wrongly assumed that in the developing continents the primary danger, as in Europe, would be communist movements manipulated by Moscow and Peking. It was some years before we came to see that the revolutionary wave sweeping Africa and Asia was in fact generated by political and economic forces deeply rooted in Western concepts of nationalism, economic progress, and self-determination. We credited the communists with having created a vast political wave which in fact they were only trying, often rather ineffectively, to ride—a wave which had been created by the indigenous forces to which I have referred.

Whatever influence the USSR and China exert today in Asia, Africa and Latin America, and in some areas it is considerable, is not primarily because of their communist ideology but because they are strategically placed major powers, highly sensitive to the social, political and economic forces which are making history.

Under the impact of this wave of nationalism, the British withdrew with dignity from their far-flung empire. The Dutch left Indonesia; the Belgians pulled out of the Congo; and the French were driven out of Indochina and Algeria and finally withdrew from their remaining African possessions.

OUR belated recognition of this massive political, economic and social upheaval ushered in the second of the four post-war phases of American foreign policy. In dealing with these new global forces our conditioned reflex was an attempt to adopt our successful European experience to a totally different set of problems. A primary element of this effort was to draw nations which would agree to accept our leadership into military alliances, with few if any qualms about their political systems.

In Asia this approach limited our military-political relationships to a number of friendly, but relatively weak nations. With their inadequate support we set out to "contain" Communist China while the four largest non-communist nations, Japan, India, Indonesia and Pakistan, sat on the sidelines in various attitudes of neutrality.

This is not to ignore some notable accomplishments. Our effort to help build a stable, dynamic, friendly Japan was brilliantly successful. We rallied to the support of South Korea and led a massive UN effort to re-establish its independence. Indeed, in all parts of Asia, with the unhappy exception of French Indochina, our support for the new independence movements was unequivocal.

Similarly in Africa, despite our NATO ties with the then major colonial powers of Europe, we generally supported the anticolonial forces. In Latin America our acceptance of the forces of change, while often timid, was a major improvement over our pre-war posture.

Also on the positive side of the ledger was our realization that the challenge posed by the developing nations had important economic and social dimensions. Out of this understanding came President Truman's Point Four, the World Bank, our support to the specialized agencies of the UN, and the Economic Assistance Programme, which was launched in India in 1952.

Yet on balance it is evident that during the 1950's the United States Government lacked a clear concept of developmental techniques and priorities. Instead of concentrating our economic assistance on those countries most willing and able to help themselves, our aid programmes often came to be used to bolster pro-American leaders who lacked effective political roots among their people. In some cases political unrest led to military dictatorship supported by misguided American military assistance programmes.

This misdirection of much of our early overseas developmental efforts was accompanied by our failure to educate the American people, press and Congress in regard to the nature and dimensions of the new world challenge.

For instance, it has been generally assumed that our efforts to strengthen the nation of the developing world would be a relatively short-range affair similar to the reconstruction of Europe.

This was a serious misconception. In the case of the Marshall Plan we were dealing with long established European nations with highly developed industrial skills, sophisticated concepts of Government, modern technologies and traditions of military organization and cooperation.

In much of Asia, Africa and Latin America, we were working with new nations, which by and large had not yet generated the habits of thought, the codes of behaviour, the literacy, education

and social integration essential for the establishment of free institutions and rapid economic progress.

It was also assumed that our economic assistance would automatically generate a feeling of warmth and gratitude toward the
United States; consequently we expected those nations we had
assisted to support our foreign policy objectives and to stand by
our side in the United Nations. When they failed to do so, we often
scolded them for their "ingratitude."

These assumptions and reactions reflect our failure fully to understand either the political and psychological forces which have been
shaping the developing countries or the limitations and purposes of
economic assistance. After long years of colonial rule the people
and leaders of the new nations are acutely sensitive to any action
by a foreign government which appears to infringe on their sovereignty. Their posture on many foreign policy questions is determined
by an overriding desire to prove that they are their own masters,
regardless of how many American toes they may step on in the
process, or how much they may be acting contrary to what we
believe to be their nations' interests.

My experience in the developing countries has convinced me that
there is only one realistic justification for providing foreign economic
assistance: to make it possible for those developing nations which
are prepared to adopt enlightened economic policies to become
politically and economically viable and prepared to contribute their
growing strength and influence toward the creation of a more
stable world.

It is the task of the historians to strike a balance between the
successes and failures of U.S. foreign policy in this second post-war
stage. Our immediate concern is to consider the third phase which
was ushered in by the election of the Kennedy-Johnson Administration in January 1961.


WITH SOME, but by no means all, of the lessons of the 1950's
in mind it may be said that we have made significant but by
no means adequate progress.

On the plus side there are many highly important achievements.
These include the transition, still incomplete, to a new, more realistic relationship with the nations of Western Europe, the launch-

ing of that exciting expression of youthful dedication, the Peace Corps, the Alliance for Progress, a more patient and realistic view of Africa, a new recognition of the overriding importance of improved relations with Eastern Europe and the USSR, the imaginative use of our vast capacity to produce food for export and an understanding of the urgent need to provide adequate development assistance to those nations which are genuinely prepared to help themselves.

On the positive side, too, there is now a much better understanding achieved at a heavy cost in money, blood and goodwill, of the limitations of military power and of the overriding importance of the forces generated by political and social change.

It is not within the scope of this article to discuss the pros and cons of our position in Vietnam. However, it is fair to point out that much of the anguish which we have faced in that tragic area reflects our earlier failure fully to recognize the political and psychological forces at work in the underdeveloped continents.

The initial mistake occurred immediately following the war when we permitted the French to re-establish their colonial position in Vietnam. A few years later, when the Viet Minh rose in rebellion, we supported the colonial French with hundreds of millions of dollars worth of military supplies.

If the French had left Vietnam when the Dutch and the British withdrew from their empires in Asia and Africa, a half million American troops would never have been called upon to fight in Vietnam and the people of Southeast Asia would have been spared their tragic ordeal.

However, if the Vietnamese crisis has convinced our Congress, press and people that political stability in Asia, Africa and Latin America can be created only by the people themselves and that in the absence of such stability costly and unpredictable armed conflicts are inevitable, at least lessons have been learned from the tragedy.

A S WE move into the decisive fourth phase of our post-war foreign policy, it is essential that we keep these lessons firmly in mind. What we need to understand is not only our strengths, which are formidable, but our limitations which are also real, coupled with a more realistic set of national priorities.

We have been spending some $30 billion a year on an effort to establish a more politically stable Southeast Asia. Once this war is over will we be prepared to spend even one-third of this sum in preventing future Vietnams in South Asia, Africa and Latin America ?

Can the American people who spend tens of billions of dollars each year on cosmetics, night clubs, cigarettes and bubble gum be persuaded to support the enlightened policies which are required to build a world in which their children and the children of their contemporaries abroad can live in peace, comfort and dignity?

Our answers to these and other relevant questions will constitute an acid test of American political leadership in the 1970's. In this context let us consider the choices we now face in Asia where a majority of mankind lives.

In the next few years I believe one of three developments will almost surely occur:

1. A frustrated and embittered United States will withdraw from Asia allowing China and/or Russia to fill the vacuum,

2. The United States will become engaged in a costly and im-possible-to-win war with China, or

3. A non-communist, indigenous political consensus will gradually evolve in Asia solidly based on the areas of primary weight and influence. I refer to India, Japan, Australia and Indo-nesia, which in cooperation with Pakistan, Thailand, New Zealand, the Philippines, Taiwan, Singapore, Malaysia and South Korea are alone capable of providing the essential Asian counterweight to China.

Will we come to see that only through such an indigenous politi-cal-defence balance in Asia can we be relieved of the present heavy pressure on us—a question that is underscored by the decision early this year of the British Government to withdraw from practically all of its military commitments 'east of Suez?' Will we understand that any such free Asian coalition, however anti-communist, cannot accept American control and direction without losing the support of its own people? Will we also realize that its creation will take time, money and infinite patience?

In this framework I believe that the emergence of a politically stable and economically viable India is of decisive importance. If the massive democratic experiment in India should fail, there is little hope for peace and stability in Asia. The reasons are clear.

—India's population is greater than that of Africa and Latin America combined. More than half of the non-Communist people of Asia live in India.

—India has survived twenty years of political freedom and has thus far maintained a genuine Parliamentary democracy underscored by four general elections. When we remind ourselves that scarcely a dozen nations in all of Africa, Asia and Latin America are still governed democratically, this in itself is a major accomplishment.

—If India's attempt to create a politically stable and economically viable society fails and this complex and often frustrating nation, with one-sixth of the human race, starts down the same slippery slope that China did a generation ago, all the blood and dollars which we have been pouring into our efforts to stabilize Southeast Asia will have been in vain.

But what of China itself? A non-communist Asian coalition, anchored at the two ends by India and Japan, may for a decade or two provide an effective Asian counterweight to an embittered and irresponsible China. But for the long haul it is essential that China gradually be drawn into a rational relationship with the rest of mankind.

Although the door is now closed we should seize whatever opportunities may arise to re-establish contacts of trade, culture and diplomacy. By so doing we may hasten the day when that great and tragic nation can again become a partner in the community of peaceful nations.

We must also recognize the decisive importance of our relations with the USSR, particularly in the next decade. In the USSR as in America we may assume that a political tug of war is in progress between advocates of international cooperation and understanding and those who are more at ease in a cold war setting. In the years immediately ahead, much will depend on the ability of American political leaders to establish a greater measure of cooperation and understanding with the Soviet Bloc provided, of course, that Soviet leaders are prepared to meet us halfway.

Here as elsewhere a flexible approach to world problems and pressures is of great importance. A notable aspect of international relationships in the last twenty years has been the often decisive impact of unpredicted developments. I refer to such events as the dramatic recovery of Japan and Germany, the break in Soviet-Chinese relations, the sudden collapse of European colonialism in Africa and the like.

We must assume that the next ten years will be characterized by equally dramatic happenings which will surprise the most competent observers. This calls for a resiliency that combines a capacity to deal with current problems coupled with an ability to adapt quickly to brand new situations.

It should now be clear why I believe that the fourth post-war period, which is now in its beginning stages, will be decisive for generations to come. What is required of us is a capacity to understand how hundreds of millions of people—speaking different languages, worshipping different gods and living under different conditions—think and feel, and then to act effectively on this understanding.

There is nothing new about their poverty, illiteracy, slums and ill-health; what is new is the deep, worldwide, growing conviction among these masses of underprivileged rootless human beings that better answers must soon be found.

These awakening peoples want something more than schools, houses and "things". Above all else they are seeking the sense of personal involvement and dignity which has thus far been denied them. Economic development experts who ignore these primary human goals and assume that an increase in gross national product automatically produces a similar increase in gross national stability are dangerously wrong.

It is understandable why so many of those with the greatest stake in the status quo view these vast political uncertainties with fear and confusion. But I believe history will determine that they reflect the churning of economic, social and political forces which hold enormous promise for all mankind.

For two decades fantastic new technologies have been literally tearing apart old societies, upsetting the traditional rhythm of individual lives, and generating new hopes among hundreds of millions of underprivileged people who have come to see poverty, ill-health and slums as man-made evils which can and must be eliminated.

History is littered with examples of once great empires whose leaders and peoples assumed that they could somehow exist and progress as islands of power and affluence in a sea of misery, envy, frustration and violence.   Thus one by one they failed the primary test of national survival: the capacity to recognize, understand and cope with political, social and economic change.   After brief periods of prestige, power and glory, some were overwhelmed by their less fortunate but better adapted neighbours, while others were simply by-passed as irrelevant.

This leads us to the central, overriding question:   Is our generation of Americans wise enough, courageous enough and above all sensitive enough to cope effectively with the new forces which are stirring mankind ?   In other words, are we Americans relevant to tomorrow's world?

Many members of the younger generation are openly sceptical; while our military power and our gross national product soar, our influence, they point out, continues to shrink. Tens of millions of Asians, Europeans, Africans and Latin Americans who revere the ideals of Jefferson, Jackson, Lincoln and Roosevelt as any American, share their concern.

Acting in the framework of this new, turbulent but infinitely promising world, it is the task of the President, his envoys, his Administration and the Congress to disprove the doubters, to relate our policies and our actions to the values on which our nation is based, and thus  prove that modern America is in fact dramatically, dynamically, supremely relevant to the freedom, dignity and progress of man in the latter decades of the twentieth century.

# 26. What Kind of World?

*Ambassador Bowles divided world critics into Partisans of Despair and Partisans of Hope. Here are his observations which were published in his* American Reporter *column of March 27, 1968.*

EVERYWHERE—east, west, north or south—there is a growing awareness that our world is approaching a crisis as governmental institutions, designed for a less turbulent world, strive to cope with the explosive by-products of the new technological revolution.

In response to these new forces which are shaping tomorrow's world, concerned people in all countries tend to divide into two groups: Partisans of Despair and Partisans of Hope.

In the United States and other developed countries the Partisans of Despair point to a formidable set of obstacles to a better and more secure life.

Most of our rivers and lakes are being dangerously polluted by industrial waste and sewage. Even the very air we breathe is being poisoned by the noxious exhaust gases given off by millions of automobiles and thousands of factories in crowded urban areas.

At the same time, automation is eliminating millions of unskilled jobs and creating a massive need for workers who are highly trained and educated. As our urban areas expand in response to these pressures, housing, schools, and medical facilities lag far behind the needs.

Meanwhile, world tensions are increasing the pressure in both communist and non-communist nations to produce "bigger and better" missiles and bombs. What now passes for "world peace" is, in fact, a peace assured by mutual terror based on the capacity of the two major powers to destroy each other.

In the developing countries, the Partisans of Despair see even more formidable obstacles to progress.

Although they admit that the miracle of improved foodgrain seed and fertilizer is beginning to ease the spectre of massive famines, a decreasing death rate and a continuing high birth rate, they assert, will double the population of the world within 30 years. This will create impossible problems. The fact that most developing nations are prevented by ancient traditions, caste, tribal loyalties, and habits of mind, from coping adequately with these problems, compounds the dilemma.

Because of these and other factors the pessimists maintain that the rich nations will inevitably become richer (although not necessarily happier places in which to live), while the poorer nations will lag further and further behind.

On the other hand, the Partisans of Hope, while admitting these awesome difficulties, see the future from a much more affirmative perspective.

In developed nations such as the United States they point to the growing public realization that national priorities are both out of balance and the consequent demand for an adequate response.

Already, they admit, there is a dramatic awakening to the urgent need to rebuild and reorganize our cities to eliminate the tensions, insecurity, and bitterness which now beset so many of them.

At the same time, heavy public and governmental pressure is being brought to bear on industries and communities to purify the air we breathe and the water we drink.

Experts predict that in the next decade the gasoline and diesel-powered trucks and cars, which contribute massively to air pollution, will begin to be replaced by electric-powered vehicles.

Racial and religious discrimination in the United States are at long last recognized as evils with which there can be no compromise. A few years ago, it was thought that no Roman Catholic could be elected President; today, the question of religion is not relevant. Several cities have elected Negro Mayors; the state of Massachusetts has elected a Negro Senator.

Our millions of university students are increasingly turning from negative criticism of their elders to come to grips with the problems which face us.

Although the arms race continues, an agreement has been reached by the two great nuclear powers to eliminate the testing of nuclear weapons in the atmosphere, to preserve the Antarctic and outer space for peaceful purposes, and to ban the proliferation of nuclear weapons.

In the developing countries, the Partisans of Hope see even greater reasons for an affirmative view of the future.

Although medical science is still extending the average lifespan, new techniques of family planning may soon make possible a sharply reduced birth rate, thus bringing population growth under control.

The prospects for the production of cheap nuclear power are unlimited. When we are able to extract hydrogen from the sea, electric power will be available to all countries at a very small fraction of present cost.

We already know how to take the salt out of sea water. It may soon be possible through nuclear energy to provide fresh water from the Arabian Sea, Bay of Bengal, and the Indian Ocean for less than one rupee per 1,000 gallons.

In the meantime, agriculture techniques, including the possibility of massive harvests from the sea continue to improve; the consequent greater availability of high-protein foods will assure better balanced diets.

The ultimate answer to the key question, "What kind of world?" will depend, in my opinion, on the capacity of governmental institutions in both developed and developing countries to bring now new technologies to bear on our current problems.

In the meantime, the Partisans of Despair and Hope may be expected to continue their debate with the former saying, in effect, that the glass is already half empty and the latter insisting that it is already half full.

As a Partisan of Hope I believe that the future of mankind is unlimited in scope, frightening in its possibilities, but infinitely hopeful in its potential.